The War in Heaven Continues

The War in Heaven Continues

Satan's Tactics to Destroy You, Christianity, the Family, the Constitution, and America

Gary C. Lawrence

Author of *How Americans View Mormonism* and *Mormons Believe ... What?!*

Published by
Parameter Publishing, LLC
1450 N.Tustin Ave., Suite 150
Santa Ana, CA 92705

office@parameterpublishing.com
GaryCLawrence.com

This work is not an official publication of The Church of Jesus Christ of Latter-day Saints. The views expressed herein are the sole responsibility of the author and do not necessarily reflect the position of the LDS Church.

ISBN-13 978-0-9906342-0-1

Printed in the United States of America

Dedicated

To all members of
The Church of Jesus Christ of Latter-day Saints
who carry the flag of the Gospel of Jesus Christ into
the five battlefields in the continuing war that began in heaven.

Contents

PREFACE

"Hell is empty and all the devils are here."

– William Shakespeare,
The Tempest

If you do not believe Satan is a real being, this book is not for you.

But if you do, then you probably already believe that there was a war in heaven. And that it continues here on earth.

Same participants, same issues, new location.

Up there … Satan drew away a third of our spiritual siblings even though we had a perfect knowledge of God's plan and His wish that we follow it.

Down here … why shouldn't Satan use the same successful tactics plus more?

That topic has animated my thinking for years.

When I was deciding which graduate school to attend, I visited with a professor at Stanford who explained that most Ph.D. programs produce specialists – those who learn more and more about less and less. His communication program, on the other hand, encouraged doctoral students to learn more and more about more and more. The vehicle was to study attitudes – how they are formed, how they are measured, how they can be changed, and how they drive behavior. Sounded good to me and off I went to Stanford.

In the 40+ years since then, I have been a public opinion pollster involved in hundreds of persuasion campaigns from politics to marketing. My job is to analyze the populations my clients want to reach and figure out what might persuade them to vote, purchase, or behave a certain way. Just as importantly, I also analyze the opposition and deduce their probable plans, tactics, and messages.

This book is the result of applying those methods to our ultimate opponent, Satan. Its purpose is to tell you what he is up to and how to recognize his tactics in this epic continuation of the war in heaven.

As I discuss each of five battlefields, I will give examples I believe point to Satan's role and influence. I do so as a conservative, as a defender of the Constitution, as an active member of The Church of Jesus Christ of Latter-day Saints, and as a very, very concerned father and grandfather. Should you view the world through a different monocle, however, you may find alternative explanations more satisfying. But if my analyses resonate with you … then we have work to do.

I hope this book will help you to better recognize and resist Satan's cunning, his wiles, and his snares, and not only strengthen your defenses, but give you the courage to lob a few grenades of truth into the battle.

– Gary Lawrence
Orange County, California
Summer 2014

Introduction

One who fails to study his enemy can hardly be expected to defeat him.

We are in the final days of not only the earth's probation, but Satan's as well. His days are numbered. He rules over this world. He will not give it up quietly. Things are going to get rough.

Funny, isn't it, that some can discern coming events in the slightest of signals, while others refuse to accept stark evidence in plain sight.

In the first group are poker players who look for clues that signal what kind of hand a player holds and his intentions. Known as a tell, it can be a change in breathing, the force with which chips are placed, fidgeting, eye movements, tone of voice, among numerous others.

We also have baseball players who watch for inadvertent signals from the pitcher – body language, angle of the glove, a wiggling of a finger – that tip the batter to what pitch is coming.

In the second group, those who don't see the obvious, we have comfortable businesses. Why didn't IBM see the signs and become Apple? Why didn't Kodak invent, or run with, digital photography? Why didn't Sears become Wal-Mart?

Not paying attention to the signs can especially infect nations. Japan refused to believe that the United States had cracked its naval code even though the Chicago Tribune broke the story as the Battle of Midway was ending, and how this breakthrough led to our victory.[1] They ignored the almost treasonous leak and continued to use that code for the remainder of World War II, which ironically enough gave us to know the flight plans of Admiral Isoroku Yamamoto, perhaps the most influential believer in the invincibility of the code, and shoot him down ten months later.

Great Britain in the 1930s is an even better example as Winston Churchill repeatedly warned of the evil emanating from Germany. He saw amassed power in the slavish worship of one man, free speech extinguished in the book burnings, racism and subjugation in the fiction of a superior Aryan race, the cessation of reason in the hysteria of torchlight parades, an excessively deep cobblestone base that made the autobahn strong enough to accommodate tanks, the Hitler Youth Movement as surreptitious infantry training, Hitler cleverly skirting Versailles Treaty sanctions against a German air force by training pilots with glider aircraft, and that Hitler was building justification for violence by scapegoating Jews as the villains and cause of Germany's troubles. All signs that Germany was preparing for war.

But Great Britain laughed at him. Windy Churchill's crackpot theories, they mocked, despite a trail of hints that cause historians to wonder why they couldn't see what was happening.

Well, **they couldn't see because they wouldn't see**.

Although the signs of the coming disaster were all around them, they were too comfortable, even in the middle of the Great Depression. They had already fought Germany and put her in her place. They actually believed the Kellogg-Briand pact that outlawed war would work, and that the sanctions of the Versailles Treaty would surely protect them. In short, they refused to look at the evidence. They paid dearly for their willing blindness.

Because of opposition in all things, there will always be a competitor, a challenger, an opponent, a rival, an enemy, or an adversary trying to beat us. Those who refuse to analyze and understand the guy on the other side … will lose. Or at least pay a high price for their ignorance.

As we know, Lucifer was an angel "in authority in the presence of God,"[2] who rebelled against the Father and was expelled from heaven, thereafter to be forever known as Satan. The name Lucifer means "Light carrier or bringer," which harmonizes with his description as a son of the morning – positive connotations all. Therefore, his rebranding was necessary and he became Satan, which in Hebrew means, appropriately enough, adversary.

While God and His Son are the embodiment of good, Lucifer *chose* to become the embodiment of evil. He lives here. He has only one other place to go. He is desperate to bring us into his misery before he is banished.

Though today's elite – those who are "ever learning, and never able to come to the knowledge of the truth"[3] – contend that Satan is a fictitious character, a majority of Americans fortunately disagree. Unfortunately, this majority has been cowed by the others that it is not politically correct to discuss him.

But discuss him and his plans we must, just as poker players, athletes, and nations' intelligence services study their opponents.

Our time is short. The Lord promised that in the last days He would hasten His work, and with it an attendant acceleration of earthquakes, pestilences, sickness, wars and rumors of wars, and general commotion. Who does not sense that the pace is quickening, serious geopolitical events are converging, economies are shaking, and things could explode any day? Things will get grim, as prophesied. (Sort of reminds you of the pessimist who says, "Things can't get worse," and the optimist who replies, "Oh yes they can.")

Satan's plan to bring millions of us into his misery has kicked into full battle mode. This book is about recognizing the patterns, tells, and tips that give us to know what he is up to. Its intent is to show how religious principles interact with current events, such as the stories in the Book of Mormon *selected* by Mormon and Moroni who saw our day and **knew what we would face**. It is about understanding what Satan is doing on five battlefields to defeat God's plan.

Though we may be mocked for seeing boogeymen under the bed, it is a plea for us to connect the dots and speak boldly about what is happening in the world and especially in America.

* * *

SECTION I

THE WAR TO DESTROY YOU

"The adversary is subtle. He is cunning. He knows that he cannot induce good men and women to do major evils immediately, so he moves slyly, whispering half-truths until he has his intended captives following him."

– Spencer W. Kimball

Chapter I

Nice Try, Pinocchio

"And there was war in heaven: Michael and his angels fought against the dragon; and the dragon fought and his angels, And prevailed not; neither was their place found any more in heaven."

– Revelation

My mind at times wanders back to another sphere and wonders what the war in heaven was like. Perhaps yours as well? It would be interesting to have the full details – presumably there were debates, conferences, lots of individual conversations – but we can glimpse insights from what God has revealed.

Our Father convened the Grand Council in heaven and presented His plan for our progress. That "the morning stars sang together, and all the sons of God shouted for joy,"[1] rather than asked for time to think it over, indicates that we were aware of and had **longed for such an opportunity**.

The Father's plan of salvation – aka plan of redemption, plan of happiness – points to one supreme strategy: Provide the setting and the conditions that would give us the greatest chance to progress and achieve exaltation.

- He would give us agency – the power to choose and be held accountable.
- Through the Son, He would create an earth upon which we can experience and learn to discern good and evil.
- He would provide mortal bodies for those who choose to follow His plan.
- He would establish the institutions of marriage and family.
- He would establish laws and justice.
- Knowing that we would fall short of perfection, He would provide a Redeemer and the Atonement, and establish mercy contingent upon repentance and following His commandments.

Then came the pivotal question – who should God send to be that Redeemer? Given their answers, the two spirits who responded had obviously had time to think about it. One selflessly thought in terms of doing the Father's will; the other saw it as an opportunity for mutiny and gain.

> And the Lord said: Whom shall I send? And one answered like unto the Son of Man: Here am I, send me. And another answered and said: Here am I, send me. And the Lord said: I will send the first. And the second was angry, and kept not his first estate; and, at that day, many followed after him.[2]

All heaven broke loose.

Other scriptures add detail. God told Moses that "Satan … came before me, saying – Behold, here am I, send me, I will be thy son, and I will redeem all mankind, that one soul shall not be lost, and surely I will do it; wherefore give me thine honor."[3]

A couple of points here. We don't know whether Lucifer's pitch for the Father's power happened during the Grand Council or in a later attempt to bargain, but it is obvious that he wanted more than an "Attaboy, Luce" pat on the back for redeeming all mankind. Lucifer wanted the Father's *honor*, which we know from D&C 29 is God's *power*.[4] **It was a naked power play.**

Next, when Lucifer became angry and abandoned his first estate, "at that day" many followed him, which seems to suggest that pre-recruiting was underway before Lucifer pulled the trigger.

A little deductive reasoning also suggests that Lucifer had to have guaranteed his followers they would have everything God was offering but without the risk and the hard work. Otherwise they would not have followed him. The clincher in his argument had to be the promise that they would have bodies, even though he knew he didn't have the power or the know-how to create them.

His deceit: His followers would not have their own bodies, but would occupy the body houses God would create for His followers. House squatting of the first order. That this "father of all lies"[5] couldn't even deliver that is now obvious. As Hobbes once said to Calvin, "Nice try, Pinocchio."

The revelation to Moses continues:

> Wherefore, because that Satan rebelled against me, and sought to destroy the agency of man, which I, the Lord God, had given him, and also, that I should give unto him mine own power; by the power of mine Only Begotten, I caused that he should be cast down."[6]

Lucifer's arrogant ambition sparked the war in heaven. He coveted the Father's power, sought to destroy the agency of man, wanted to displace Jesus Christ as the Only Begotten, and rebelled against everything the Father stood for. God reaffirmed that Jesus Christ was chosen from the beginning (Jehovah had already created many worlds under the direction of the Father) and, to underline that point, caused that Lucifer be cast down "by the power of mine Only Begotten."[7]

In other words, for emphasis of Who is in charge, He had Christ deliver the message and personally cast him out.

Isaiah similarly records Lucifer's ambition:

> How art thou fallen from heaven, O Lucifer, son of the morning! how art thou cut down to the ground, which didst weaken the nations!
>
> For thou hast said in thine heart, I will ascend into heaven, I will exalt my throne above the stars of God: I will sit also upon the mount of the congregation, in the sides of the north:
>
> I will ascend above the heights of the clouds: I will be like the most High.[8]

Had Lucifer been successful, do you really think he would have endured suffering and humiliation, and have given his own life on the cross so we could be empowered, progress, and become like God? Are you kidding?

In contrast to this arrogance, the Savior said simply, "Father, thy will be done, and the glory be thine forever."[9]

In this continuing war that started in heaven, some participants have bodies but no memory; others are without bodies but apparently retain a memory of the pre-mortal existence. Before Jesus cast the evil spirits into the herd of swine, as recorded in Matthew 8, they appeared to know who Jesus was and had a knowledge of their eventual fate for they said, "What have we to do with thee, Jesus, thou Son of God? Art thou come hither to torment us before the time?"[10]

We don't remember them, but they remember us. Their memory of who *we* are makes our job tougher.

* * *

Fortunately, however, as Joseph Smith taught, "All beings who have bodies have power over those who have not. The devil has no power over us only as we permit him."[11]

Chapter 2

ALONE ON THE SEAS OF LIFE

"Well if I were You-Know-Who, I'd want you to feel cut off from everyone else. Because if it's just you alone, you're not as much of a threat."

– Luna Lovegood
in J. K. Rowling's *Harry Potter and the Order of the Phoenix*

Satan wants to destroy all God-given institutions – especially Christianity, the family, the Constitution, and America – but whatever the outcomes of those battles, he will settle for destroying *you!*

In the spring of 2010, 16-year-old Abby Sunderland of Marina del Rey, California, attempted to sail around the world in her 40-foot sailboat. Alone. When a rogue wave broke the mast and left her adrift in the southern Indian Ocean, critics howled. "What is wrong with these parents? She is 16, a child."

Abby's father Laurence Sunderland defended his family's actions: "I've never advocated this for 16-year-olds. I've advocated this for experienced sailors [and] Abby is a fine sailor."[1] In other words, she was ready.

The criticism continued. After all, what kind of parents would send out a child to sail storm-churned oceans alone?

Well, Heavenly Parents, that's who. The parallel differs only in scope.

When the Father's plan was presented in heaven, you can imagine the whiny arguments of the third part of the hosts of heaven:

- How can you send your children on a journey from which they may not return? It's unfair.
- How can you be so heartless to cut off your children from the only world they've ever known, and extinguish their memory of it as well?
- Why take the risk? It's not worth it. You should guarantee a satisfactory outcome.

Sound familiar? That's because the two schools of thought in our pre-mortal existence are still with us.

On the one hand are those who want a cocoon society where everyone is entitled to the security of food, housing and medical care even if paid with the sweat of other people's brows. These are the wimpy souls who want rewards without effort, success without risk, and accolades conferred by fiat instead of deeds. And who criticize those who encourage their children to dream and to dare and to do.

These timid cowards rarely risk deeds that lead to greatness, but are only too happy to control the lives of others in **worship of equality of outcomes** – the great levelers who make sure no one fails. And if that means commensurately that no one excels, so be it.

Then there are those who work *with* life's risks instead of *against* them. These are they …

- … who willingly, even excitedly accept risks;
- … who measure the odds and then leave hearth and home to create, compete, and conquer;

- … who are confident in the skill sets they learned from their Parents or parents;
- … who with their deeds advance society.

These are they who, directly or intuitively, know that our Heavenly Father sent us to fulfill specific missions and to gather experiences that strengthen character – real-life knowledge that **can only be achieved by exercising agency with its attendant risks**, not surrendering it to the siren-song statists who would destroy it.

If God's intent had been to provide us a cushioned life of ease, there was an offer on the table He could have accepted. He didn't.

DESPAIR AND DEMONIZATION

The Father's work focuses totally – *totally* – on us. (Ponder that in a quiet moment.)

As a necessary part of His plan, we are physically separated from Him. We also suffer a spiritual separation during our time of testing in that our spirits also are not in the presence of God. This separation need not be isolation, however. Just as Abby Sunderland had a satellite phone, we have prayer.

Built into our spiritual DNA is the desire to commune with the Father. Satan seeks to break this spiritual connection and block any influence from heaven. He wants us to feel the despair of being isolated and alone.

Enter earthly tyrants who employ the same technique.

Tyrants want unattached subjects fearful to speak with one another. They atomize their societies. No volunteer associations, no religious meetings, nothing outside state-sanctioned groups. (Which is why freedom of assembly is one of the five prime rights in our First Amendment.) Planting spies in every family and neighborhood to rat on budding dissidents, they govern through fear. No one knows whom to trust. Russia did a masterful job of it, but East Germany, with Teutonic efficiency, showed Russians to be amateurs in the craft. When that government was overthrown in 1989 and secret files opened, people were shocked to find out who among them were the Stasi snitches.

Tattlers can make an individual feel isolated and weak, but it intensifies when he is ignored, belittled, put down, abused, his friendships betrayed, or his warts magnified. Such emotional deprivation – feeling worthless and alone in the world – brings despair and the urge to **fix blame and take revenge**.

Thus does Satan prepare people to believe demonizing and polarizing propaganda. Hitler, for example, gathered the misfits in an otherwise cultured and educated society and branded the Jews as their tormentors. Same with Lenin, Mao, Castro, Khomeini, Guevara, and all other tyrants – find the despairing and vulnerable, and stir them to hate.

There has never been a war in which each side did not view the other as culpable, guilty, evil, stupid, and unworthy to live. Derogatory names are essential, examples of which could be given if this weren't such a politically correct book. One blog lists almost a thousand slurs (18 for the French, 46 for the Italians, 118 for Asians, etc.) and that's just in the English language.[2] According to the military practices of many countries, viewing the enemy as having a few character flaws is not sufficient. Coupled with claims of a superior cause, soldiers must be brought to believe they are killing someone who is less than human, someone who doesn't deserve to live. Extreme isolation.

For the average person, personal demonizing is most visible in politics, war being only an extension thereof. If you oppose the president, you're racist. If you favor natural marriage, you are a bigoted homophobe. If you oppose abortion, you hate women. If you want secure borders, you're heartless and cold. So predictable from those who "make a man an offender for a word."[3] In presidential campaigns, Mitt Romney was demonized as rich and out of touch, Michael Dukakis and George McGovern as soft on crime, Ronald Reagan as a trigger-happy cowboy. Effective? Well, as Barry Goldwater said of himself after he had been severely demonized in the 1964 presidential election, "If I hadn't known the man better, I wouldn't have voted for the #&@$!! either."

Misuse the body

If we cannot be enlisted to abuse others, Satan tempts us to abuse what he will never have, a body house that clothes our spirit.

The pattern is all too familiar. We hear the enticements: "It's no big deal. Everyone's doing it. A little visit to the world's pleasure pots won't hurt. Try it, you'll like it. You can repent later." And what happens if you give in? Boom. Satan exaggerates what he once tempted as "no big deal" and the magnitude of the sin explodes: "You've done it now, pal. It's over for you; no going back; you're stuck. Might as well keep doing it. No use trying to change."

Personal cleanliness fortifies us against the isolation and despair of the world, but there are deeper reasons as well, as Elder David A. Bednar explains:

> Our physical bodies make possible a breadth, a depth, and an intensity of experience that simply could not be obtained in our premortal existence. ... [Satan] does not have a body, and his eternal progress has been halted. ... He cannot learn the lessons that only an embodied spirit can learn. ... Because a physical body is so central to the Father's plan of happiness and our spiritual development, Lucifer seeks to frustrate our progression by tempting us to use our bodies improperly.... The very tool he does not have is thus the primary target of his attempts to lure us to spiritual destruction.[4]

We rarely think of the **body as a source of knowledge**, but it is. Satan hinders this great means of gaining knowledge if we swallow his deceptions that sexual relations are for pleasure only; there is no need for commitment or fidelity; homosexuality is as good as heterosexuality; abortion is merely ridding oneself of a mass of unwanted cells, like a dermatologist freezing off a mole; and a precious child from God is just "a kid."

Improper use of procreative powers can not only cause us to lose hope, it robs us of intelligence-building experiences.

Entropy

The physical laws that govern this telestial world also contribute to isolation and despair. Known as entropy, it says that, in this world, things move from an ordered to a disordered state – the molecules from an open perfume bottle will never reorder themselves into that bottle, for example. Left alone, things deteriorate and problems arise from the disorder. In other words, **God created the earth so things would go wrong**.

The gift of work is the antidote to this despair-causing entropy. Sounds funny, but if nothing ever went wrong, why would we work? And if we didn't work, how would we grow? As we struggle against entropy, we learn, we experience, we progress, and exaltation can be our reward. But absent entropy, there would be no problems, no trials, no opportunities to prove ourselves, no progress, no exaltation, no eternal life – and God's work and glory would come to a halt.

When things get tough, as entropy dictates they must, Satan wants us to give up. He uses naturally occurring problems as well as our sins to discourage us ("God doesn't care about you or this wouldn't have happened"). He inundates our senses with stories of depravity, decadence, and debauchery. He sows confusion and sets the whole earth in commotion.[5] He sends "murmuring voices that conjure up perceived injustices" and "cynical voices that destroy hope."[6] He wants us to be as miserable as he is: "…to be alone in the dark and without hope."[7]

Whether despair and depression are caused by sin, financial problems, marital discord, wayward children, gossip, a bad hair day, or the clouds of war, in our spiral-down moments he whispers, "Give up."

* * *

Winston Churchill countered clearly: "Never give up; never, ever, give up."

Chapter 3

Calling Shots and Pulling Strings

"[They] have become free forever, knowing good from evil; to act for themselves and not to be acted upon ...."

– Lehi

The non-scriptural phrase *free agency* overemphasizes freedom, whereas *agency* without the adjective clearly suggests that *power* is the best synonym. Agency powers our progress. Not exercising it is the same as not having it.

When you hear the word agency, think *agent.* Just as one hires an attorney to be one's agent in a legal matter, we in essence hired ourselves to be our own agents when we entered mortality. We decide matters, act as we will, and are answerable.

I learned that quite nicely one Sabbath and it wasn't in church. I was working my way through college as a rock-and-roll disc jockey in Provo, Utah – Beatles, Beach Boys, top-60 hits, enthusiasm, punchy comments, go go go. Tiring as can be. It was in the day when stations signed off at 1:00am and came back on the air at 5:00am, and one Sunday it was my turn to open up. Well, it had been a bad week

– mid-terms, social life a fizzle, not much sleep, and now I have to be a top-of-my-game DJ? I thought, "This is crazy. Who in the deepest heart of Mormondom wants to hear rock 'n roll at five o'clock on a Sunday morning?" So I went into the stacks, found a long Brahms concerto (don't ask me why it was even on the premises), put it on the turntable … and took a nap.

Action. Consequences. Turns out there *were* people who wanted rock 'n roll on a Sunday morning before dawn. And they told the boss. Scratch one radio career.

A fine clear-cut lesson in agency.

The unbreakable links

My good parents taught me that actions and consequences are inseparably connected – that by choosing my actions, I have automatically chosen the consequences. But only over time did I begin to see the total interconnectedness of agency with all eternal principles:

- With agency came power to act
- With power to act came laws
- With laws came justice
- With justice came consequences – rewards and punishments
- With rewards comes progress
- With punishments comes the opportunity for repentance
- With repentance comes the mercy of the Savior's Atonement

Satan knows he cannot rescind agency, but if he can prevent the consequences of that agency, laws become moot. And if laws are not, then justice is not. And if justice is not, well, here's how Alma explains it in Alma 42, one of the most profound treatises, not only in scripture but in all of philosophy:

> Therefore, according to justice, the plan of redemption could not be brought about, only on conditions of repentance of

> men in this probationary state, yea, this preparatory state; for except it were for these conditions, mercy could not take effect except it should destroy the work of justice. Now the work of justice could not be destroyed; if so, God would cease to be God.[1]

He details the linkage:

> And also, if there was no law given against sin men would not be afraid to sin.
>
> And if there was no law given, if men sinned what could justice do, or mercy either, for they would have no claim upon the creature?
>
> But there is a law given, and a punishment affixed, and a repentance granted; which repentance, mercy claimeth; otherwise, justice claimeth the creature and executeth the law, and the law inflicteth the punishment; if not so, the works of justice would be destroyed, and God would cease to be God.[2]

Alma then emphasizes that mercy (falsely seen by many today as an escape from justice) can claim the penitent because of the atonement, but cannot rob justice: "Nay, not one whit. If so God would cease to be God."[3]

All told, Alma tells his son Corianton three times that **without justice, God cannot be God**. And if that happens, guess who stands on the sidelines ready to fill the vacuum? In fact, it was Satan's plan from the beginning.

Because of Lucifer's boast prior to the war in heaven "that one soul shall not be lost" were he chosen to be the Son of God, some have assumed that his plan was to force mankind to do good, thus rescuing them and bringing them all back to live in the presence of God – one big happy family.

This doesn't hold up. As Mormon explained:

> But whatsoever thing persuadeth men to do evil, and believe not in Christ, and deny him, and serve not God, then ye may know with a perfect knowledge it is of the devil; for after this manner doth the devil work, for *he persuadeth no man to do good, no, not one;* neither do his angels; neither do they who subject themselves unto him.[4] [Emphasis added]

To think otherwise is to grant Satan an undeserved sliver of sympathy. Can anyone really think that Satan was willing to do the Father's will, would have paid for our sins, would have redeemed us, would have given his life for us? No. There was and is no love in that being. The good and the commendable have no place in his kingdom. The letters are the same, but Satan is not Santa. Satan is a destroyer – an unadulterated, unalloyed, uncompromising destroyer.

So how did he persuade a third part[5] of the hosts of heaven to follow him? It doesn't make sense that people would have chosen to be forced to do anything. They didn't. They followed Lucifer because he peddled the whopper that they could indulge their pleasures and he would guarantee they would all return to heaven. This **"do whatever you want" enticement** – this separation of consequences from actions – is laid out at least four times in the Book of Mormon: [Emphases added]

- Nephi taught that "there shall also be many which shall say: Eat, drink, and be merry; nevertheless, fear God – he will justify in committing a little sin; yea, lie a little, take the advantage of one because of his words, dig a pit for thy neighbor; *there is no harm in this*; and do all these things, for tomorrow we die; and if it so be that we are guilty, God will beat us with a few stripes, and at last *we shall be saved* in the kingdom of God."[6]
- Moroni prophesied that "there shall be many who will say, Do this, or do that, and *it mattereth not,* for the Lord will uphold such at the last day."[7]
- Korihor, the antichrist, taught that "every man fared in this life according to the management of the creature; therefore every man prospered according to his genius, and that every

man conquered according to his strength; and *whatsoever a man did was no crime.*"[8]

- Another Book of Mormon villain, Nehor, implied there would be no consequences to actions, no matter the number or severity: "And he also testified unto the people that all mankind should be saved at the last day, and that they need not fear nor tremble, but that they might lift up their heads and rejoice; for the Lord had created all men, and had also redeemed all men; and, in the end, *all men should have eternal life.*"[9]

The same supposed escape from consequences is also embedded in the idea that men will be saved *in* their sins rather than redeemed *from* their sins.[10]

No consequences. Squishy justice and warrantless mercy. A guaranteed return ticket, an easy short cut, salvation without effort, something for nothing, risk-free sin. It definitely appealed to the lazy, the gullible, and the free-lunch crowd – billions of them.[11]

And still does.

WHO PULLS THE STRINGS?

In an upcoming *Journal of Book of Mormon Studies* article,[12] Craig Nelson points out that the famous second chapter of Second Nephi is in actuality a condensation of the pre-earthly happenings – the Grand Council, the Father's plan, and Satan's counter. I find it intriguing that Lehi, as he counsels his son Jacob in that chapter, explicitly mentions "act and not be acted upon" three times, and implicitly a fourth.[13]

Why this emphasis? President James E. Faust gives us the reason:

> Being acted upon means somebody else is pulling the strings.[14]

That's the puppetry visual. When we act, we call our own shots and pull our own strings – the essence of agency. The more such decisions we make, the greater our experiences, the more we learn (especially from our mistakes), and the more we progress toward eventual exaltation.

When we're acted upon, on the other hand, we are puppets. Those who love bossing others around – from well-meaning busybodies to tolerable authoritarians to outright tyrants – pull the strings. Each is a danger to your being your own agent and **you are in danger of becoming dependent upon them**. Does presumptuous government come to mind?

Satan wants anybody and everybody to pull your strings except you.

Taking responsibility

We exercise agency when we act, but also how we *react*.

I love the story of chief judge and governor Pahoran's reaction to mistaken accusations from his chief captain. As you will remember, Captain Moroni, one of the most righteous soldiers in history, is off in the boonies fighting the Lamanites and has not been resupplied by the government in Zarahemla. Off goes a stinging epistle to Pahoran – soldiers are suffering and hungry, you have withheld provisions, thousands have died who might have been saved, you sit upon your thrones in thoughtless stupor and idleness while enemies spread death, government slothfulness and great neglect, you may even be traitors to your country, and so on, strong letter to follow. Moroni then threatens to return to Zarahemla and mop up the place.[15]

What would have been your reaction had you sat in Pahoran's chair? Wouldn't you have felt justified reaming out Captain Moroni for not understanding that you were just a mite busy fighting the king-men who wanted to overthrow government and church? Perhaps moan about the hand you've been dealt? A falsely accused victim if there ever was one.

But Pahoran exercises mature agency. He gives a status report, but it's not a whiny excuse: the king-men have taken over the city and have allied with the Lamanites, and so he has fled and established a government in exile. He then pens these amazing words:

> And now, in your epistle you have censured me, but it mattereth not; I am not angry, but do rejoice in the greatness of your heart. ... I do joy in receiving your epistle...[16]

Step back from this story a moment. Ever notice how emotions begin small and intensify? "That remark offended me," one person in a discussion might think. What happens in the next few seconds determines the type of person he is becoming by which **staircase of emotions** he chooses. He might choose to feel hurt, then step through dismay, resentment, revenge, anger, and arrive at hate. Or he might cut the offender some slack – "Maybe he's had a bad day" – followed by empathy, compassion, sympathy, kindness, and love.

If the first reaction is a negative emotion and is not curbed, Satan, knowing the corrosive nature of bad emotions, has his playing field. The verb "to stir" (we might use the phrase "to whip up") perfectly captures the escalation pattern. Which is why there are at least 15 scriptures that caution us, such as the Savior's direct warning, "... he stirreth up the hearts of men to contend with anger, one with another."[17]

Pahoran chooses the positive staircase and then exercises even better agency by suggesting a set of steps to solve the problem, which he and Moroni then execute.

Elder Dallin H. Oaks declared:

> Satan would like us to believe that we are not responsible in this life. That is the result he tried to achieve by his contest in the pre-existence. A person who insists that he is not responsible for the exercise of his free agency because he was "born that way" is trying to ignore the outcome of the War in Heaven. We are responsible, and if we argue otherwise, our efforts become part of the propaganda effort of the Adversary.[18]

* * *

When God gave us the gift of agency, He gave us more than *freedom* to choose. He gave us the ***power*** to achieve exaltation, conditioned upon our actions, aligned with accountability, in harmony with justice and the grace of the Savior.

Chapter 4

You Work; I'll Eat

*"There has never been but one question in all civilization –
how to keep a few men from saying to many men:
You work and earn bread and we will eat it."*

– Abraham Lincoln

Welfare that does not require something from the recipient robs people of dignity, but also and more importantly, robs them of their agency and their chance to progress and become what their Father in heaven wants them to be.

This chapter boldly claims that **free goods destroy the individual**. Free food fills the tummy, but corrodes the soul.

Borrowing an analogy from Dinesh D'Souza, if a man is hungry and you give him a sandwich, it's a moral transaction and both of you feel good. But if a third party forces you to give the man a sandwich, the *food* result is the same – the man gets a sandwich – but the *moral* result is vastly different. You resent it, the recipient soon comes to expect another sandwich, and the third party, who doesn't give a sandwich of his own, rides off proclaiming himself to be a morally wonderful human being.

"Whenever the government is involved, there is an element of compulsion, and the effect of compulsion is always to strip the virtue out of the transaction."[1]

HUNGER AND AGENCY

When Adam and Eve were banished from the Garden of Eden, their first concern was getting enough to eat in a lone and dreary world where food did not spontaneously grow on trees. As their posterity multiplied, two opposing thoughts arose that continue to this day:

- I will get enough to eat by my own labors
- I will get enough to eat by taking from the labors of others

As mankind organized, almost all societies developed rules against the latter. Frederic Bastiat, 19th century French economist-philosopher, laid it out this way:[2]

- Life, liberty, and property are gifts from God, precede all human legislation, and are superior to it.
- Man seeks to satisfy his desires with the least possible pain.
- Man can satisfy his wants by labor. This is the origin of *property*.
- Man can also satisfy his wants by consuming the products of the labor of others. This is the origin of *plunder*.
- Man will resort to plunder when it is easier than work.
- Plunder stops only when it becomes more painful and dangerous than labor.
- The law is the collective organization of the individual right to lawful defense.
- The proper use of law is to protect property and punish plunder.

There are two types of plunder. If an *individual* takes someone's fruits of labor, the law punishes this obvious illegal plunder. But what if the *law itself* "takes from some persons what belongs to them, and gives it to other persons to whom it does not belong"? Such can only be called **legal plunder – stealing under color of authority**.

Now here's the threat to agency and the individual. The most popular fallacy of our time, Bastiat writes, is that the law should not only be just, but must be philanthropic. "These two uses of the law are in direct contradiction to each other. We must choose between them. A citizen cannot at the same time be free and not free." One cannot use the law both to protect liberty and advance fraternity; the latter will destroy the former.[3]

A Midwestern governor tweaked his opponents, "When you die and go to heaven, St. Peter is probably not going to ask you what you did to keep government small. But he is going to ask you what you did for the poor."[4] Nice debate tactic, but it falsely implies that helping the poor is directly correlated with the size of government, and that only government can provide resources. The role of agency and individual benevolence is conveniently ignored.

If God's purposes for hunger are to be realized, **helping others must be voluntary**. If voluntary, the poor are fed and the givers enjoy the growth that comes from exercising agency. Both feel thankful for their blessings – food for one and sufficiency to give for the other. If, on the other hand, helping is not voluntary but dictated by authoritarian leaders, the poor may still get fed (minus oh-so-reasonable administrative fees), but who grows? No one. The conscripted giver, unable to exercise agency, is resentful, and the recipient, not knowing whom to thank, in time views the gift as an entitlement for which he need not work.

The Church welfare difference

No one who has been around the Church for long can help but compare our welfare program to the give-them-money-and-food-stamps approach of government. Why does Church welfare work so well while government welfare is so wasteful?

Two reasons: First, our goal is to help people out of poverty; feeding them is just the first step. We are goal focused, not process focused, and we are guided by a direct commandment: "Thou shalt not be idle; for he that is idle shall not eat the bread nor wear the garments of the laborer."[5]

Second, we do not work from a formula – that so much income, so many assets, so many dependents determines welfare. We **insert the judgment of a real person** into the mix who can take into account attitude, motivation, education, marketable skills, etc. and can determine what will best assist that person. Many bishops – *judges* in Israel – discover they handle cases that may appear identical to an outside observer, but, because they are working with the deeper person and not surface requirements, have been prompted to help one through a food order and the other through different means. Yet both are helped toward self-sufficiency.

The Church system involves a real person making a qualitative judgment instead of an apparatchik checking boxes in a formula; involves others to help the member improve his marketable skills; provides for on-going assessments of need; and works with the person so he, exercising his agency, is led to solve his own problem.

Benjamin Franklin affirmed a timeless gospel principle when he said, "In my youth I travelled much, and I observed in different countries, that the more public provisions were made for the poor, the less they provided for themselves, and of course became poorer. And, on the contrary, the less was done for them, the more they did for themselves, and became richer."[6]

Safety net or hammock

If doing good is forced by law, we have false philanthropy. Those who pass such laws will claim they are only organizing what citizens should be doing in the first place, but are not doing consistently or broadly enough. Using the law in this way is enticing: lawmakers gain power giving out goodies and feel good about themselves at the same time. I can imagine, sometime and somewhere, even a group of LDS lawmakers gathering together and singing "Have I Done Any Good in the World Today" as self congratulation for using government power to "do good."[7] The end result is still plunder: the promiser and the beneficiary both gain; the producer of the good loses.

An overwhelming majority in America agrees that the able should give to those who are not able, and the scriptures are replete with admonitions to that end. The argument is whether the state with its police power should be the enforcing mechanism. Once that ominous step is taken – that the law should not only tell man what he *must not* do, but also what he *must* do – then the squabbles consume us: who are the rich, who are the poor, who is able, who isn't, how much, from whom, what is fair share? Where should the line be drawn so a safety net does not become a hammock? The intensity of such definition disputes obscures the greater problem: **forced philanthropy defeats the gift of agency**.

In his March 4, 1925 inaugural address, President Calvin Coolidge said:

> I want the people of America to be able to work less for the government and more for themselves. I want them to have the rewards of their own industry. That is the chief meaning of freedom. Until we can re-establish a condition under which the earnings of the people can be kept by the people, we are bound to suffer a very distinct curtailment of our liberty."

(That was almost a hundred years ago. What would he say today?)

Force curtails our liberty and our agency because individuals make fewer decisions for themselves while the string pullers – who actually believe they have the omniscience to decide what is best for us unenlightened rubes – make more. This works against God's teaching process – that we learn by making decisions and either benefit or suffer from the consequences. With fewer opportunities to decide matters for ourselves – for example, looking a hungry person in the eyes and deciding what we will freely do with our own resources – we have fewer of the vital real-life choices that we were sent here to experience.

Bastiat hammers this home like a gospel doctrine teacher:

> But when the law, by means of its necessary agent, *force*, imposes upon men a regulation of labor, a method or a subject of education, a religious faith or creed – then the law ... substitutes the will of the legislator for [people's] own initiatives. When this happens, the people no longer need to discuss, to compare, to plan ahead; the law does all this for them. Intelligence becomes a useless prop for the people; they cease to be men; they lose their personality, their liberty, their property.[8]

One nibble at a time.

Excessive rules and diminished justice

Laws by nature restrict behavior. The proliferation of laws, however, feeds the idea that government must *control all* our behavior, which soon becomes the dangerous philosophy that government is *responsible for* our behavior. As this seeps through society, people lose self-accountability, and life becomes a game of "it's not wrong unless you get caught."

The original purpose of law was to protect against injury. These *defensive* laws told us what we must not do as well as what we must do to protect ourselves, such as pay taxes for the common defense and to assure domestic tranquility. Justice applied penalties to those who injured others.

Then came a second type of laws, call them *offensive* or redistributive laws, which became the legal plunder discussed above. Too often, legislation may be little more than a congressional wish (think clean air, clean water, equality) and the actual live-by-it-daily laws are legislated by D&C-121 types who itch to tell others what to do. Ensconced into comfy corners of government, they grind out directives away from the spotlight of accountability. We grant those thousands of pages a deference they do not deserve. We hesitate to question. In short order, **legal plunder becomes *organized injustice*.**

It is further abetted by:

- The tendency of many to avoid responsibility – blame others – and to separate consequences from actions, such as abortions of convenience.
- Hidden-purpose legislation – things that look noble on the surface but foster authoritarian mischief underneath.
- The mindset of string pullers who see us as raw clay to be molded.

As government grows, mediating institutions that cushion the individual from the incursions of the state shrink. The individual stands increasingly isolated in the face of government power.

Lousy as living under such smothering state power may be, the true danger is how it undermines both agency and justice. The longer such stifling conditions persist, the more one is lulled into inaction. It becomes harder to find truthful information, harder to fight against the string pullers, and harder to protect the right to choose and to act. It becomes easier to go with the flow, turn problems over to self-anointed decision makers, and, in short, forego the experiences God sent us here to gather.

Too focused on what sounds good than what really works, authoritarian leaders and their rule-writing supporters don't realize, or don't care, that their arrogance mocks God. In taking over so many decisions for the public, they are saying, "You are incapable of running your life, so we will make decisions for you." Which is to say, "You cannot handle and do not deserve agency." Which is to say, "God made a mistake by giving you agency."

God made a mistake? That's what they imply.

The light in this muddle is our hoped-for future because the celestial kingdom will have the fewest rules and regulations. Why? Because those who inherit it will have learned to *govern themselves*. No string pullers needed. Pure agency and pure justice.

Not having to spend eternity under a mile-high stack of regulations should be incentive enough to get there.

* * *

When we in the hereafter have access to the perfect statistics of this life, it will be interesting to discover how many people fell short because they were given too much and how many succeeded because too little.

Chapter 5

LULL, FLATTER, RAGE: THE SECRETS OF NEPHITE VILLAINS

"The louder he spoke of his honor, the faster we counted the spoons."
– Ralph Waldo Emerson

Just as lullabies are sung to an infant, the goals of lulling are the same for an adult: relax, you can trust me, there's nothing to worry about.

On May 29, 1919, Einstein's theory of relativity received its first empirical support through photographs of a solar eclipse confirming that "the planet Mercury deviated by forty-three seconds of arc a century from its predictable behaviour under Newtonian laws of physics."[1]

Whoa! If the laws of the physical world were relative to time and circumstances, many reasoned, why should relativity not apply to the metaphysical world and such things as morality? Coming at a time when philosophies from Marx to Darwin to Freud were challenging the accepted order of things, suddenly everything was shaky and nothing seemed certain. Doubts that anything can be absolute had been set in train.

The battle continues a century later. Moral relativism runs counter to God's plan that we must learn to distinguish truth from error, right from wrong. Relativism has made it easier to discount sin, consequences, justice, mercy, and even the Atonement itself, and offers a convenient hide-behind for those wanting to escape responsibility for their actions. If someone buys that good and evil are imaginary constructs – that nothing can be absolutely true but only relatively valid or invalid depending upon a frame of reference and circumstances – then that someone will fail a major test of mortality.

For those who lull, flatter, and entice people to sin, moral relativism has made their job immensely easier.

First comes lulling

"Oozing charm from every pore, he oiled his way around the floor" goes Henry Higgins' description of his adversary in *My Fair Lady.* The observation also applies to Satan. Elder James E. Faust warned in the October 1987 conference:

> [Satan's] voice often sounds so reasonable and his message so easy to justify. It is an enticing, intriguing voice with dulcet tones. It is neither hard nor discordant. No one would listen to Satan's voice if it sounded harsh or mean.

Claims that there is no devil and if there were he would have horns, tail, and cloven foot are clever deceptions. Lucifer is cunning and charming. It wasn't an uncharismatic klutz who persuaded a third of our Father's children to follow his nefarious plan. As Shakespeare described him in *King Lear*: "The prince of darkness is a gentleman." And others of the ilk in *Hamlet*: "That one may smile, and smile, and be a villain…."

If a poll had been taken as the war in heaven moved toward the climactic decision, I am convinced that the spirits who chose to follow Lucifer would have said that he cared more about them than did the Father. After all, who follows someone they perceive to be uncaring?

God wanted His children to take the risky and sorrowful path of mortality, whereas Lucifer promised that not one soul would be lost. What could be more caring than that? A guarantee to beat all guarantees, had it been true.

Caring is also easy to fake. All you have to do is give away free stuff, as many politicians have discovered, in contrast to requiring work. So it was that billions of the Father's children were taken in by Satan's temporary solicitude and cotton-candy lures instead of recognizing the **true caring embedded in the Father's plan of agency**, personal responsibility, and then rewards beyond our imagination.

Taken to its logical conclusions, the reassurance that all is well means no effort is necessary, and we'll all end up in heaven no matter what we do. Easy street. Here is how Nephi warned of this tactic:

> And others he will pacify, and lull them away into carnal security, that they will say: All is well in Zion; yea, Zion prospereth, all is well – and thus the devil cheateth their souls, and leadeth them away carefully down to hell.[2]

As quoted earlier, Nephi also warned of the eat-drink-and-be-merry types who will say there is no punishment save a few stripes. But if so, it means that the punishment is not equal to the infraction, which means that justice has been diminished. Applied broadly enough, justice diminished is justice destroyed.

Then flattery

After people in a world with shaky foundations have been lulled and reassured, then flattery comes on stage telling them to do whatever they want because there are no absolutes and there will be no consequences to their actions.

Hugh Nibley observed: "Every great mischief in the Book of Mormon starts out with a person who is a master of many words, who is very clever and has a cunning knowledge of the language, and who is above all expert at flattering speech." Further: "If you want to organize a movement, you start out and end up with flattering words, and they always work. Flattering words are those the people want to hear...."[3]

Flattery is associated with more Book of Mormon villains than any other trait: Korihor, Amalickiah, Jacob (the anti-Christ king of a secret combination), Morianton, the Zoramites, Sherem, King Noah and his priests, Jared (not the one of "brother of" fame), the kingmen, the well-known Gadianton, and early Alma who "did speak much flattery to the people."[4] In virtually every case of successful flattery, there was also powerful eloquence:

> Sherem: "And he was learned, that he had a perfect knowledge of the language of the people; wherefore he could use much flattery, and much power of speech *according to the power of the devil*."[5] [Emphasis added]
>
> Gadianton: "... who was exceedingly expert in many words..."[6]
>
> Alma (pre-conversion): "And he was a man of many words...."[7]
>
> Korihor: "And he did rise up in great swelling words ... pleasing unto the carnal mind."[8]

Flattery leads to pride, pride leads to a feeling that one is above the law, which in turn leads to the belief that there is no law – in fact, no sin, no punishment, no heaven, no hell, and especially no devil. The flattery-besotted minds of those – especially the intellectual elites – who seek seers who "speak unto us smooth things"[9] are anxious for such reassurance. Nephi again:

> And behold, others he flattereth away, and telleth them there is no hell; and he saith unto them: I am no devil, for there is none – and thus he whispereth in their ears, until he grasps them with his awful chains, from whence there is no deliverance.[10]

It may surprise that **flattery is more than a schmoozing puff job**.

Indeed, it is a deviously disguised attack on the principle upon which all existence depends – that there is an opposition in all things.[11] Thus, if there is no hell, there is no punishment; if there is no devil, how can there be a God? The flattery level among atheists must be off the charts.

As French poet Charles Baudelaire said 150 years ago, "The devil's finest trick is to persuade you that he does not exist."

Then rage

If lulling and flattering are soft falling leaves, rage is a leaf-blower. As one wag put it, we have enough blood to think or to be angry, but not enough to do both at the same time.

Satan's famous hissy fit is recorded in Moses 1. Moses was transfigured so he could speak face to face with God and behold His glory, which prepared him for battle with Satan. After Moses received his natural strength again (visions are draining, as Joseph Smith found on several occasions), "Satan came tempting him, saying: Moses, son of man, worship me."[12]

Satan's was undoubtedly a polite but firm request at first, but also a "you're nothing special" put down: son of *man*. In my mind's ear, I hear a soothing, charming voice guarded not to be gruff. When Moses refused – "where is thy glory, that I should worship thee?" – out came the fireworks:

> Satan cried with a loud voice, and ranted upon the earth … And now Satan began to tremble, and the earth shook … And it came to pass that Satan cried with a loud voice, with weeping, and wailing, and gnashing of teeth…."[13]

Satan's goal was to so unnerve Moses with temper-tantrum anger that he would accede to Satan's demand. Didn't work, but the tactic has not disappeared. Shortly before the birth of the Savior, rage was taking its toll on the Nephites:

> Satan did stir them up to do iniquity continually; yea, he did go about spreading rumors and contentions upon all the face of the land, that he might harden the hearts of the people against that which was good and *against that which should come*."[14] [Emphasis added]

We also will experience more of this all-purpose weapon that stirs contention, attacks the good, and tempts people to seek authority and riches:

- "...he that hath the spirit of contention is not of me, but is of the devil, who is the father of contention, and he stirreth up the hearts of men to contend with anger, one with another."[15]
- "For behold, at that day shall he rage in the hearts of the children of men, and stir them up to anger against that which is good."[16]
- "The ends of the earth shall inquire after thy name, and fools shall have thee in derision, and hell shall rage against thee."[17]
- "Satan had great power, unto the stirring up of the people to do all manner of iniquity, and to the puffing them up with pride, tempting them to seek for power, and authority, and riches, and the vain things of the world."[18]

A pattern from the Book of Mormon, which was written for our time, shows **rage as a path to power**. It begins with an argument that escalates: Sherem contended with Jacob, calling his teachings blasphemy and a perversion of the law of Moses.[19]

Then anger: Amlici, intending to deprive the people of their religious rights and privileges, and to destroy the church, stirred up anger and caused "much dispute and wonderful contentions."[20] (Such British understatement.)

And finally violence: Lawyers in Ammonihah, among whom Zeezrom was prominent, "...did stir up the people to riotings, and all manner of disturbances ..."[21] Nehor "endeavored to enforce [priestcraft] by the sword..."[22] and slew Gideon in the attempt. And in the wake of rage-addled characters such as Amalickiah, Ammoron, and the king-men, there had been "murders, and contentions, and dissensions, and all manner of iniquity among the people of Nephi ...."[23]

A letter from Giddianhi demanding the surrender of Lachoneus, the Nephite chief judge, demonstrates an elaborate interplay between lull, flatter, and rage – and toss in mock, threaten, and bribe. This leader of the Gadianton robbers begins his demand with flattery and then in stages ... mocks, pities, threatens, struts, justifies, threatens again, flatters again, demands surrender, threatens a third time, sweetens the deal by promising an equal share of the spoils, lulls by promising no harm, threatens a fourth time, distorts the situation by upside-down logic, justifies the good works of his robbers, and ends by demanding compliance.[24]

It would be difficult to find any surrender demand in history that surpasses its complexity, intricacy, and brass.

* * *

The Nephites fought connoisseurs of villainy. We should learn from them.

SECTION II

THE WAR TO DESTROY CHRISTIANITY

"I think we will witness increasing evidence of Satan's power as the kingdom of God grows stronger. I believe Satan's ever-expanding efforts are some proof of the truthfulness of this work. In the future the opposition will be both more subtle and more open. It will be masked in greater sophistication and cunning, but it will also be more blatant. We will need greater spirituality to perceive all of the forms of evil and greater strength to resist it."

– James E. Faust

Chapter 6

The Epitome of Sibling Rivalry

"Nobody ever comes down on Buddhists;
it's always Christians that get a punch in the eye."

– Alice Cooper

If there is anything virtuous, lovely, or of good report or praiseworthy ... Satan cheapens, debases, and perverts it.

In March 2013, an instructor at Florida Atlantic University caused an uproar when, following an *approved* curriculum, he told students to write the name JESUS in big letters on a piece of paper, place it on the floor name side up, and then stomp on it. This juvenile exercise was supposed to teach students to think of the importance of symbols in culture.[1]

So typical of the steps in the mockery formula: Paint the target as laughable, silly, and ridiculous, or as lowly, despicable, and repugnant. Discourage association by sticking "Do Not Touch" labels on persons, beliefs, and practices. Instill shame to be associated with Jesus Christ, and fear to share His teachings.

SATAN'S UNDYING HATRED

Satan "directs his most strenuous opposition at the most important aspects of Heavenly Father's plan of happiness. For example, he seeks to discredit the Savior and the priesthood, to cast doubt on the power of the Atonement, to counterfeit revelation, to distract us from the truth, and to contradict individual accountability."[2]

Early in the Savior's earthly ministry, Satan came with the Big Three temptations[3] using the doubt-producing preface "IF":

- If thou be the Son of God, turn these stones into bread.
- If thou be the Son of God, cast thyself down … and [angels] shall bear thee up, lest at any time thou dash thy foot against a stone.
- All these [kingdoms of the world] will I give thee, if thou wilt fall down and worship me.

Food when hungry, fame when obscure, power when seemingly weak. The Savior's double-entendre answer: "Get thee behind me."

Then came the astonishing attack on Christ's divine birth. The alternative nativity story common among the profane in the 2nd and 3rd centuries, as chronicled in the debate between Origen and Celsus, was that Christ was the illegitimate son of a Roman soldier named Panthera and a promiscuous Mary.[4] Vile as can be.

As Origen put it, "It was to be expected, indeed, that those who would not believe the miraculous birth of Jesus would invent some falsehood." And posed the question "whether He who sends souls down into the bodies of men, degraded Him who was to dare such mighty acts, and to teach so many men, and to reform so many from the mass of wickedness in the world, to a birth more disgraceful than any other, and did not rather introduce Him into the world through a lawful marriage?"[5] Powerful debater, that Origen. (Note also that the doctrine of the pre-mortal existence, eventually jettisoned in the Great Apostasy, was still being taught 200-plus years after Christ's birth.)

What defamation of parentage could be worse than comparing Jesus' Father not to a hard-working carpenter, which most people assumed, but to a philandering Roman soldier – a three-way slap at Father, Son, and Mary, the fair and chosen vessel of God. Giving the soldier a name especially made the story seem accurate.

Through the centuries, Satan has never ceased to vent spleen and bile against the Savior and every aspect of His work.

- Jesus Christ. Merely another itinerant preacher, no one special, but smart enough to capitalize on the frenzy of Jews looking for a messiah who would rescue them from Roman rule. His miracles were sorcery, detractors claimed,[6] and His body was not resurrected but was stolen by His followers when the soldiers who guarded His tomb fell asleep.[7]
- Religion. Opiate of the masses, the product of frenzied minds, the silly superstitions of fools, outdated and boring.
- Sin. An outmoded concept. Everything is relative depending on the person. There are no absolutes. Sex is for pleasure only.
- Hereafter. There is no life after death. Live for today.
- The restored Church. Not a Christian denomination, a cult (only 34% in one of my national surveys are definitely sure that we are not), doesn't accept the Bible, believes in a different Jesus, believes Satan and Jesus were brothers.
- Members. Hicks from the sticks, loonies from the boonies, superstitious rubes out in the desert, downscale intellects, naïve, ignorant, and hopelessly not with it. Uncool. So misled they believe they can become gods and have their own planets.
- Prophets: Cult of the personality. Power seekers – "suits" – who pretend to hear the voice of God.
- Scriptures: The Book of Mormon musical. 'Nuf said.
- Temple ordinances: Foolish traditions, sinister, magic underwear, vain hopes, product of frenzied minds, pretended mysteries.

- Priesthood: A sexist cabal run by oppressive males who treat women as second-class citizens.

Satan's efforts have accelerated immensely since 1820. A rich study in propaganda.

Offended by the name
Of the Savior,
But not by profane
And coarse behavior,

What explanation can there be, other
Than the jealous little brother
In the epitome
Of sibling rivalry?

The intensity increases

The Florida stomping incident is sad evidence of the increasing intensity of hatred toward our Lord. What were they thinking? Were there no other symbols whose role in society could be discussed without poorly hidden hatred? Wouldn't a decent non-believer respect the beliefs of others? Never let a convenient excuse to humiliate the Savior go to waste, must be their slogan. To me it is proof that the intellectual elite cannot abide the idea that there is a higher power than their own minds.

Incidentally, it was a good member of the Church who stood up against the instructor (who professed to be a good Christian, if you can believe it) and refused the exercise. He was suspended, charged with a violation of the student code of conduct, and ordered not to return to class. FAU initially denied he had been suspended, but eventually admitted the attempted punishment, apologized (due to the public exposure, no doubt), and dropped all charges against him.[8]

Tolerance, apparently, is a one-way street.

Many, but not nearly enough, were rightly shocked several years ago when a photographer mocked the Savior by putting a small plastic crucifix in a jar of urine. He was feted for his creativity, and won prizes and public funding.[9] Another artist, if I may loosely use the term, recently ruined a fresco of Christ in a Spanish church, depicted the Savior as a hairy monkey, and was signed to a lucrative royalty deal for merchandising her art.[10]

And how often in common conversations we hear the name of Jesus Christ taken in vain. Though a despicable violation of a commandment, it may be a backhanded affirmation of His divinity. After all, who in our culture uses the name of Allah, Isis, Zeus, Jupiter, or Buddha as a profane interjection?

Of course, there is also mockery of God, Himself:

- When environmental agencies flush a year's supply of water for 500,000 people down a river to lower the temperature to benefit fish, while nearby residents and farmers suffer water shortages, they are mocking God. Fish are more important than God's greatest creation?[11]
- When people pray to Mother Earth (the Gaia hypothesis), they are mocking God for they worship the suit instead of the tailor.
- When activists demonize fossil fuels, they are mocking God who created energy-dense liquids for our benefit and the spread of the gospel. (Ever fly on a battery-powered airplane?)

God is the Father of our spirits and empowers males to become fathers of earthly bodies for those spirits. Satan, bodiless and impotent, can never become such a father, only a father of lies, so he mocks the concept, the Giver, and those who have the privilege of procreation. Feminists say a woman needs a man like a fish needs a bicycle. And have you noticed in movies and advertising that children are wiser than adults and everyone is smarter than dad, often portrayed as a bumbling fool? Is the mockery of fathers in our culture happenstance, or an intentional pattern to disparage a prime and defining characteristic of God – His fatherhood?

So who are the mockers?

Three enemies plagued the Church in the 1830s and 40s: frontier rabble, religious ministers, and apostates. The apostates were the most toxic because as former insiders they were supposedly in the know. Same today. Satan wants mockers who are disaffected saints because they have street cred.

President Boyd K. Packer has said that "cynical mocking … is typical of those who are not faithful and not truly converted."[12] (As many have pointed out, apostates leave the Church, but they cannot seem to leave it alone.) And they surely will be sniping at us until Brunhilde warbles, but the mocking momentum is shifting to atheists. President Packer again:

> Atheists and agnostics make nonbelief their religion and today organize in unprecedented ways to attack faith and belief. They are now organized, and they pursue political power. You will be hearing much about them and from them. Much of their attack is indirect in mocking the faithful, in mocking religion.[13]

Elder Neal A. Maxwell had a great observation: "Why do the disbelievers who line that spacious building watch so intently what the believers are doing?"[14] I love this question because it points out the comedy in our detractors' actions, which in turn suggests that **humor can be an effective tool on our side**. In fact, Psalms 2 says that when kings and rulers take counsel against the Lord, He "shall laugh" and "have them in derision."[15]

* * *

When those who hate Jesus Christ mock us believers as foolish and naïve, why not counter, "Why is someone smart if he uses the five senses to learn, but someone is stupid if he employs those five plus one more?"

Chapter 7

SECULAR RELIGION AND ITS THREE-POUND GOD

"When people stop believing in God, they don't believe in nothing – they believe in anything."

– G. K. Chesterton

Lehi counseled us not to put our trust in the arm of flesh.[1] That should also include the gray-matter flesh between the ears.

In a future public opinion survey, I intend to ask this question:

> "Who or what do you think is the highest power in the universe – God or the mind of man?"

Now, we pollsters know people will at times give socially acceptable answers instead of their true feelings, and I can predict which of these two choices will win a majority. What I will know for sure is that those who say man's mind is the highest power really believe it.

The most universal bondage or subjugation of man, said Elder Quentin L. Cook, is "ideology or political beliefs that are inconsistent with the gospel of Jesus Christ. Substituting the philosophies of men for gospel truth can lead us away from the simplicity of the Savior's message." He further stated that "gospel truths are often rejected or distorted to make them intellectually more appealing or compatible with current cultural trends and intellectual philosophies. If we are not careful, we can be captured by these trends and place ourselves in intellectual bondage."[2]

Intellectuals prideful in the prowess of their minds will always disparage religion, that annoying competitor.

A modern golden calf

If an individual admits that God is the highest power, he must align himself within that belief. But if he can be brought to believe that the highest power is man's mind – a tempting morsel for those with high IQs – then it's trash the silly commandments and bring on the competition to see who will sit at the top of the totem pole.

That is why many intellectuals, infatuated with their brilliance and convinced they are born to rule, reject God, embrace worldly wisdom, and persecute those they consider less cerebrally endowed. **Anyone who worships God interferes with their view of the universe**, and specifically their hoped-for role as one of its masters.

While traditional royal systems put titles in front of a name (King George, Sir John, Lady Margaret, Earl of Sandwich, Duke of Earl), the intellectual aristocracy puts them as initials at the end: MD, Ph.D., J.D., Ed.D., DDS – and that's just the doctorates. Gaining knowledge is good; flaunting it isn't. To be distinguished by ranks is the obvious game as anyone who has attended a university graduation ceremony can attest. Looks like a bomb went off in a paint shop – each color, tassel, and stripe carrying somber significance.

Hugh Nibley nailed it in his opening prayer at BYU's1960 commencement ceremony: "We have met here today clothed in the black robes of a false priesthood."[3] True prophets encourage us to learn truth from all sources, but to beware the "intellectual voices that profess sophistication and superiority."[4] (Ever notice how many think complexity rather than clarity is a sign of intellectual stature?)

Jacob warned:

> O that cunning plan of the evil one! O the vainness, and the frailties, and the foolishness of men! When they are learned they think they are wise, and they hearken not unto the counsel of God, for they set it aside, supposing they know of themselves, wherefore, their wisdom is foolishness and it profiteth them not. And they shall perish.[5]

Now, once this premise of intellectual superiority takes hold, worshipers of the intellect **seek organizations through which to parade skills and exercise power**. One author notes that the market economy does not reward intellectuals "according to their own estimation of their obvious social worth" so intellectuals gravitate toward power and they love the idea of a hierarchy apart from the free market, one that will worship their IQs. Today they "play leading roles in the bureaucracies of the state, as advisors, experts, and administrators, and increasing the power of the state means increasing the power of the intellectuals" – "a place in the sun, in which their cash rewards are almost certainly higher, and in which power rewards are undoubtedly higher."[6]

Thus, the rise of the pretentious non-religious intellectual has been fostered by the rise of the administrative state, and the state in turn uses the supposed omniscience of this intellectual priesthood to claim supremacy. Archbishop of Chicago Francis Cardinal George warns that "this tendency for the government to claim for itself authority over all areas of human experience forms the secularization of our culture. If God cannot be part of public life, then the state itself plays God."[7] G.K. Chesterton adds, "Dethrone God and the state becomes God."[8]

Secular religion – the cult of the state

The first freedom mentioned in the First Amendment was written to protect religion from the power of the state, not vice versa, and that government would favor no particular denomination.

Instead of having ***a*** state religion, such as the Church of England or the Church of Sweden, the irreligion of the intellectual elite has become ***the*** state religion, a secular religion wielding political power. Elder Neal A. Maxwell *in 1978* prophesied its rise.

> [We] shall see in our time a maximum if indirect effort made to establish irreligion as the state religion. It is actually a new form of paganism that uses the carefully preserved and cultivated freedoms of Western civilization to shrink freedom even as it rejects the value essence of our rich Judeo-Christian heritage. … Brothers and sisters, *irreligion as the state religion would be the worst of all combinations.* Its orthodoxy would be insistent and its inquisitors inevitable. Its paid ministry would be numerous beyond belief. Its Caesars would be insufferably condescending. … Your discipleship may see the time come when religious convictions are heavily discounted. M.J. Sobran also observed, "A religious conviction is now a second-class conviction, expected to step deferentially to the back of the secular bus, and not to get uppity about it."[9] **This new irreligious imperialism seeks to disallow certain of people's opinions simply because those opinions grow out of religious convictions**. Resistance to abortion will soon be seen as primitive. Concerns over the institution of the family will be viewed as untrendy and unenlightened.
>
> In its mildest form, irreligion will merely be condescending toward those who hold to traditional Judeo-Christian values. In its more harsh forms, as is always the case with those who dogmatism is blinding, the secular church will do what it can to reduce the influence of those who still worry over standards such as those in the Ten Commandments. It is always such an easy step from dogmatism to unfair play – especially so when the dogmatists believe themselves to be dealing with primitive people who do not know what is best for them. It is the secular bureaucrat's burden, you see.[10] [Emphasis added]

That predicted future is now here.

The battle over religious freedom is thus no longer between religion and non-religion; it is between God-oriented religion and state-oriented religion. Between freely chosen religion and state-ordered official ideology that brooks no dissenting opinions (think fascism, communism, global warming).

Here's the kicker. Both religions want the freedom to believe, act, assemble, and speak. But **while one religion seeks only the right to *persuade*, members of the other seek to *impose* their will** through the state's police and taxing powers. It's like a basketball game except one team has three extra players – the referees.

Secular religion mirrors traditional religion – the president as prophet-cum-messiah, the cabinet as apostles, the bureaucratic elite as high priests using the power of a legislative-judicial-executive trinity, the Federal Register as scripture, all financed by double or triple-rate compelled tithing. But its impact is quite different. The secular state religion …

- Turns hearts away from God and toward the intellect.
- Promises more immediate fulfillment of wants through government largesse.
- Thwarts our missionary work in other countries because the Church is seen as a competitor, and diplomatic assistance may be discouraged.
- Provides an outlet for the intellectual elect to pursue their dreams of power and control. It dangles the irresistible promise of power to those who think they've been short-changed, as tyrants such as Amalickiah have always known.[11]
- Allows false messiahs to more easily appear. No self-proclaimed messiah would get far unless he has his hands on at least a few knobs and levers of power.
- Undermines trust in the Savior – that He is the light and life of

the world, and "without me ye can do nothing."[12] **Government counterfeits that teaching when it says, "You didn't build that"** – in essence, you cannot do anything without government.

Government beyond the Founders' intent replaces God as the giver of blessings, the center of society, and the object of adoration. To hide their agenda, however, intellectual elites give token lip service to Christianity to calm those they consider Duck-Dynasty-meets-Larry-the-Cable-Guy types.

Just as Christianity has a variety of denominations, so too secular religion. These God-less faiths are differentiated by the god they choose to worship – intellect, power, wealth, fame, beauty, sex, environment, and so on. Their names may not be emblazoned on buildings, but if they were and if truth in advertising prevailed, we'd see such names as ...

Church of the Omnipotent State

Church of the Intellectual Elite

Church of Gaia our Mother Earth

Church of Sexual Libertines

Church of Equality

Church of the Greens

Church of Hollywood Fame

Church of Lucre

Church of the Occult

Church of Leisure

Church of Cave 17

All hating competition from on high.

Here's the danger. A state that plays God will soon have a leader who becomes deity-in-chief. Having clawed his way to the top of the power pile, he will turn paranoid and then tyrannical. He will demand loyalty and worship. Tyrants, almost by set formula, will always seek to destroy traditional religion because **religion is the worship of a Competitor the tyrant cannot match**. And the tyrant, narcissistic as can be, cannot stand it.

As one columnist put it, "It's one of the peculiar ironies of history that the people most eager to hang the priests are those most eager to replace them."[13]

The great and abominable church

A few chapters into the Book of Mormon, Nephi writes of a vision in which an angel tells him that there are two churches only: the church of the Lamb of God and the church of the devil, aka the great and abominable church.[14] What we know from the 13th and 14th chapters of 1 Nephi is that this second church …

- Was founded by the devil, is the mother of abominations, whore of all the earth, sits upon many waters, has dominion over all the earth.
- Slays, tortures, and brings down into captivity the saints of God.
- Desires gold, silver, all manner of precious clothing, and harlots.
- Seeks the praise of the world by destroying the saints of God.
- Took away many plain and precious things from the Bible causing many to stumble and Satan to have great power over them.
- Will gather together multitudes upon the face of all the earth to fight against the Lamb of God and there will be wars and rumors of wars among all the nations.

The age-old self-focused desires of man are all there: power, wealth, and fame, all to be used to destroy the work of God. Reading later from the plates of brass, Nephi tells his brethren that the kingdom of the devil includes "all churches which are built up to get gain, and all those who are built up to get power … become popular … seek the lusts of the flesh and the things of the world…."[15]

In a landmark article on this topic,[16] Stephen Robinson persuasively demonstrates...

- That "the term *great and abominable church* means an immense assembly or association of people bound together by their loyalty to that which God hates."
- That contrary to the supposition of some members, the Roman Catholic church could not be the great and abominable church because "Roman Catholicism as we know it did not yet exist when the crimes described by Nephi were being committed." And further, "no single known historical church, denomination, or set of believers meets all the requirements for the great and abominable church...."
- That "membership" in the church of the devil is "based more on who has your heart than on who has your records."
- That the "Mother of Harlots ... can represent the false beliefs and ideologies that often capture and motivate governments."

So where today is there an immense association of people bound together by their loyalty to that which God hates – an association that worships the mind instead of God, that seeks power, enjoys a luxurious lifestyle, and competes for the plaudits of the world?

Is it just possible that Nephi described today's intellectual elites, those who have wormed their way into positions of power? And isn't this power being increasingly employed to the detriment of religious freedom? Just as early Christianity was a victim of Hellenization – the polluting of Christ's teachings with Greek philosophies – is not religion today similarly corrupted by man's shallow philosophies?

Secular intellectualism of today is the same great and abominable church as Hellenized Christianity of the second century.

Stephen Robinson concludes:

> The historical abominable church of the devil is that apostate church that replaced true Christianity in the first and second

> centuries, teaching the philosophies of men mingled with scriptures. It dethroned God in the church and replaced him with man by denying the principle of revelation and turning instead to human intellect. As the product of human agency, its creeds were an abomination to the Lord, for they were idolatry: men worshipping the creations, not of their own hands, but **of their own minds**." [Emphasis added]

Spot on.

* * *

If someone claims the human mind is the greatest power in the universe, ask him to create a blade of grass.

Chapter 8

The Miter and The Gavel

"Nothing is more dreaded than the national government meddling with religion."

– John Adams

Secular religionists ache to put traditional religion in its place – subservient to government, docile and deferential. They refuse to stand when Handel's "Hallelujah Chorus" is played lest they be deemed supportive of Christianity, but let the latest Hollywood bimbo step on stage and you'd think they were suddenly sitting on tacks.

In the summer of 1954, Senator Lyndon Johnson of Texas swayed the U.S. Senate into changing one little item in the Internal Revenue Service code. On a voice vote. Without debate. It has bedeviled religions ever since.

Let me use a parallel. Imagine that someone offered to pay you if you would not say certain things. You would reject it. Same thing if someone said they would pay you if you did say certain things. You can't be bribed, right?

But what if it happened this way? You are told you qualify for a better tax rate than your neighbor and, because it seems harmless enough, you accept it. Then after you have come to be dependent on the savings, government comes along and says, "You have had the benefit of a tax break for lo these many years. You will lose that tax exemption if you say X." Now what?

Most would cave. And that is exactly what happened to religion on that summer day 60 years ago.

Religions had enjoyed tax-exempt status since the introduction of the income tax in 1913, but Johnson itched to curb the influence of non-profit organizations, including churches, in his re-election campaign. Having been elected to the Senate in 1948 in what many now concede was a fraudulent victory, he feared that the churches would endorse his opponent. So Johnson pressured solons to ban non-profits from not only opposing any candidate, but from endorsing as well. Known as the Johnson Gag Order, it remains part of the IRS code to this day. Threatened with denial of tax-exempt status, churches buckled.[1]

That is the reason a letter from the First Presidency is read from the pulpit every election year to confirm that the Church complies with this regulation. Not that the Church would endorse candidates absent the gag order, but some religions would, and the First Amendment says they have that right without being penalized. The restriction obviously violates religious freedom, chills free speech, and weakens America.

Distort the meaning of separation of church and state

The relationship between government and religion is clearly stated in the First Amendment: "Congress shall pass no law respecting an establishment of religion, or prohibiting the free exercise thereof…" – commonly known as the Establishment Clause and the Free Exercise Clause.

Having felt the pressure of religion abetted by state power, the Founding Fathers were firm that **no religion should become the state**

religion – that is, no Church of America along the lines of the Church of England, of Sweden, of Norway, etc. When Thomas Jefferson originated the phrase "a wall of separation between Church & State" in a letter to the Danbury Baptist association in Connecticut in 1802[2] (the phrase is not in the Constitution), it was fully in harmony with the intent of the First Amendment – that churches would be protected from the power of the state, not that the state needed to be protected from the power of the church, and that people would be protected from a state-sponsored favorite church. No one would own both miter and gavel.

Those conditions so stated, the Founding Fathers never intended for religion to be shunted to the sidelines. Elder Neal A. Maxwell warned, "Our founding fathers did not wish to have a state church established nor to have a particular religion favored by government. They wanted religion to be free to make its own way. But neither did they intend to have irreligion made into a favored state church."[3] But with the distortion of "separation of church and state," a vocal minority clamored for **no religion at all in the public square**.

To some extent they have been successful in curbing the influence of religion in public policy. They have created a vacuum in that religious voices historically heard in public debate are no longer there. Those who believe they are intellectually superior, and deserve the accouterments thereof, are filling that vacuum and wielding political power.

The Book of Mormon warns that pride of intellect leads to persecution of those of humble religious beliefs and less favored with education opportunities,[4] which can morph into restrictions on religion. M. J. Sobran, quoted by Elder Maxwell, described how society has gravitated from support for religious freedom to indifference to hostility:

> It takes a special ingenuity to wring out of [the First Amendment] a governmental indifference to religion, let alone an aggressive secularism. Yet there are those who insist that the First Amendment actually proscribes governmental partiality not only to any single religion, but to religion as

> such.... It is startling to consider that a clause clearly protecting religion can be construed as requiring that it be denied a status routinely granted to educational and charitable enterprises, which have no overt constitutional protection. Far from *equalizing* unbelief, secularism has succeeded in virtually *establishing* it.
>
> [She continues:] What the secularists are increasingly demanding, in their disingenuous way, is that religious people, when they act politically, act only on secularist grounds. They are trying to equate *acting* on religion with *establishing* religion. ... the consequence of such logic is really to establish secularism ... to internalize the major premise of secularism: that religion has no proper bearing on public affairs.[5] [Emphasis original]

Some people think that separation of church and state means that religion-based opinions may not influence public policy, but that the state may tell religions what they may and may not do.

A sly substitution

When the Employment Non-Discrimination Act (ENDA) was voted out of a Senate committee, some complained about the "egregiously broad religious exemption" in the bill "that would leave too many jobs outside the measure's protection...." They complained that the "exemption extends way beyond houses of worship encompassing personnel at *hospitals and universities who perform no real religious function....*"[6] [Emphasis added]

Notice how **they cleverly substitute freedom of *worship* for freedom of *religion*** – that no real religious function can be performed beyond houses of worship. If one accepts their sly deception, then religion becomes nothing but worship and must be contained within churches, chapels, synagogues, temples, and mosques. Buildings. Confined space and the only space where religion should exist. That religion has multiple facets beyond worship services escapes them.

Putting aside for the moment that if legislation can grant an exemption, later legislation can rescind it, the question becomes: What is religion and how far does it extend? Does religion extend to affiliated entities such as hospitals (14% are Catholic affiliated) and universities?

- Does religion cover the church custodian, the gardener, the scoutmaster of a church-sponsored Boy Scout troop? What about professors or surgeons at church-related universities or hospitals?
- May the Catholic Church refuse to allow an on-site wedding ceremony in a Catholic hospital if a gay man is dying of AIDS and desires a wedding ceremony with his partner as a final expression of their love?
- If Indiana legalizes same-sex marriage, may Notre Dame refuse to allow an open-air gay wedding ceremony in a picturesque corner of its beautiful campus?
- May BYU refuse to hire a qualified professor who is actively gay?
- What about soup kitchens, clothing stores such as Deseret Industries, religion-based welfare assistance, counseling services, and so on? Do these count as elements of religion?

How exactly is religion defined, and more importantly, **who gets to do the defining?**

The state seems to have claimed that territory by its actions against religion-affiliated and faith-guided entities. Consider these current religious liberty cases:[7]

- The HHS contraception mandate. The Affordable Care Act (aka Obamacare) requires employers to provide contraceptive coverage in their health plans. Why should a business be required to provide products that are cheap and readily available throughout society, save it be to establish state domination and as a slap to certain religions' doctrines? Further, government says businesses do not have religious freedom rights. Opponents such as Hobby Lobby say business owners have religious freedoms and shouldn't be required to check them at the door before doing business. (Fortunately, so far at least, the Supreme Court agrees with the Hobby Lobby stance.)

- Adoption agencies. Catholic Charities ceased to provide adoption services when Massachusetts mandated that same-sex couples also qualify as adoptive parents, and other churches now offer only adoption counseling rather than facilitate actual adoptions.
- Abortion drugs. More states are requiring all pharmacists to fill prescriptions for abortion-inducing drugs even though a pharmacist may be conscientiously opposed and another pharmacist is available to provide the drug.[8]
- High school commencement ceremonies. A school district in Wisconsin rented a church for a high school graduation ceremony. Lawsuit time. Government endorsing a religion, you know the drill. What would have happened had the church turned down the offer to rent its property?
- The pledge of allegiance. Even though federal courts have upheld the "under God" phrase in the pledge of allegiance, atheists in Massachusetts are suing to have it removed, arguing that it violates Massachusetts's equal rights act by casting atheists as unpatriotic second-class citizens.[9] And where did this idea come from? According to one of the plaintiffs, "It's an approach that has been successful in challenging traditional marriage statutes in other states."[10]
- Tax probes. The IRS has audited religious groups out of all proportion to their incidence, especially pro-life ministries. It has even demanded to know the content of a pro-life group's prayers! Other denominations have been ordered to turn over their membership lists.[11]

Our society is built upon the rule of law; our law is built upon the Constitution; the Constitution is built upon the religious faith of the people – religion and morality being indispensable to political prosperity, as George Washington phrased it.[12]

That is the reason that religious freedom is the first freedom mentioned in the Bill of Rights. It hangs together with four others: speech, press, assembly, and right to petition. Destroy this linchpin and all others will crumble.

To be successful in this battle between miter and gavel, we must become to the First Amendment what the National Rifle Association is to the Second Amendment, defense attorneys are to the Fifth Amendment, and states are to the Tenth Amendment.

Runaway speech codes

Silencing all individual conversations is impossible, but squelching sermons is a real possibility and will be a major battlefield in the years ahead. Universities have become test markets for freedom of speech theories by censuring students who utter what they deem hate speech, lest some poor soul feel offended. Their rules are now spreading into society at large and lap at the doors of our churches. The problem? By definition, preaching against sin will always offend someone, namely the sinner.

University radicals spilling into the streets once came mainly from the political science and economics departments. Not any more. The push for speech codes, trigger warnings about reading material for certain classes, definitions of hate speech, cordoning off free-speech zones, and many other restrictions now originate from English professors more than any other academic discipline. (Perhaps words being the weapons in the war in heaven might have something to do with it.)

The campus, with its suppressing, politically correct speech codes, has become the least free zone in America, not counting prisons. It has also become our early-warning indicator of what the secular elite would impose on society as a whole.

While it is generally accepted that speech can be curtailed if it blatantly incites violence, we now find one-sided speech restrictions based solely on perceived disrespect or annoyance. University classes on the filthiest sexual deviancies hide behind free speech and are praised as modern, artistic, and liberating, but a cross on a necklace, a Bible verse on a dorm door, and references to Christmas are somehow offensive.

The rules of this game seem to be that it is okay to cite Nietzsche, Hegel, Keynes, Marx, Darwin and the goofballs of Comedy Central, but reference God, Christ, or the Bible and the non-religious elite react as if you had flashed a Luger at a garden party. Comedian Bill Maher can call God a psychotic mass murderer who drowns babies (referencing the movie *Noah*) and people shrug, but let a preacher call certain behaviors a sin and watch the clamor to silence him.

That's the problem with runaway speech codes. To preach repentance as commanded, the sin for which repentance is needed must be identified. Identifying that sin requires precise words – words that people increasingly find offensive. **Speech codes and preaching repentance can never coexist.**

Not many ticks of the clock before pharisaical bureaucrats borrow pages from university speech codes and give them the force of society-wide regulations, especially targeted at Christianity.

An ally in the fight to protect religious freedom, our friend Cardinal Francis George, predicted that "the greatest threat to world peace and international justice is the nation state gone bad, claiming an absolute power, deciding questions and making 'laws' beyond its competence."[13]

Not welcome in the public square

Shopkeepers in Germany during Hitler's reign hung the sign, "Juden unerwünscht" – Jews not welcome. If today's public square were a storefront and certain elites had the way, the signs would say, "Religions not welcome." Values molded by religious beliefs, they say, have no place in the public square – "You're forcing your beliefs on us" or "You want a theocracy." Tiresome mantras.

Let's look at three examples.

First, no public prayers. Commenting on a case then before the U.S. Supreme Court, a major newspaper editorialized that governments such as city councils should not have "a blank check to pray in a whole community's name with language drawn from a particular faith" – that people shouldn't have to endure routine official prayers 'in the name of Jesus' as the price of participating in local government."[14]

Here we go again. Funny how the great champions of diversity want conformity, and how preachers of tolerance reverse course when it comes to religion.

The elite seem to believe the public isn't smart enough to understand that a town council prayer by a clergyman is not a government endorsement. There can be few (perhaps the town drunk) who are not aware that people take turns – last week a Catholic priest gave the prayer, this week it was a Mormon bishop, and next week a Wiccan priestess. Do the elite really think people are so ignorant and gullible that a flavor-of-the-week prayer will drive them to that church on Sunday? If having the honor of invoking God's blessings on a city council's proceedings really had an endorsement impact on the petitioner's denomination, then show me that attendance at each religion's weekly worship services waxes and wanes with who gave the prayer at Thursday's council meeting. You will find no such correlation.

These don't-taint-me-with-religion wusses hold that all public prayers should be nonsectarian, that is, stripped of language preferential to a particular denomination. But how can a Christian offer a sincere prayer if he must delete all references to Christ, if he cannot close in the Savior's name? How can one even begin a prayer without expressing a religious preference in the form of the Addressee – God, our Father, Allah, Isis, etc.?

Those who love to tell others what to do want to sanitize public prayers so they won't offend sensitive ears. Just mumble a jumble of mushy platitudes. I say that such hollow prayers offend God's ears, and the whining is directed almost exclusively toward one religion. Think about it. Who among us is offended if a Muslim references

Mohammad or Allah, or if a Wiccan speaks of "Mighty mother, daughter of the Nile"? We'll even respect an atheist's moment of silence if that is his "prayer." So if someone cannot stand to hear the word "Jesus," that someone needs a life.

The editorial noted that in the council meetings of the town at the center of the Supreme Court case (Greece, New York), two-thirds of prayers concluded in Jesus' name, with "references to 'Jesus Christ,' 'Jesus,' 'Your Son' or the 'Holy Spirit'" sprinkled throughout. Oh, the ignominy. The town is probably more than 67% Christian and yet it is somehow unfair for Christians to be proportionately represented. A minister should not be forced to pray in a way he usually does not, or prevented if he does.

As it turns out, the Supreme Court in May, 2014, supported public prayer: "The First Amendment is not a majority rule, and government may not seek to define permissible categories of religious speech. Once it invites prayer into the public sphere, government must permit a prayer giver to address his or her own God or gods as conscience dictates, unfettered by what an administrator or judge considers to be nonsectarian." A 5-4 decision.[15]

I'm afraid it will be back and the new attack will seek to prevent city councils from inviting "prayer into the public sphere" in the first place.

Second, it would be hard to top San Antonio's 2013 antics regarding employment in the public square. When this city council deliberated expanding non-discrimination protections based on sexual orientation and gender identity, there was much in the ordinance beyond complaint. But the policy precluded anyone being appointed to office or granted a city contract if they had ever "demonstrated a bias, *by word or deed*" against any person on the basis of sexual orientation or gender identity.[16] Ever.

So if someone had opined against homosexual behavior, say, in a sermon or class at church, that person's words would have disqualified him from appointed city office and competing for business with the city.

Free speech? And in Texas to boot.

Fortunately, the punishment for past words was taken out before passage, but it revealed the **naked intent of the drafters to silence all religious speech** against gay behavior. If they could have made it stick, they would have. The phrase "by word or deed" remains, but this time it only applies to words spoken while a sitting city appointee.[17] That's a relief? Past free speech won't be prosecuted, only new "free speech." Censorship still reigns and no city official or employee dares voice an opposing opinion … even in church.

Pity the poor bishop or teacher who works for San Antonio Monday through Friday and speaks against sins on Sunday. They are not only muzzled in the public square, but also in church circles. And if speaking against homosexuality is verboten today, which of the Ten Commandments will be safe from speech police tomorrow? Might such thinking spread and prevent missionaries from proselytizing with their local-government-prohibited offensive messages?

Third, even the military, consistently ranked as the public institution people have the most confidence in (Congress is lowest),[18] has exhibited worrisome behavior that we would not have thought possible a few years ago.

Two chaplains were told they cannot pray in the name of Jesus.[19] The Air Force Academy told a cadet he could not post a biblical passage of inspiration on his personal whiteboard (fortunately rescinded when many classmates posted Bible and Quran verses on theirs).[20] An officer was told to remove the Bible from his desktop lest someone be offended, no matter that it had been in the easily accessible spot for 18 years.[21] And the Defense Department revoked permission for a printing company to include the logos of service branches on Bibles it prints for sale on military bases.[22]

Gone are the days when a president, Franklin Roosevelt, would write the prologue to the Gideon Bibles given to servicemen: "As Commander-in-Chief I take pleasure in commending the reading of the Bible to all who serve in the armed forces of the United States."

Elder Neal A. Maxwell again:

> ... if people are not permitted to advocate, to assert, and to bring to bear, in every legitimate way, the opinions and views they hold that grow out of their religious convictions, what manner of men and women would they be, anyway?[23]

* * *

So how do the secular religionists get the gavel to dominate the miter?

1. Begin with a class of supposed victims of discrimination and stir up sympathy.
2. Introduce noble-intention legislation to correct the problem.
3. Grant religion an exemption so the bill will pass, but make it as narrow as possible.
4. Use the legislation to establish the power of government to define what constitutes a religion.
5. Label religious opposition as unfair and hateful.
6. Demand that religions not participate in public policy discussions and that faith-based opinions be barred.

Coming to a city near you.

Chapter 9

Send in the Clowns

"Who are you going to believe, me or your lying eyes?"

– Groucho Marx

Satan works in devious ways, his miseries to perform.

What better way to deceive and mock than sending false messiahs to dilute the claims of the true One.

When I asked my go-to history expert, Brian Thomassen, for the most interesting messianic clowns, he suggested Sabbatai Zevi, a 17th century Sephardic Jew who lived in Turkey. Sabbatai proclaimed himself the long-awaited Messiah and in the wake of pogroms that had wiped out a third of European Jewry, the remainder being of a mind to consider messianic claims, his fame spread.

Well, the Ottoman Turks didn't cotton to this threat to their power for some reason, so the sultan devised a test. Sabbatai could face a volley of arrows and come through unscathed, or he could convert to Islam. Facing second thoughts about his claims, he thought it better to be a live Muslim today than a dead messiah tomorrow. He converted.[1]

Why take a chance?

The ultimate identity theft

False messiahs come in two packages: those claiming to be *the* Messiah and those more humbly posturing only as *a* messiah.

Wikipedia lists over 40 Jewish claimants to be the original Messiah, and more than 30 Christians who have claimed to be the Messiah of the Second Coming.[2] (Even Muslims join in with seven contenders.) If we include secular leaders and celebrities whose followers, if not themselves, consider them to be a messiah, then the list expands considerably.

There was a George Baker who redesigned himself as Father Divine, God Himself (perhaps the earliest TV evangelist). More recently we had Sun Myung Moon, founder of the Moonies, who labeled himself the Second Coming of Christ anointed to finish Jesus' mission. And always present have been those claiming to be the reincarnation of Christ, even including a woman.[3]

The true Messiah will return again to save the world from evil. It follows that **ordinary messiahs must also promise to save the world** ... from something. That something could be war, economic collapse, oppressive political systems, environmental disaster, and any other imaginable catastrophe. Current examples include Al Gore, whose oft-stated goal is to save the planet, and Prince Charles who said, "My duty is to save the world."[4] A segment of President Barack Obama's followers have cast him as a messiah. I am unaware of a demurral. (As a side note, the Beatles didn't seek to save the world from anything, but nonetheless elevated themselves to messiah status when John Lennon said, "We're more popular than Jesus."[5])

Then there are the unintentional false messiahs such as Rachel Carson. This author of *Silent Spring* – there might be a springtime when birds don't chirp and animals don't frolic – became the fad messiah for the movement to save the environment by outlawing the pesticide DDT that kills malaria-bearing mosquitoes.

The debate has raged for five decades and this is not the forum to consider mounds of material on the topic. But what we know is … (1) that as DDT use goes up, malaria goes down … (2) but that it carries environmental consequences … (3) that someone or something fanned the thin-bird-eggshells hysteria … (4) that this delayed an intelligent cost-benefit analysis and a balanced use policy … and (5) that it resulted in millions of children dying needlessly.[6]

I find it difficult to believe that the adversary was not involved.

Near the end of his mortal ministry, the Savior warned that "there shall arise false Christs, and false prophets…."[7] Nephi also warned of such false messengers and the futility of Jews looking for other than the true Messiah: "… for there should not any come, save it should be a false Messiah which should deceive the people…."[8]

So what are the traits that distinguish a false messiah from the Savior? I submit that the most important red flag centers on a me-complex:

The True Messiah	A False Messiah
Love one another	Love me
It's all about the Father	It's all about me
The glory be thine	The glory be mine
Do what is right	Do what I want
No blessing is beyond reach	No blessing, period
All that the Father has shall be yours	All that you have shall be mine
I will save mankind so they may have power	I will claim to be saving the earth so I gain power
I have come that they may have life more abundantly	They are here so I may have life more abundantly

Imagine a want ad in the Satan Sentinel:

> *Wanted: false messiah. Must be charming, persuasive, and a convincing liar, able to feign caring and fake sincerity. Ruthless, cunning, and narcissistic traits a plus. High salary, full benefits, and cult of the personality worship. Applications for false prophets also being accepted. No past experience needed; on-job training provided. Job description: destroy Christianity.*

Such false messiahs will not seem evil at first, but will be charming and solicitous of the people. As Alexander Hamilton warned in Federalist 1: "Of those men who have overturned the liberties of republics, the greatest number have begun their career by paying an obsequious court to the people ..."

Sooner or later, messiah pretenders overplay their hand. The worship of the people is too heady. They claim too much. Their prophesies become spectacular flops. The signs will eventually be obvious to all.

False teachings

The non-corporeal clowns Satan dispatches are his angels who whisper false teachings. Along with the normal tripe that the Church employs foolish ordinances to enslave people, opposes progress, usurps power, and denies people their rights and privileges, the apostate doctrines are well known:

- Modern-day revelation is denied.
- Prophets and apostles are no longer needed.
- Feeling oneself called to the ministry is sufficient authority.
- Reincarnation replaces the story of our pre-mortal existence.
- The Trinitarian doctrine muddies an understanding of the Godhead.
- Indulgences substitute for repentance.
- Baptism by sprinkling destroys the symbolism Christ intended.
- Infant baptism is an abominable distortion of Christ's Atonement.

- The concept of grace has been cheapened.
- Many offices in the original Church have been changed.

Then come the smears to demean the Savior's re-established original Church. A fear in the 19th century was that Mormons would "steal Christian bodies and souls through kidnapping and conversion..."[9] and a secret conspiracy to take over government lingered into the 2012 campaign when prominent writers "pondered what it would mean to have someone in the White House whose religious leaders dictate his behavior."[10]

I have experienced the nonsense first hand. As my companion and I were going about our missionary labors in Esslingen, Germany, someone showed us a pamphlet that warned people against us. It told the story of a woman who ostensibly joined the Church, moved to America, became disillusioned, returned to Germany, and tearfully told her minister her odyssey. Poorly written and obviously rushed into print, it went from one salacious episode to another and finished up with the woman sobbing (as close as I can remember the words), "The final humiliation was when the Mormon priests pushed me out of the second story of the Salt Lake temple into the Great Salt Lake to be baptized."

I didn't know whether to laugh, punch a hole in the wall, or find the woman and recruit her for the Olympics. The related rumor is that Mormons have secret tunnels that lead directly to the Salt Lake temple through which missionaries spirit away young ladies. Returned missionaries who served in countries as far away as Denmark and New Zealand have told me they heard people in those lands seriously declare it to be true.

Tunnels from Denmark! How could any person in the 1960's ever think such absurd things? Well, maybe for the same reason that people 50 years later still believe the preposterous about us.

All part of destroying restored Christianity.

* * *

Book of Mormon villains share seven traits in common – eloquence, flattery, pride, lying, cunning, deceit, and contention. All come together in false messiahs who deceive and blind with their subtle craftiness and cunningly devised fables.[11]

Dangerous clowns.

SECTION III

THE WAR TO DESTROY THE FAMILY

"The family is ordained of God. Marriage between man and woman is essential to His eternal plan. Children are entitled to birth within the bonds of matrimony, and to be reared by a father and a mother who honor marital vows with complete fidelity. Happiness in family life is most likely to be achieved when founded upon the teachings of the Lord Jesus Christ."

– The Family
A Proclamation to the World

Chapter 10

Cisgender Heteronormative Created He Them?

"The real issue in the Proposition 8 debate – an issue that will not go away in years to come … – is whether the opponents of Proposition 8 should be allowed to change the vital institution of marriage itself."

– Dallin H. Oaks

Adam and Eve were married before the Fall. Marriage came before death. That God created marriage before man created governments not only buttresses the doctrine of eternal marriage, but also tells us … don't mess with it. Man cannot change eternal institutions.

But Satan keeps trying. He attempts to undermine the family by confusing gender, promoting sexual relations outside of marriage, ridiculing marriage, and discouraging childbearing by married adults who would otherwise raise children in righteousness.[1]

The National Rifle Association once asked me to team up with a Democratic firm to do a comprehensive national study of the gun-control issue. The rules were that both pollsters had to agree on methodology, sample, and question wording. Each would have veto power and each could analyze and publicize results as desired. Fair as can be. Yet the Democratic pollsters contacted turned it down because, as each said, "I don't agree with the mission of the sponsor."

Now compare that to the story of a New Mexico photographer. Because of her religious beliefs, Elaine Huguenin refused to use her creative talent to photograph a same-sex commitment ceremony saying that her work and her presence would imply approval. She was sued. Her attorneys established that the market was not closed to the lesbian plaintiffs; numerous photographers were willing to memorialize the occasion with a quality at least equal to that of the photographer in point. She simply didn't agree with the mission of the couple.

To no avail. The New Mexico Supreme Court ruled against her – a concurring judge wrote that the photographer had to channel her conduct "so as to leave space for other Americans who may believe something different,"[2] – and the U.S. Supreme Court in 2014 refused to hear her appeal.

Please tell me how Ms. Huguenin's rationale differs from that of political pollsters who only work for candidates and on issues they agree with? Are pollsters' political beliefs superior to her religious beliefs? May I reject customers because of my political beliefs but she can't reject them because of her religious beliefs? Because she lost in court, why should I not be required to accept business from Democrats, or my counterparts forced to accept business from Republicans?

To extend the parallel, what if a same-sex-marriage organization asked me to conduct research for them? If I refused, would a judge fine me for discrimination? Why haven't we pollsters on both sides of the aisle been taken to court?

Well, it turns out that ceremony pictures in the New Mexico suit were not the goal. The plaintiffs wanted a test case to bring to court. They wanted someone to be forced, by her presence, to appear to approve of what she did not approve of. They wanted her punished for her religious beliefs and practices.

Why can a same-sex couple command space in the marketplace against the religious rights of others, but space for a Christian must stop at the inside walls of his church?

The stage

From the *Proclamation on the Family*, we learn that "marriage between a man and a woman is ordained of God and … is essential to His eternal plan." Its critical importance could hardly be more clearly articulated.

Satan has tried three methods to thwart God's purposes:

> Mock – make marriage ***negative*** through ridicule. It's old fashioned, stupid, archaic, a symbol of male oppression, out of date, restrictive, unequal, and bigoted because it excludes other arrangements of love.
>
> Ignore – make it ***neutral*** by skipping it. Erase the stigma of cohabitation by claiming marriage is unneeded, superfluous, no big deal. A recent report from the Centers for Disease Control and Prevention estimated that half of all American women are cohabiting.[3]
>
> Expand – make it ***positive*** by adding definitions. If marriage is so good, let others in on it. Apply the label to any and every combination of desires and orientations. Smother it with love, dilute it, weaken it, and, in time, destroy it.

He also cheapens the noble purpose of procreative power and wants everyone to believe any and all sexual behaviors are normal. What must be a new record in successful deception happened when a gay member of the Church exulted that a judge's ruling legalizing same-sex marriage in Utah "means that the path toward godhood is opened."[4] Talk about addlepated reasoning.

EQUALITY, ELASTICITY, EXTINCTION

Same-sex marriage is not Satan's end goal, but merely one step in a cleverly disguised process. Instead of the complementarity of the sexes and their procreative powers as a couple, he makes commitment and love the sole basis for marriage. Then it's legalize same-sex marriage ("If they love each other, why can't they be married?"). Then expand marriage to include other combinations. Soon everything is marriage and nothing is marriage.

In the wake of the U.S. Supreme Court hearings on the federal Defense of Marriage Act (DOMA) and California's Proposition 8 held in the spring of 2013, one editorial observed:

> "...for the Court to transform the definition of marriage for one group fundamentally restructures it for all groups and makes it harder for society through its representatives to rule out anything that adults want to call 'marriage.'"[5]

The lesbians and gays of the LGBT community may initially be satisfied if same-sex marriage is legalized, but then comes the question, "If we accommodate the Ls and the Gs, how can we not accommodate the Bs?" The clamor for bisexual marriage (in the name of equality, of course) will rise and we will have ... threesomes (there's already a word for it: *throuples*). And if threesomes, can foursomes be far behind? Goodbye golf term.

Satan insidiously uses the coercive gay rights movement to achieve his real goals: marriage extinction and normalization of homosexual behavior. One lesbian leader candidly admitted the equality-elasticity-extinction thinking at a Sydney Writers Conference in 2011:

> "It's a no-brainer that we should have the right to marriage but equally I think that it is a no-brainer that the institute of marriage should not exist. That causes my brain some trouble. Part of the reason that it causes me trouble is that fighting for gay marriage generally involves lying about what we are going to do with marriage when we get there.

> Because we lie that the institution of marriage is not going to change. It's going to change and it should change. And again it should not exist."[6]

One person's rantings? We shall see. At the very least, Satan sows confusion with increasing variations of marriage so that the institution loses its meaning.

Normality and equivalence

More than wanting to legalize same-sex marriage, the activist LGBT community wants society's unreserved approval of their behavior – to christen it normal in every respect and even endorse it. This is why gays and lesbians not only demand that we grant same-sex marriage, but want us to cease calling gay behavior wrong and join them in calling it right.

This dust-up is similar to Lincoln's battle with slaveholders prior to the Civil War. In his Cooper Union address, Lincoln asked rhetorically what would satisfy the south regarding slavery, and then answered: "This, and this only: cease to call slavery *wrong*, and join them in calling it *right*. And this must be done thoroughly – done in *acts* as well as in *words*. Silence will not be tolerated – we must place ourselves avowedly with them. … Holding, as they do, that slavery is morally right, and socially elevating, they cannot cease to demand a full national recognition of it, as a legal right, and a social blessing."[7]

Reminds one of what Isaiah said:

> Woe unto them that call evil good, and good evil; that put darkness for light, and light for darkness; that put bitter for sweet, and sweet for bitter![8]

We know what happened when Gadianton robbers demanded Nephite agreement with their practices – "yield yourselves up unto us, and unite with us"[9] – and we know what demands for total capitulation to "slavery is good" led to after 1859.

Not only do LGBT leaders want same-sex marriage to have the same status as natural marriage, **they want unconditional approval of homosexuality**. They want society's imprimatur. What they don't want known is that such societal approval makes it easier for them to propagandize children in the schools.

Deception through equivalence plays an integral role. The idea is to claim that one's cause is comparable to a more favored cause, and kidnap the luster. Thus, proponents of same-sex marriage argue that discrimination against gays and lesbians is equivalent to racial discrimination. It is a false equivalence and it is obvious that while there are "no differences between black and white human beings, there are enormous differences between male and female human beings."[10] Nonetheless, the LGBT community continues to talk about marriage in terms of civil rights, a hijacking resented by most African-American voters as witnessed by the 70% who voted for Proposition 8, the highest of any ethnic voter bloc.

Every great moral thinker has opposed racism, but try to name one who has ever advocated same-sex marriage.

A related example of deceptive equivalence was the message posted on the billboard outside an Anglican church in Ontario, Canada: "Jesus had two dads and he turned out just fine," suggesting equivalence between a gay couple raising a child and the Son of God's one-of-a-kind circumstances. Cheeky? More like blasphemous.

The point is that **Satan takes a counterfeit and raises it to equivalence of something wholesome, good, and right**: Communism is just like the law of consecration, same-sex marriage is equivalent to marriage between a man and a woman, pornography is just a healthy outlet for the natural attraction of the sexes, government power is no different than priesthood power, any group of people can be a family, and on into the night.

Tolerance and love

Although we are taught to be patient and understanding, this does not and cannot mean blanket tolerance. In fact, the word *tolerance* appears nowhere in the scriptures. The twisted use goes something like this: "If you were compassionate, you would be tolerant. If you were tolerant, you would accept me as I am. If you accept me as I am, you would approve of what I'm doing." So now tolerance is distorted to mean acceptance; in fact, in heated corners, *required* acceptance.

President Thomas S. Monson teaches: "The face of sin too often wears the mask of tolerance."[11] The old saying comes to mind: First we abhor, then tolerate, then embrace.

Love is similarly misunderstood. How often we hear that if we follow Christ's admonition to love one another, we would approve of same-sex marriage. Nothing could be further from the truth. **It is a fallacy to equate love and approval**. God loves all of His children. He obviously does not and cannot approve of all they do. Nor can we.

The greatest love we can experience is the Savior's love for us and our love for Him. But if we truly reciprocate His love for us, we will keep His commandments. That includes fidelity to the holy order of matrimony that God – not man – created. Satan would have us mistake Christ's love as justification for the counterfeit of gay marriage.

If same-sex marriage becomes the law of the land, don't be surprised if you hear little if anything about tolerance and love for those of opposing viewpoints. It will prove to be another of many one-way streets in this war.

Consequences of redefining marriage

In a brief filed in appeal against a judge's ruling legalizing same-sex marriage in Utah, veteran Supreme Court and appellate expert Gene Schaerr identified 15 consequences of redefining marriage that even a non-believer can understand.[12] Among them, redefined marriage would …

- Break the critical conceptual link between marriage and procreation.
- Result in more couples having children without the stability of marriage.
- Lead parents to make fewer self-sacrifices and remain married.
- Undermine the social norm that those who wish to have children should first get married.
- Lead to more fatherless households with their manifest ills.
- Encourage more father abandonment.
- Reduce birthrates.
- Make it difficult to resist other innovations that would lead to additional children being raised without a father or mother.
- Pressure governments to revoke the tax-exempt status of religions that don't agree with the redefinition.
- Increase conflicts between public schools and parents regarding what is taught about sexuality and marriage.

Award-winning columnist Richard Larsen adds: "Merely 'definitionally' reducing marriage to nothing more than a state legitimized relationship between 'people that love each other' is antithetical to the factual basis to our existence as a civilization. The fact is, marriage has always been about protecting society, at least in part, through the possibility of propagation, protection and the creation of family units."[13]

Demonizing natural marriage advocates

One of the most shocking diatribes ever issued in a Supreme Court holding happened in June 2013 when Justice Anthony Kennedy, writing in the Windsor case for a 5-4 majority, **assumed that opposition to same-sex marriage automatically means hatred of gays**, and that the Defense of Marriage Act (DOMA), passed by large bi-partisan majorities in 1996, has "no legitimate purpose." That somehow there is no difference between marriage as established by God and variations established by man, that all marriages must be treated equally, and that DOMA improperly declared that same-sex marriage "is less worthy than the marriages of others."[14]

Justice Kennedy blasted supporters of traditional marriage for supposed bigoted motives – that our presumed intent is to disparage, injure, degrade, demean, humiliate, and place same-sex couples in second-tier marriages by "refusing to acknowledge a status the State finds to be dignified and proper."

Dignified and proper? How far we have traveled.

Justice Antonin Scalia attempted to restore a bit of reality to that august body by arguing in dissent, "[To] defend traditional marriage is not to condemn, demean, or humiliate those who would prefer other arrangements, any more than to defend the Constitution of the United States is to condemn, demean, or humiliate other constitutions. … In the majority's judgment, any resistance to its holding is beyond the pale of reasoned disagreement. … All that, simply for supporting an Act that did no more than codify an aspect of marriage that had been unquestioned in our society for most of its existence – indeed, had been unquestioned in virtually all societies for virtually all of human history."

Justice Scalia continued: "By formally declaring anyone opposed to same-sex marriage an enemy of human decency the majority arms well every challenger to a state law restricting marriage to its traditional definition. Henceforth those challengers will lead with this Court's declaration that there is 'no legitimate purpose' served by such a law, and will claim that the traditional definition has 'the purpose and effect to disparage and to injure' the 'personhood and dignity' of same sex couples …"[15]

(Sadly, there was not one mention of God by either side. Not one.)

Justice Kennedy and his cohorts fell for the claim that marriage is about love and commitment more than about procreation and stable families headed by a man and a woman. So did the federal judge who overturned California's Proposition 8: "Indeed, the evidence shows Proposition 8 does nothing more than enshrine in the California Constitution the notion that opposite sex couples are superior to same-sex couples."[16]

If love and commitment were indeed the prime movers and features of marriage, then the superiority of one form over another could not be argued because no human metric exists that can objectively measure such things to the satisfaction of all parties. And that's precisely the conclusion gay leaders wanted the justices to reach – all forms of marriage are equal.

However, marriage is more than love and commitment. It is the institution through which children are to be brought into the world.

The word *superior* may be offensive to the equality-obsessed, but how can one argue that what God has created is not superior to what man creates? To say that a same-sex union is equal to a union of a man and woman is false on its face. **One person cannot continue the species alone, and a third person isn't necessary**. A man-woman union is superior to any other arrangement because it is the only one that can naturally produce children and form the family unit God designed. (Again, simple things are anathema to those who believe complexity and sophistication march hand in hand.)

Don't expect such logic to trump the emotions and goals of the other side. Expect on-going demonization. No matter how many times we explain that we don't hate gays – that opposing same-sex marriage is vastly different than being anti-gay – leaders of the gay religion will continue to posture their followers as victims of malice and oppression.

The Lord knew that religious liberty, marriage, and the family would be threatened in our latter days. That's why religious freedom is the first freedom of the First Amendment, its front-and-center placement in the pantheon of Creator-given freedoms is not happenstance. Yet we have law professors today who, believe it or not, can say, "When religious liberty and sexual liberty conflict, I'm having a hard time coming up with any case in which religious liberty should win."[17]

Note to law professors and judges: The First Amendment reaffirms the primacy of religious liberty; the Constitution says nothing about sexual liberty. Unfortunately, due to woozy legal theories, the day may not be far off when voicing support of natural marriage will be evidence of hateful bias and punishable by speech-code laws now being formed.

Manipulating words

In his famous book, mentor of radicals Saul Alinsky (who incidentally gives an "over-the-shoulder acknowledgement" to Lucifer who rebelled so effectively that he won his own kingdom) lists among his key rules: "Do what you can with what you have and clothe it with moral garments."[18]

For those who advocate same-sex marriage and behavior, manipulating words is crucial to their success. They twist words and symbols by kidnapping, relabeling, and diluting.

- There are many pejoratives about homosexuality, but decent people have refused to use such labels, settling on the clinical and neutral term homosexual. But even that is not good enough for those with same-sex attraction. They kidnapped the word gay in the 1930's, solidified the term by 1965, and made it commonplace in the 1980's.[19]
- God gave Noah the symbol of the rainbow as a promise that the earth would never again be destroyed by flood. The LGBT community swiped it and flies rainbow coalition flags to symbolize a spectrum of support for their agenda.
- If a man and a woman fall in love and decide to marry, though each is already married to another, this abandonment of spouses and families was labeled by the *New York Times* as "honest to their feelings" and "brave."

- If a married man comes out as gay, taking up with a same-sex partner has been called "being true to himself."

"Male and female created he them" goes the biblical phrase. But that was before Facebook, which now presents over 50 gobbledygook definitions to choose from when it asks your gender. Cisgender heteronormative, for example, is the supposedly sophisticated way of saying male and female – cis being the opposite of trans, and gender, hetero, and normative more or less self-explanatory.

To distort such basic words as male and female, and make them just one category in a list of many variations, dilutes and cheapens God's highest creations. And makes it easier to change society's thinking about marriage.

If important words lose meaning, so do the concepts for which they stand.

A battle until the Millennium

The ripples from the gay marriage rock tossed into the public pond will splash against all things religious for years to come. No development in history has provided Satan a greater opportunity to destroy several God-given institutions simultaneously.

The pitch is equality and fairness – that no one's love is different than another's, that natural marriage and same-sex marriage are equivalent, that no one should be a second-class citizen. If the nation accepts this thinking, then conformity becomes a societal good and agency something less.

Now comes the gospel of Jesus Christ with its admonitions to stand apart from the world, to live the commandments, to be a different and unique people, and to accept that God-ordained marriage is indeed superior to man's creations. Once these points become clear, gay marriage can only be seen as a flat-out threat to God's plan and religious freedom. (How can the dilution or destruction of a key pillar of society not impact our freedoms?)

In March, 2014, the First Presidency and the Quorum of the Twelve Apostles published a letter to Church leaders which read in part:

> Changes in the civil law do not, indeed cannot, change the moral law that God has established. God expects us to uphold and keep His commandments regardless of divergent opinions or trends in society. His law of chastity is clear: sexual relations are proper only between a man and a woman who are legally and lawfully wedded as husband and wife.[20]

Elder Neil L. Andersen added: "While many governments and well-meaning individuals have redefined marriage, the Lord has not."[21]

One cannot both embrace the restored Church and approve same-sex marriage. **There can be no compromise; any co-existence will be short-lived.** Further, because advocates of gay marriage will use the issue to silence religious leaders, members who approve a redefinition of marriage cannot effectively defend against other attacks on religious freedom.

Whether the Supreme Court legalizes same-sex marriage will no more end this battle than *Roe v. Wade* ended the abortion argument. It will see-saw back and forth until the Savior's foot splits the Mount of Olives.

It will be unpleasant. We will be attacked for defending natural marriage. Careers have been and will continue to be lost because we take a stance the world doesn't agree with. The person out of step with man's wisdom will be labeled hateful – hate that can be justifiably returned, will go the rationalization of the secular religion, who will clothe themselves in moral garments as they unleash their pseudo-righteous vituperation.

President Ronald Reagan saw it in 1984: "Those who are attacking religion claim they are doing it in the name of tolerance, freedom, and open mindedness."[22] And Nephi, son of Helaman, noted how those who usurped power condemned the righteous because of their righteousness."[23]

Elder Dallin H. Oaks counsels us:

> In this determination we may be misunderstood, and we may incur accusations of bigotry, suffer discrimination, or have to withstand invasions of our free exercise of religion. If so, I think we should remember our first priority – to serve God – and, like our pioneer predecessors, push our personal handcarts forward with the same fortitude they exhibited.[24]

God commands us to love everyone, but He has never commanded anyone to practice same-sex marriage. Our duty is to frame the battle in the larger eternal perspective and not shy from referring to God's plan. "Take God off the table and then let's discuss it," said one loudmouth TV hostess. Nope. Without antagonism toward any individual, we must point out the distortions, deceptions, and faulty reasoning of our opponents as necessary to defend God's institution of marriage. We must take what abuse may spew and give the Holy Ghost a chance to work on man's mind – especially on those in the peripheral audience who are undecided observers.

* * *

To any who are not sure, two simple questions: "Who created the sexes?" and "Do you think it occurred to God to define the male-female relationship?"

Chapter 11

Families Are Whatever

"You don't have to have an 'ideal family' to preserve the ideal of the family."

– Carol Soelberg
United Families International

The integral importance of the family in civilization cannot be overstated. As John Adams said, "The foundation of national morality must be laid in private families."

Ah, the family. People who love you, accept you, help you. A dad to protect, a mom to nurture; Christmas morning; freshly baked bread; all the warm and fuzzies associated with the word.

Of course, strangers can protect, nurture, give, bake, and even tuck you in at night. But somehow it's not the same. Why? Because there is a **natural convergence of strengths between a man and a woman, and an intangible tug between those parents and their children**, whether natural or adopted.

The world dilutes the concept. It argues that the traditional family is outdated, boring, narrowly defined, and needs to be modernized and more inclusive. It points to departures from the ideal family such as divorce and death and uses them as excuses to redefine family in artificial and strange ways.

Families, in their thinking, should be whatever people want them to be.

The Proclamation on the Family

Along with an increasing number of astute social observers, George Will warns that disintegration of the family is one of the two greatest threats to America today (the other is not living within our means). "We know the importance of a father in the home. We know that the family is the primary transmitter of what's called social capital, that is the habits, mores, customs, values, dispositions that make for success in a free society."[1]

Our leaders have seen it for years.

In September of 1995, the First Presidency and Council of the Twelve Apostles published a proclamation to the world about families, only the fifth such proclamation since the Restoration in 1830.[2] Not a few members wondered at the time why our leaders were stating the commonsense obvious and why such a proclamation was necessary.

It was because they saw the future where the obvious would not remain obvious. A future where 41% of all babies are born to unmarried mothers.[3] A future where 91% of men and 86% of women have had premarital sex.[4] A future where 43% of children live in fatherless homes.[5]

Let's look again at the wisdom and guidance in that prescient document:

- The family is central to God's plan for His children
- Gender is an essential characteristic of our identity and purpose
- Family relationships live beyond the grave

- Parents have a solemn responsibility to their children
    - To rear them in love and righteousness
    - To provide physical and spiritual needs
    - To teach them to love and serve one another
    - To observe the commandments of God
    - To be law-abiding citizens
- Fathers are to preside, provide, and protect
- Mothers are primarily responsible for the nurture of their children
- Both are obligated to help one another as equal partners

Nine critical principles for success are listed: "Successful marriages and families are established and maintained on principles of faith, prayer, repentance, forgiveness, respect, love, compassion, work, and wholesome recreational activities."

The *Proclamation* acknowledges, "Disability, death, or other circumstances may necessitate individual adaptation" and then states, "Extended families should lend support when needed."

The direction is clear: Parents bear the responsibility for rearing their children and will be answerable to God for their actions.

State versus parents

The deterioration of the family has been addressed in hundreds of books and articles more extensively than I can review in a few Cliff-note pages here. Researchers seem to have examined every conceivable pressure on the family: death, divorce, infidelity, cohabitation, postponing marriage and children, abortion, child abuse, spouse abuse, elder abuse, financial pressure, unemployment, poverty, illness, old age, sexually transmitted diseases, childlessness, same-sex attractions, you name it.

But there is one threat that has not been given the attention commensurate with its insidiousness, in my opinion. The state.

The family is a competitor to the state. It is a counterforce against intrusive power. It is the bulwark against tyranny.

Of course, no one argues that there are never times when society's intervention may be necessary to protect a child, but one must also note that nowhere does the *Proclamation* even hint at bringing in government to take over any of the core parental responsibilities.

Those favoring more state say-so in family matters argue that young parents do not yet have sufficient wisdom to make proper decisions; that they need help; and that if parents always have the last say, what will stop abuse or even death of a child? They say that if more government action saves only one life, it is worth it. (Of course, if saving one life is the goal, we could save 35,000 a year by outlawing cars.)

Those favoring less state intervention, on the other hand, contend that parents, being closest to the situation, are in the best position to decide necessary actions: that increased state involvement decreases parental agency; and that a third party with its one-size-fits-all regulations will not necessarily make wiser decisions. Further, if the state succeeds in eliminating all adverse decisions two parents may make, say hello to the destruction of the family and goodbye to God's plan of progress.

Blurred roles

The state also threatens the family when it fails to reinforce traditional parental roles. It has somehow become a badge of distinction in sophisticated circles to prattle that there are no substantive differences between men and women – that a woman can do a man's job, and vice versa. Government has shown itself susceptible to lobbying by such groups who blur the roles of man and woman – homogenize the differences – under the guise of equality or fairness or reparation for alleged past offenses. Two mothers can do the job, two fathers as well, or a single parent of either sex. Mix or match, doesn't matter, the argument goes.

Those who want same-sex *marriage* play the *negatives* – discrimination, second-class citizens, etc. – but find it tough to argue the *positives* of a same-sex *family*. They point to individual cases where children from gay or lesbian households succeed in life, but they cannot assemble compelling statistics overall. We know the probabilities of successful outcomes increase when children are raised by both a father and a mother.[6]

In contrast to that unisex wisdom of the world, having a father and a mother in the home verifies for the children that men and women were created with different but complementary traits such that together they can progress higher, become more successful, and have more happiness than either could alone. Proof is that neither one alone can create life nor achieve exaltation. This God-given arrangement also allows children to observe each parent's unique traits, and to realize that one parent can never adequately exhibit the traits of the opposite parent, no matter how feminine the male or masculine the female.

After all, if families headed by two moms or two dads were really a better arrangement, wouldn't God have instituted it? Or, if you prefer a more secular argument, why haven't history's great philosophers lined up in support of such a structure? In fact, no historical philosopher or moral teacher of note has ever advocated that the fundamental building-block of society should be based on something other than a married father and mother.[7]

GENDER CONFUSION

Satan adds to parental problems by confusing children about gender. For example, the previously mentioned ENDA legislation says that no one shall be discriminated against in employment opportunities because of sexual orientation or gender identity.

Sounds reasonable; who could possibly oppose fair employment practices? Well, the reason this noble-sounding legislation languished before Congress for over three decades is that what appeared to be one thing on the surface hid mischief underneath: whatever provisions applied to sexual orientation also had to cover gender identity, which was, and still is, a fuzzy concept. It wasn't clear what accommodations gender-conflicted employees might demand of their employers, and some said it would even lead to men using women's restrooms. Heavens to Murgatroyd.

Well, wouldn't you know it? While assurances were mouthed in Washington that ENDA legislation would not lead to such distortions, California passed a law that requires all public schools to allow transgender K-12 students to use whichever restroom and locker room they want, consistent with their *feelings* of gender identity.[8] This means that if an anatomical boy "feels deeply" that he is a girl, he must be allowed to use girls' restrooms. And participate on girls' athletic teams. And shower in their locker rooms.

How silly are things going to get? Hard to think of another piece of legislation that scores worse on the giggle test. Letting high school boys use girls' restrooms and dressing facilities is like letting Russians wander through CIA headquarters if they promise they really, truly, cross-my-heart feel like Americans. As YSA Bishop Larry Eastland remarked, "What normal, healthy, over-hormoned, curious teenage boy is not today high fiving every other buddy on his way to the principal's office to confess his dual personality?"

Fake families

When Stalin atomized his society, the last holdout was the family. Even the churches caved. The state encouraged children to tattle on their parents' conversations and become a Hero of the Soviet Union. Fear reigned; no one knew whom to trust. Families ceased to be unified. Then came mass arrests of opponents, real or imagined, followed by show trials and executions. By the beginning of World War II, "Soviet society was atomized and the people so fearful of reprisals that mass arrests were no longer necessary."[9] A key was disconnecting children from parents, inculcating loyalty to the state that became a false family with Stalin as the father, or at least avuncular Uncle Joe. The formula is still a threat today.

Family is too useful a word not to be hijacked. Loaded with warm fuzzies and comfy cozies, why not, a string puller might muse, use the positive term for political objectives? And claim that government is the only thing we all belong to, thus substituting it for the family?

In the summer of 2013, the federal bureaucracy apparently began informally field-testing the term "federal family" to see how people would react. It's a blatant pitch that government is a family and that we're all in this together. It cheapens the God-instituted family and replaces it with a man-made version.

- HHS Secretary Kathleen Sibelius in a news release commemorating National Preparedness Month: "While our federal family is becoming better prepared to support the nation, we know that being truly resilient requires the whole community coming together."
- An ATF agent: "It's as close as you're going to get to blue-collar law enforcement in the federal family."
- DHS assistant secretary, referring to how a town recovered from a tornado "in partnership with the federal family."
- Deputy Administrator of FEMA: "This determination resulted in enhanced attention to the event across the federal family…"[10]

It's not Big Brother any more; it's Federal Family.

* * *

The *Proclamation* again:

> We warn that the disintegration of the family will bring upon individuals, communities, and nations the calamities foretold by ancient and modern prophets.

Chapter 12

It Doesn't Take a Village, Idiot; It Takes a Family

"Well, it's one a.m. Time to go home and spend some quality time with the kids."

– Homer Simpson

Certain leaders would have us believe that the traditional family is unequal to the task of raising a child in today's fast-paced modern society. That it takes a village. Perhaps a comforting thought to some, but others question, "If the village is in charge of raising my children, who's in charge of the village?"

If you happened to be watching MSNBC on April 8, 2013, perhaps you might have found a little something to disagree with in this commentary by anchor Melissa Harris-Perry:

> We have never invested as much in public education as we should have because we've always had kind of a private notion of children. Your kid is yours and totally your responsibility. We haven't had a very collective notion of these are our children. So part of it is we have to *break through our kind of private idea that kids belong to their parents* or kids belong

> to their families and recognize that kids belong to whole communities.[1] [Emphasis added]

Jolting stuff. A private notion about children? How quaint.

Ownership of children

What this says about our society is disturbing. We're not talking about a crackpot guest on a TV show, but rather a news anchor, an employee of the network, who would feel sufficiently supported that she could mouth an extremist ideology.

Oh, we could argue her points and pose our own counters:

- We haven't had a very collective notion. (Who decided that a collective notion should be the ideal?)
- We haven't invested enough in public education. (Will the education sector ever feel adequately funded?)
- Kids don't belong to their parents, but to the whole community. (Try making that case to the mother who suffered the labor pains.)

But let's cut to the nub. She has called for Americans to embrace a **bogus system that would destroy the family** as God intended it.

Village thinking is counterfeit thinking. That instead of parents being sealed to each other and children sealed to the parents (able to call on extended family to help as needed), we should all be one big mushy village family with no clear lines from generation to generation and person to person. Shades of hippie communes. A newborn becomes one of the crowd, his parents have diminished responsibilities, and everyone salutes the overarching philosophy that the only thing we all belong to is government.

Hard to believe someone would advocate such collectivism in a nation founded on individual freedoms. Even communists weren't that blatant about it. Their utility word *proletariat* derives from the word *progeny* indicating that children were the only things the downtrodden owned. If the communist revolution happened today rather than 1917, the would-be tyrants would have to use a new vocabulary. (Perhaps the term *breeders* would work, as certain allies of today's "Staat-uber-alles" types derogatorily call parents.)

Whatever discussion, pro or con, may ensue about these ideas will only embolden kiss-it-better government to take over tasks that by virtue of agency and God's plan rightfully belong to parents. If the traditional family weakens, village string pullers will take over ownership like a dormant bank account escheated to the government.

Not convinced of the danger? Ms. Harris-Perry concluded, "We as a society, expressing our collective will through our public institutions, including our government, **have a right to impinge on individual freedoms** in order to advance a common good." [Emphasis added]

Someday, Ms. Harris-Perry, you may stumble onto a guiding document we call *A Proclamation on the Family*. God's apostles and prophets did not write one called *A Proclamation on the Village.*

The child-protection hide behind

Get a load of this sign in a Michigan hospital:

> "Attention parents of adolescent children age 12y-17y- New Michigan Medical Records access laws have been put in place. This will require a nurse to have a short 5 minute private conversation with your child."

As explained to one mother, the child would be allowed to access his/her medical records online and would be allowed to block a parent from viewing the website. No opt-out policy. No parent allowed.[2]

So the parent only gets to view a teen's medical records if the teen grants permission? Why is he an adult in this situation but his name can't be printed in the paper if he holds up a gas station? What might the teen be worried that his parents might see? And isn't it the right of parents to know the medical condition of their children?

What topics do you think the nurse might possibly ask about? Birth control, perhaps? Other matters that only parents have traditionally handled? What if the nurse doesn't share a parent's traditional values about abstinence before marriage? If the nurse encourages the teen to take some condoms (your parents won't know), can experimenting be far behind?

Hiding behind the minor chance of ferreting out child abuse, the state substitutes itself for the parent. Using this phony hide-behind, the state can introduce information earlier on the timetable than the parent planned, or worse, suggest ideas opposite to parental teachings.

Government power overwhelms parental authority because it threatens doctors and nurses with loss of license if they do not implement regulations. And, in this case, parents can lose their children to child protection services if they do not comply with such "no parents allowed" interventions.

Child protection has become the vehicle to expand the role of the state – well-intentioned by some, cynically exploited for power by others – and in due time *substitute itself for the family.* With the state applying its own set of morals.

When a child cannot protect himself against abusive parents, for example, laws allow government to remove him from their home. Once society employs such child-protection power, however, it then looks around for what else might constitute harm. The terrain gets slippery.

- Should the state step in if a parent disciplines a child with an occasional spanking? Or metes out other punishments such as restrictions on what the child is allowed to do? Do extended time-outs or go-to-your-room punishments qualify as harm? Who decides?
- We all want children to have adequate food, but should the state get involved if parents don't quite meet that goal, or provide a poor quality diet? At the other end of the scale (so to speak), is it government's duty to solve an obesity epidemic, to outlaw 16-ounce sodas?

- Peaceful calm in a family is ideal, so is a raised voice evidence of harm? When does animated discussion become verbal abuse? Do disapproving glances constitute harm to psyche or ego?
- Ignorance is harmful, so how should we judge the lack of books or other reading materials in a home? Any actionable harm on this front?

My point is **there is virtually nothing that cannot be defined as harmful** by somebody somewhere. All parents make mistakes, children will misbehave, and family life will at times resemble Red Bull-saturated occupants of the clown car at the circus. As the definition of harm expands, the belief grows that all parental mistakes must be eliminated or children will suffer. And as that gains traction, people – some undoubtedly well intentioned – will use even picky violations as reasons for government intervention. Officials eager to justify their own jobs will respond.

Ascendancy of offensive laws

As discussed in Chapter 4, defensive laws – those that say "you shall not" and are designed to protect against, punish, or deter injury – were the primary laws to first bring order to a society. As civilization progressed, offensive or assertive laws – those that say "you shall" and are designed to command behavior in ways legislators think will benefit society as a whole – became more prevalent.

These include laws to redistribute goods produced by others and, germane to our focus here, laws that mandate effort. To command which actions citizens must perform means that the commanding authority looks at all options and makes a choice. By making such a choice, the state usurps agency because it decides how we must spend our time and efforts.

It is a major warning signal to the autonomy of the family when the preponderance of laws shifts from defensive to offensive.

Education, for example, is necessary to function in today's society, but who decides what is adequate and who should deliver it? Should the state require children to attend public schools, as is the case in Germany? What about those who would choose to expend effort to homeschool their children, or spend their resources to send them to private schools? Who has the agency here?

If the state prevails and universal attendance at public schools is mandated, is it not then the state's prerogative to decide what a child shall and shall not be taught? And is curriculum control not but a short step to indoctrination, of hearing only one side of an issue? Which may have figured in the calculations of one pro-indoctrination author whose article in Slate was titled, "If You Send Your Kid to Private School, You Are a Bad Person."[3]

Or take nutrition. Is it government's role to require parents to provide so many calories a day to their children? And if they can't or won't, is this grounds for penalties? Is a law outlawing those villainous 16-ounce sodas a defensive law to prevent harm, or an offensive law in disguise so the state makes the decisions that should be left to parents? If so, can a law to feed children broccoli be far off?

Or population control. If the Malthusians gain power, will their fears of a population explosion lead to a directive for people to stop having so many children, absolutely counter to the "multiply and replenish" commandment we have received?

If the state can require X, what is to stop it from requiring Y? Where do "you shall" laws end?

Look at it this way. Let's say that two parents are real clods – clueless as can be. God knows they are clods, but does He deny them the right to have children? Does He deny them the right to decide how best to rear those children? How much agency does He give them? Wouldn't we have to say they have the same agency as non-clods?

Now, clods and non-clods alike must face the consequences of their mistakes. But what is important in God's way of doing things is that none will be deprived of valuable learning experiences. The state, on the other hand, would deprive people of all painful experiences if it could, and it surely seems to be trying. That in itself defeats God's purposes and our progress.

Has the village taken over? A test is whether you have the *right of exit*, which means that if a system is not working for you or your children, you have a right to go somewhere else. However, if there is a monopoly, especially a government monopoly, there is nowhere else to go.

Satan loves monopolies because by definition there is less agency. He would have us look to government instead of ourselves for solutions to problems. Excessive government robs us of the progress we would make if we had to solve problems on our own, or together with our families.

It's axiomatic: The greater the say-so of government, the greater the monopoly of government over that part of life. The greater the monopoly, the more diminished the agency of the individual. And no right of exit.

Welcome to the village.

* * *

When the annals of agency are written, the following incredible denial of God's gift to His children will be cited for what went wrong with America:

> "We just think people will be too focused on saving money and they won't get the [health] care for their children and themselves that they need. … The money has to go to the federal government because the federal government will spend that money better."[4]
>
> – Hillary Clinton

Chapter 13

Just a Blob of Unwanted Cells?

"I've noticed that everyone who is for abortion has already been born."

– Ronald Reagan

If abortion doesn't destroy the family, it at least destroys a family that could have been. As Mother Teresa said, "The greatest destroyer of love and peace is abortion."[1]

I have rarely been as upset about an incident as I was when I read about a late-term abortion in Philadelphia, and how the infant, born alive, was swimming in the toilet desperately struggling to live. Despicable beyond words. How depraved have we become?

I'll tell you how depraved. In 1979, atheist philosopher Peter Singer wrote, "Human babies are not born self-aware, or capable of grasping that they exist over time. They are not persons, therefore the life of a newborn is of less value than the life of a pig, a dog, or a chimpanzee.[2]

A child of God is of less worth than a *pig?!* Twenty years later, this pro-infanticide champion was awarded Princeton University's first tenured professorship in bioethics. Not far removed from this philosophy, Joseph Stalin said: "If you have a problem, there is a man. No man, no problem."

Thus would Satan destroy God's plan: If no spirits enter mortality, the plan of salvation is empty. No man, no plan, no honor for God. Three intersection points:

- Stop man as the giver of life
- Stop woman as the producer of life
- Stop children from growing up

Stopping the man from fulfilling his role is difficult (though the gay movement is doing its best), while stopping the woman's role is much easier as Satan has nine months to entice her to abort the body house under construction, or have the expectant mother herself destroyed – a twofer. Then, if the little spirit finally makes it into mortality, years of helpless infancy and dependency await – during which the child needs a loving mother and father – before he or she can join defenders of the kingdom on the parapets.

Hiding behind exceptions and positive words

God's authorized religion acknowledges that abortion can – with spiritual guidance and competent medical advice – be justified in cases of rape, incest, danger to the life of the mother, or a deformed and unviable fetus. But only a very small percentage of abortions are performed for these reasons. Upwards of 99% of all abortions are for convenience, to escape the natural consequences of sexual intercourse.

Government encourages this deception by spending over $500 million a year funding abortions, and over 55 million abortions have been performed in America in the last 40 years. Those are the dry statistics, but the brutality of abortion doesn't penetrate. An abortion doctor is brought to trial for the murder of viable babies who had the cheek to survive botched late-term abortions. The gruesome realities – spines being cut by scissors or an infant drowning in a toilet – are ignored by the major mass media, usually a pushover for covering gore and violence in other venues.

Word manipulation hides the truth. The Alinsky rule to clothe evils such as abortion in moral garments begins with downplaying the seriousness of sex outside of marriage. Note the common words to disguise the sin:

- Cheating – equivalent to peeking at a classmate's test answers
- Stepping out – equivalent to healthy exercise
- Sowing wild oats – every society needs agriculture
- Hooking up – networking, let's do lunch
- Affair – in the same company with public affairs and foreign affairs

Diverting shame through clever relabeling, and disguising lust for love, Satan would have us call it anything but its true name.

Then come phrases that combine two positive words to hide a negative. For example, the word *open* suggests truthfulness and transparency, and *marriage* is one of God's divinely appointed institutions. So what could possibly go wrong with an open marriage? Similarly, *friends* are wonderful and *benefits* are positive. But the combination connotes something far afield from chastity.

So it is with *pro* and *choice*. *Pro* is synonymous with positive, and *choice* is the essence of agency, but together they become a weasel euphemism for terminating life. Being pro-choice as the phrase originally meant was the essence of what we chose in heaven – freedom **and** accountability. But **pro-choice in today's vernacular means people get to choose the action and adjust the consequences later.** They conveniently forget that the choice happens the night before, not the morning after.

Canceling the consequences of one act by another act does not eliminate accountability – it doubles it.

Target: women

When politics collides with our religious teachings, we must name names, point out the behavior, and ask one simple question,

"Who approves of this, God or Satan?" Even politicians can't have it both ways.

For example, what is so disheartening in the ongoing destruction of families that could have been is having a leader unashamedly extoll abortion as a virtue. President Barack Obama once spoke to a convention of the largest organization of abortion providers and unequivocally approved their activities. He never said the word "abortion," but drumbeat the ever-handy phrase "right to choose." He demonized opponents of abortion as bigoted opponents of choice, or as opponents of women's health. He then invoked the blessings of God on these abortion providers and their activity by shameless stating: "God bless you, Planned Parenthood."[3]

God bless ... *who?!* For doing ... *what?!* It almost makes one want to check to see if the story came from *The Onion*. It is not only a fulfillment of Isaiah's prophecy that evil shall be called good, but it is hard to imagine a more warped way of taking God's name in vain.

President N. Eldon Tanner warned:

> To mothers, daughters, and women everywhere, let me stress the fact that because of your great potential and influence for good in the lives of all of us, Satan is determined to destroy you.[4]

Author Larry Barkdull writes why Satan's primary targets are women and children:

> Satan knew something that we should understand: If he could defeat the woman and remove her out of her place, he could win the war; but if he left her alone, he was doomed. Why? Because she had the power to bring forth the promised Child along with other righteous children to crush his head.[5] Therefore, Satan took direct aim at the woman to make her as miserable as possible. [His] strategy was twofold: attack her head-on and attack her through her children.[6]

Barkdull further maintains that "God lays the responsibility for the woman and her children's welfare on the man" and charges the priesthood to be their safety net.[7]

* * *

Satan might goad other nations into war against the inhabitants of this promised land, but he achieves so much more as he convinces people to destroy the children they could have had.

Chapter 14

The Destruction of Meaning: The Non-Divorce Divorce

"It's a beautiful thing, the destruction of words."

– George Orwell, 1984

If Satan, skilled master of counterfeits, can appear like unto an angel of light,[1] then why not the power to harness seemingly positive words to destroy justice and agency? Satan's tactic here is to dress his actions in righteous words, present counterfeits with aplomb, and dismissively disparage those who challenge his usage.

As the boy complained about a Garden of Eden play at church, "The snake gets all the lines."

Language changes. Terms are manipulated. Which is why fat chance and slim chance mean the same thing. And why it took etymologists years to figure out that the words *complete* and *finished* are not the same. Those who write our dictionaries concluded that if you marry the right one, you are complete, but if you marry the wrong one, you are finished. And if the right one ever catches you with the wrong one, you are completely finished.

Redefinitions

Words were the bullets in the war in heaven and still are. Changes in ammunition affect the battle.

Slippery definitions often begin in political language, which George Orwell said "is designed to make lies sound truthful and murder respectable, and to give an appearance of solidity to pure wind."[2] A few examples in today's verbal volleys:

- *Timeless principles* means turning back the clock;
- *Limiting government* means abandoning the poor;
- *Unemployment* is now liberation (from being trapped in a job);
- The invasion of Crimea was described as an *uncontested arrival* (one comedian says that manufacturers of drones would prefer they be called *surprise visitors*);
- The Arab world cannot bear to say the name *Israel* – they call it the Zionist entity;
- Mob rule of demagogues has been spruced up as an *extreme plebiscitary presidency*;[3] and
- Lies, in Churchill's mockery, are *terminological inexactitudes.*

And … used cars are now pre-owned, food storage is hoarding, and natural marriage is smeared as heterosexist oppression. As for Hollywood, filthy is now edgy, dirty is modern, swearing is colorful, and crudity is brave.

Gradual changes

This method takes a word or phrase, makes changes in small steps, and redefines it as something more positive:

- Most people sense that excess money supply leads to undesirable consequences, and a commodity that government can create for the price of paper makes many uncomfortable.[4] So *printing money* became *monetizing the debt* and is now called *quantitative easing*, a muddy phrase with airs if there ever was one. But ease is a positive word, like relaxation after work.

- Similarly, *dole* became *welfare* became *relief* became *assistance* became *entitlement.* Great irony, that. A title has value and, except for aristocratic inheritance, results from effort – such as earning a degree or working to buy a home. It is one thing to remove a stigma, quite another to make it a sought honor.
- The word *whoredom* has almost disappeared. *Whores* became *prostitutes*, then *streetwalkers*, then *"ladies" of the night*, and now are *escorts*. Talk about cheapening a noble word.

Upside downs

An airline announced that cashing in frequent flyer miles less than 20 days prior to departure "will incur a $75 USD Award." Fees are now called awards?

The greatest upside downs have been those hurled at the Savior and his anointed servants:

> "For John came neither eating nor drinking, and they say, He hath a devil. The Son of man came eating and drinking, and they say, Behold a man gluttonous, and a winebibber, a friend of publicans and sinners."[5]
>
> "And many of them said, He [Jesus] hath a devil, and is mad; why hear ye him?"[6]
>
> "Take this fellow [Samuel the Lamanite] and bind him, for behold he hath a devil."[7]

In fact, it was Samuel the Lamanite prophet who told the Nephites in Zarahemla that if a prophet testified of their sins, they would say he is of the devil. But if a man told them to do whatever their heart desires, they would say he is a prophet.[8] How true.

In our day, the adherence to the timeless principles of the Constitution is disparaged as absolutism and turned upside down. As Barack Obama put it, "We cannot mistake absolutism for principles," as if recognizing true principles cannot mean anything but. Note the clever word salad: "We cannot mistake" (double negation for emphasis) "absolutism" (extreme definition) "for principles" (the good). In other words, those who say America's founding principles are timeless are absolutists and hence extremists. Therefore, principles are never absolute – they must be open to interpretation, be changeable, moderate, and in tune with the times. One observer responded, "It's a way of redefining words so that common sense is turned upside-down and nobody knows the difference."[9]

And in our pioneer history, Satan, never passing an opportunity to taunt, even had his followers toss the Prophet Joseph into *Liberty* Jail – a pathetic oxymoron.

Dilution by modifiers

Justice is a central and vital concept in Heavenly Father's plan, as we noted in Alma 42. There are not many ways Satan can substitute a deceptive word for it, so he dilutes it through overuse of adjectives. Here are a few phrases in recent news stories that muffle the original concept:

- Social justice
- Economic justice
- Political justice
- Academic justice
- Environmental justice
- Earth justice
- Transformative justice
- Climate justice
- Gender justice
- Animal rights justice

What's next – vegetable justice? The list is as long as a list of adjectives, including a new one at recent UN proceedings: erotic justice. What mischief won't ensue with that one?

The distortion of equality and fairness

Each year that I taught early morning seminary and the topic was our pre-earthly existence, I divided the class into two groups and asked them to imagine the war in heaven as a political campaign. One side had to develop bumper-sticker arguments in favor of the Father's plan, and the other side in favor of Lucifer's.

Year after year, those working Lucifer's side always completed the exercise first and their themes invariably centered on two words: equality and fairness. Those championing the Father's plan took longer and their arguments were multi-faceted, but the key themes were obedience and trust. (One bright young man came up with the all-time winning bumper sticker: "Got body?")

Satan's use of equality to undermine agency and justice is deviously brilliant. God desires that all His children return, so Satan redefines it to imply that equality of outcome – not one soul shall be lost – is good, no matter the method. He intentionally obscures *types* of equality. God gives to no child what He isn't willing to give to each of His children, this being true equality of *opportunity*. Freedoms are also God-given – equal *rights*. But to reason from equal *opportunity* and equal *rights* that there must be equality of *outcome* is to ignore the critical intervening variable, the actions of man himself. Precisely what Satan wants.

Human nature being what it is, where there is choice, there will be unequal effort. And because not all behave equally properly before God, **equality as an end state is impossible**. (There are degrees of glory for a reason.)

Yet equal outcome is what Satan promised. Which means under his plan unequal input doesn't matter, which means that agency doesn't matter, which means that actions don't have consequences, which means no justice, no law, no punishment, no mercy … and God would cease to be God. Satan's goal.

Those who mount soapboxes to agitate for equality of outcome – the din of inequity – are in reality campaigning against the Father's plan of agency for His children. They argue that anything but equal outcomes isn't fair and that someone else is causing unfairness. What they fail to see is that seeming unfairness happens for a reason, and too often the reason is unequal effort.

Counterfeits

Under the "things are not what they seem to be" category, a Soviet-era joke claimed that communism is the path to peace, as evidenced that the Moscow zoo has a lamb and lion lying down together in harmony. When the zookeeper was asked behind the scenes how that could be, he said, "I toss in a new lamb every day."

Twists and distortions are found not only in words and phrases, but in broader concepts as well.

The Concept	The Counterfeit
Keep the commandments. They are timeless principles that will bring the most happiness.	Religious commandments once may have been useful, but are now old and useless. Our behavior depends on today's unique circumstances.
God's plan determines the future. Our actions determine our fate within that plan. Prophets help us by warning of coming events.	History determines the future. Historical determinism and the thesis-antithesis-synthesis dialectic control how events unfold. One can be on the right side or wrong side of history, but it determines our fate.

The Concept	The Counterfeit
God sends natural disasters to turn people's hearts away from immoral behavior, especially sexual sins. He commands us to worship Him.	Man's misuse of his environment is the cause of natural disasters. The only important immorality is failure to care for and worship mother earth.
When things get tough, turn to God.	When things get tough, rely on the experts who run society.

Conscious uncoupling

Satan twists words to hide the negatives of abortion; so, too, with divorce. Take away the stigma by giving it a new name as a Hollywood star and her husband did. They call it "conscious uncoupling."

Clever use of words. *Conscious* implies they are awake, logical, and know what they're doing. *Uncoupling* suggests that if marriage has been diminished as mere coupling, then **uncoupling diminishes the taint of divorce**. No big deal. Like switching railroad cars around.

The rationale: Conscious uncoupling "prevents families from being broken by divorce and creates expanded families that continue to function in a healthy way outside of traditional marriage."

The guru who guided this couple through the whitewashing process published his claims and logic thus:[10]

- We ought to redefine the construct of marriage and get rid of outdated constructs.
- The idea of being married to one person for life is too much pressure for anyone.

- Our biology and psychology aren't set up to be with one person for four, five, or six decades.
- Conscious uncoupling avoids the drama of divorce.
- Divorce will be a positive experience if approached in building up your partner's "spiritual endoskeleton."
- Conscious uncoupling brings "wholeness to the spirits of both people" and "prevents families from being broken by divorce and creates expanded families that continue to function in a healthy way outside of traditional marriage."
- Although it looks like everything is coming apart; it is actually all coming back together.
- To change the concept of divorce, we need to release the belief structures we have around marriage that create rigidity in our thought process.

The author's main point is to heal the internal spirit. No argument there. But he whitewashes, even seems to recommend, divorce as the way to get to a higher plane. Therefore, the treatise is riddled with positive terms – wholeness, healthy, building up, prevents breakage, creates expanded families, coming back together … conditioned on giving up the outdated construct of marriage. And enough psychobabble (do spiritual endoskeletons dwell in closets?) to give it a veneer of erudition.

Divorce by any other name is still the breaking of the marriage covenant.

Another newly developing movement to take away the stigma of divorce, but more to the point to weaken marriage, is to substitute the word *wedlease* for the traditional *wedlock*. As in leasing a dwelling instead of buying it, wedlease couples contract to remain with each other for a period of time, say one, five, or ten years. At the end of the lease contract, they can choose to renew, renegotiate terms, or terminate the lease. And if they terminate the arrangement before the prescribed period, they're not divorced, only lease-breakers – unleased and unleashed.

Dandy, just dandy.

* * *

The concept does not exist for which Satan does not have a counterfeit. Expect to hear more about conscious uncoupling in the future.

SECTION IV

THE WAR TO DESTROY THE CONSTITUTION

"The Constitution of the United States, as given to us by our fathers, is the real government under which individuals may exercise free agency and individual initiative."

– David O. McKay

Chapter 15

Ageless Emotions, Timeless Principles, A Moral Document

"Our Constitution was made only for a moral and religious people. It is wholly inadequate to the government of any other."

– John Adams

How does a society give leaders sufficient power to accomplish desired goals, but not so much that they become tyrants?

The Constitution of the United States of America holds the answers.

Can you name an emotion today that did not exist a hundred years ago? Or one that didn't exist, say, two or three thousand years ago?

Impossible. While fresh ways to *apply* emotions pop up, **there are no new emotions**. Love, hate, anger, compassion, jealousy, kindness, revenge, caring, lust, and a variety of desires have been with us since the fruit buffet in Eden. Adam and Eve had no more and no fewer emotions to choose from than we do.

Because emotions are timeless, so too must be the principles that control them. The principles designed to control the desire for power are embedded in the Constitution. Whether we will remain free depends on whether we honor them.

In a nutshell

Let's begin with an overview of the Constitution from the 98th and 101st sections of the Doctrine and Covenants,[1] and the document itself:

- It was established by God – "by the hands of wise men whom I raised up unto this very purpose...."
- It was not written for Americans alone – it "belongs to all mankind..." and "for the rights and protection of all flesh...."
- It affirms natural God-given rights – "supporting that principle of freedom in maintaining rights and privileges..." and "[that] every man may act in doctrine and principle ... according to the moral agency which I have given unto him...."
- It was the first step in the elimination of slavery – "I, the Lord God, make you free..." and "it is not right that any man should be in bondage one to another. And for this purpose have I established the Constitution...."
- It affirms the people as sovereign – "We the people of the United States, in order to form a more perfect union.... " and "that every man may be accountable for his own sins...."
- It establishes a limited government – self evident from the structure of the Constitution, but especially the enumerated powers clause and the Tenth Amendment affirming that non-enumerated powers remain with the states and the people.
- It is an ingenious formula for diffusing and controlling power through checks and balances – separation of power, division of power, and enumerated powers. Its principles are the antidote to abuse of power.

The brilliance of our inspired Constitution is that no longer were people to be subjects to a sovereign monarch under the clever but false concept of divine right of kings (invented to keep "lessers" in their supposed place, and a fancy way of taking the name of God in vain), but were to be sovereigns themselves – "We the People" granting government its just powers.

This great document was designed to prevent the misuse of power by tyrants, be they kings, czars, or officious overfed functionaries. Breaking away from the divine right of kings took a long time, and we can trace the influence of such philosophers as John Locke and Montesquieu on Thomas Jefferson, James Madison, and other Founding Fathers. But the impetus to and guiding hand in its creation came from God, not from man. It is a God-given work that Satan must destroy or his purposes fail. It's that serious a battle.

A necessary half step

The Constitution grants government sufficient power to accomplish necessary functions, but not so much to invite abuse (it happens unbidden anyway). It is God's instrument to maximize agency and stand as a bulwark against those who, as in the war in heaven, would minimize our latitude of action and deprive us of our God-given right to be our own agents and to make decisions for ourselves.

Note again that D&C 101:79 unequivocally states:

> Therefore, it is not right that any man should be in bondage one to another.

Then the payoff in verse 80:

> And *for this purpose* have I established the Constitution of this land, by the hands of wise men whom I raised up unto this very purpose, and redeemed the land by the shedding of blood. [Emphasis added]

The most absurd criticism is that the Constitution is a racist document. After all, the shallow reasoning goes, the Constitution made slaves worth only 3/5 of a person. If only critics knew that **eliminating**

bondage was God's purpose in establishing it. Rather than being a racist document, the Constitution is exactly the opposite – a document that would *lead* to the elimination of slavery in America.

The 3/5 Compromise was a necessary half step. If no slaves had been counted, the southern states would not have ratified the Constitution. If slaves had been counted fully, the southern states would have had disproportional influence in Congress and the Electoral College, which would have substantially delayed the abolition of slavery.

The Lord knew what He was doing. He raised up a group of wise men to take the first step, and then came another wise man, Abraham Lincoln, to finish the job, with the Daniel Websters of the interim period being the oratorical connective tissue between the two. By following God's two-step plan, America became the only civilization in history to fight a war to abolish slavery, and it took the lives of 300,000 white and black anti-slavery soldiers to do it.[2]

The child cannot define the parent

It seems to be Satan's strategy to undermine the Constitution by small bites rather than a highly visible frontal attack. In the following chapters, we will look at detailed ways those in power stretch, misinterpret, add to, and avoid the Constitution, but first a few broad strokes.

Former Attorney General Ed Meese points out deeper meanings in the Constitution that are often underemphasized,[3] paraphrased as follows:

> Federalism is critical to the **control of power**. The Framers viewed government in America as neither wholly federal nor wholly national but a composite of the two. *Division* of power between the states and the central government is equally important as the *separation* of powers between the three branches of the central government.

> Federalism contributes to a **sense of political community** and hence to a kind of public spirit. In the space left by a limited central government, the people rule themselves by their own moral and social values. Through deliberation, debate, and compromise, a public consensus is formed about what constitutes the public good. This knits individuals into a community of citizens. The liberty to determine the morality of a community, rather than have it imposed, is protected by the Constitution.
>
> Although the Constitution is "the Supreme Law of the Land," constitutional law is the **product of all three branches**, not solely the decisions of the Supreme Court. Each has a duty to interpret the Constitution in the performance of its official functions, and each official takes a solemn oath to that effect. Thomas Jefferson warned, "To consider the judges as the ultimate arbiters of all constitutional questions (is) a very dangerous doctrine indeed, and one which would place us under the despotism of an oligarchy."[4]

Meese quotes constitutional historian Charles Warren that "however the Court may interpret the provisions of the Constitution, it is still the Constitution which is the law, not the decisions of the Court." This is not to say that Supreme Court decisions lack the character of binding law; they are binding. But they need not be seen as the last word. Of its own accord or through changes in appointments, the court may come to revisit some of its doctrines and adjust its pronouncements to the *commands of the Constitution*. In other words, the Supreme Court may enjoy the adjective in its title, but true supremacy remains with the Constitution itself.

Concluding his essay, Meese emphasizes that the Constitution "is and must be understood to be the standard against which all laws, policies, and interpretations should be measured. It is our fundamental law ... against which the actions of government officials must be squared. In the end, the continued success and viability of our democratic Republic depends on our fidelity to ... our great charter of liberty."[5]

Very logical, very clear, but now look at the distortions that have crept in:

- Demise of federalism. The power of the states in relation to the federal government has eroded, much of it beginning with the 17th Amendment. Prior to its enactment in 1913, U.S. Senators were elected by state legislatures, a way for states to check the power of the central government. While members of the House of Representatives had to face the voters every two years, U.S. senators were granted six-year terms to provide the longer and more deliberative view – the saucer that cools the hot tea, in Washington's memorable demonstration to Jefferson – knowing, however, that they would be watched carefully by legislative peers back home. But with the demise of election by state legislatures, senators could ignore legislatures and the people for four years and posture as needed for two. As peer pressure from fellow U.S. senators grew and accountability to state legislatures all but disappeared, states' influence in Washington took a hit. Today, especially with the lure of federal dollars, **state governments are morphing into subservient agents** of the federal government and must claw back their powers lest a critical constitutional principle wither.
- Flexible morality. If government is not limited, there is no room for the people to rule themselves by their own moral and social values, and to call on political institutions to help them. Rather, those wielding excessive power determine what social values shall and shall not be heeded. Attacks on religious freedoms haven't helped. The restoration of a high standard of public morality is essential to the revival of constitutionalism.
- False supremacy. Higher education has taught for years that "the Constitution is what nine justices say it is" – the mantra of those who plump for a living constitution. It even happened in a constitutional law class I took at BYU, and it was a while before I recognized the flawed reasoning. If the edict of five out of nine justices were "the Constitution," what prevents

wholesale changes in the document from the bench? Why endure an intentionally complex amendment process if all one had to do was convince five justices of one's opinion? Choose which sections to apply and which to ignore and, presto, a remodeled Constitution.

That last point, a bit exaggerated for emphasis, symbolizes the upside-down thinking that has seeped into too many corners of government. What began as a sovereign people creating a fundamental document, that in turn created government, has now become the people as subjects of a government that has the power to redefine that fundamental document as it wishes.

Such thinking ignores nature. The **child cannot define the parent**; only the parent can define the parent. **The Constitution is not what the Supreme Court says it is; the Constitution is what the Constitution says it is.**

Yet Congress ignores the Constitution in its deliberations, smug in the idea that the judicial branch has the responsibility to judge whether laws are constitutional or not, and they need not concern themselves with constitutional matters. In other words, legislate however you will and it's only unconstitutional if the Supreme Court calls you out on it ... years later, if at all. Sort of like those who feel they can do anything they want with no thought of right or wrong because it's only wrong if they get caught.

Under rules adopted by the House in 2011, members introducing a bill are required to cite the section of the Constitution that grants the authority. A study of the 3764 bills introduced that year revealed shameful ignorance and/or arrogant rejection that our founding document should be any guide whatsoever in their deliberations. One congressman maintained that Congress has the authority to introduce whatever legislation it wants and it is up to the Supreme Court to determine its constitutionality.[6] In other words, drive as recklessly as you want until a cop pulls you over.

In a similar "don't bother me with details" example, then-Speaker Nancy Pelosi, when asked where the Constitution authorizes Congress to order Americans to buy health insurance, mocked the reporter, "Are you serious? Are you serious?"[7] A subsequent clarification from her office claimed the Commerce Clause as authority, an argument much in dispute. The point is her haughty attitude toward the Constitution.

* * *

Members of Congress take an oath to "support and defend the Constitution of the United States ... and bear true faith and allegiance to the same...." They should think about it more often.

Chapter 16

Old Dead White Men Versus Old Dead White Men

"The Constitution is the guide which I will never abandon."

– George Washington

Jay Leno once cracked, "They keep talking about drafting a constitution for Iraq. Why don't we just give them ours? It was written by a lot of really smart guys, it's worked for over 200 years, and we're not using it anymore."

Interviewed on Egyptian TV in 2012, U.S. Supreme Court Justice Ruth Bader Ginsburg said:

> I can't speak about what the Egyptian experience should be, because I'm operating under a rather old constitution. The United States, in comparison to Egypt, is a very new nation; and yet we have the oldest written constitution still in force in the world.... I would not look to the U.S. Constitution if I were drafting a constitution in the year 2012. I might look at the constitution of South Africa.[1]

A chance to defend the Constitution and she muffed it big time.

Applicability

Parse Justice Ginsburg's unfortunate remarks. Article 6 of the U.S. Constitution specifies that all judicial officers "shall be bound by Oath or Affirmation, to support this Constitution..." Doesn't the word *support* imply speaking well of it, appreciating it, defending it? Her remarks, on the other hand, suggest the Constitution is a shackling device under which she chafes.

Second, does "operating under a rather old constitution" mean that something newer must necessarily be better? Might not having "the oldest written constitution still in force in the world" indicate that perhaps it's working – that it contains timeless principles? Why the assumption that old must be inferior to new?[2]

Third, browse through the 90-page, 32,000-word Constitution of the Republic of South Africa Justice Ginsburg seems to venerate over ours. You will find many directives, rules, and regulations about people's rights and the powers of government, but you will not find one *principle* of governance that is superior to the principles in the U.S. Constitution in *controlling power in the hands of fallible humans*, which has been the single biggest obstacle bedeviling would-be nation builders throughout history. And the Framers did it in only 4400 words.

Consider in this vein President Barack Obama's remarks to NBC reporter Matt Lauer:

> What's frustrated people is that I have not been able to force Congress to implement every aspect of what I said in 2008. That's just the nature of being president. It turns out our Founders designed a system that makes it more difficult to bring about change that I would like sometimes.[3]

That is precisely the point, Mr. President. Our Founders designed the system so that one person's agenda, no matter how firmly he may believe its benefits, *would* be difficult to bring about – and *must* be difficult if improper uses of power are to be stymied:

- That one branch of government cannot unilaterally force its will on any other.
- That those holding power would be double-checked by other power holders in government.
- That thought, reflection, debate, and negotiations would be required among all parties of interest before a policy is enacted.
- And it surely does not say that the executive should have the power "to force Congress to implement every aspect" of that executive's agenda.

Can you imagine a member of the Church whining that following the requirements for temple attendance makes it difficult to implement his own agenda?

The Framers

The Constitution is under attack typified by the cynical jab, "What could a bunch of old white men who lived two centuries ago possibly understand about our problems today?" Further, the argument goes, how could *they* be the conveyors of true principles when George Washington owned slaves, Thomas Jefferson supposedly fathered children with one of his, Franklin had dalliances in Paris, Alexander Hamilton was prideful, Samuel Adams was a hothead, and James Madison was a geek?

As if God can only use the perfect as His instruments.

The purpose of such stories is to dissuade a fair analysis of what these men accomplished – the well-known rejection by association:

- Babe Ruth was said to cuss, booze, and philander worse than a sailor.[4] So therefore his home run records don't exist?
- Joseph Smith was called a gold digger. How does that change the Book of Mormon?
- Einstein didn't speak until he was four and didn't read until he was seven. Therefore, his theory of relativity is bogus?

On top of being old, white, and relatively well off, the Founding Fathers have been criticized as irreligious and in no position to write an inspired document. Though they may not have been active in the denominations of their time, **they almost unanimously acknowledged God's hand in their work**, which is the very opposite of the Deism – the belief in a non-interventionist God – many accuse them of. Constitutional scholar Mark Cannon, the first administrative assistant to the chief justice, concludes that some historians have misjudged our Founders' religiosity because they were critical of historical Christianity, its creeds, the triune Godhead, and self-serving ministers. Given that they were among the great and noble whom God raised up, how could their attitudes be otherwise? Cannon cites a few examples among hundreds of such quotes showing that the Framers were very spiritual men:[5]

> Benjamin Franklin: "[The] longer I live, the more convincing proofs I see of the truth – that God governs in the affairs of men."[6]

> George Washington: "The success, which has hitherto attended our united efforts, we owe the gracious interposition of heaven."[7]

> Signer Charles Pinckney: "When the great work was done and published, I was … struck with amazement. Nothing less than that superintending hand of Providence, that so miraculously carried us through the war … could have brought it about so complete, upon the whole."[8]

> James Madison: "It is impossible for the man of pious reflection not to perceive in it a finger of that almighty hand which has been so frequently and signally extended to our relief in the critical stages of the revolution."[9]

After intellectual elites have attributed all human frailties to one or another of the Founding Fathers, then comes the ludicrous such as refusing to even utter the term, Fathers being a so sexist word. The

White House once posted a link to a government website with the headline, "The Papers of the Founding Founders Are Now Online."[10] Founding Founders? Such can be the silliness of political correctness unchained. (Mirthifully, the phrase was later scrubbed.)

A living Constitution?

One of Chinese general Sun Tzu's favored tactics was to heap scorn and ridicule on an opponent's choicest values and traditions. It weakened opponents' will to fight five centuries before Christ and is still employed today, its longevity evidence that it works.

So the Constitution will not be seen for what it is – a God-given roadmap to control power – Satan heaps scorn on it as an evil roadblock against progress. For example, a Georgetown University law professor recently stated that what he calls our broken system of government stems from the Constitution "with its archaic, idiosyncratic and downright evil provisions."[11] Evil provisions? And downright evil to boot?

Woodrow Wilson, the first president to publicly criticize the Constitution, spoke of grave defects in "this miserable delusion of a republic,"[12] and throughout his political career was often openly hostile against the Constitution calling it pre-modern, cumbersome, and open to corruption.[13] Yet he was an admirer of William Gladstone who had the opposite impression of its character describing it as "the most wonderful work ever struck off at a given time by the brain and purpose of man."[14]

Wilson and his allies Louis Brandeis and Oliver Wendell Holmes, Jr. (he who bragged, "All my life I have sneered at the natural rights of man."[15]), pushed the idea of a "living Constitution." Carried forth by Richard Ely, John Dewey, and Herbert Croly, among others (all together a fine set of old dead white men), the phrase implies that the Constitution is an organism that evolves over time. Of course, the Constitution is living in the sense it can be changed through an amending process, but the Wilsonites use the "living" idea to stretch original wording to cover the latest social engineering theories and schemes – that the Constitution should "be understood as a vehicle for change rather than a means of constraint."[16] They claim that there are no timeless principles – that natural rights constitutionalism is archaic, that we must guide ourselves solely on the social warp and woof in which we live, as determined by whichever group's fads and fancies are in fashion.

Our response to such sophistry is, as noted in the previous chapter, that there are no new emotions. Each emotion triggers a generic or innate behavior embellished only by the circumstances of the day. There may be unique applications of that behavior, but the emotion-behavior connection has remained remarkably consistent throughout history – hate and anger lead to violence, love and compassion lead to nurture, and so forth.

Therefore, timeless core behaviors driven by timeless emotions must be addressed by timeless principles – a characteristic of the Constitution Mr. Wilson failed to grasp. Two presidents later, however, Calvin Coolidge affirmed it:

> If all men are created equal, that is final. If they are endowed with inalienable rights, that is final. If governments derive their just powers from the consent of the governed, that is final. ... If anyone wishes to deny their truth or their soundness, the only direction in which he can proceed historically is not forward, but backward toward the time when there was no equality, no rights of the individual, no rule of the people. Those who wish to proceed in that direction can not lay claim to progress.[17]

The origin of rights

The basic struggle between the Constitution and those who would replace, diminish, or destroy it centers on the rights of the people. Where do they come from – God or man, nature or government?

Some ideologues with their favorite historians in tow claim that the Constitution differs from the path the Declaration of Independence pointed us. They argue that the Declaration had it right, but the Framers of the Constitution eleven years later went a different direction. This crafty distortion implies that the Founders weren't sure of themselves and made mistakes. And if they weren't on solid footing, then people two centuries later can be excused for taking latitude with the document.

The Declaration of Independence is replete with references to natural rights: the laws of nature and nature's God; all men are endowed by their Creator with certain unalienable rights; governments derive their just powers from the consent of the governed; if government becomes destructive, it is the right of the people to alter or abolish it; and so declared with firm reliance on the protection of divine providence.

The Constitution carries that same thrust: "We the People … do ordain and establish this Constitution for the United States of America." (Love the word *for*.) Again, Ed Meese:

> Part of the reason for the Constitution's enduring strength is that it is the complement of the Declaration of Independence. The Declaration provided the philosophical basis for a government that exercises legitimate power by "the consent of the governed," and it defined the conditions of a free people, whose rights and liberty are derived from their Creator. The Constitution delineated the structure of government and the rules for its operation,, consistent with the creed of human liberty proclaimed in the Declaration."[18]

Only a person who ignores the role of natural law in both documents, who fails to see the connection between the laundry list of offenses listed in the Declaration and the Constitution's focus on the limitation of powers, and who cannot see the avowed goal of representation and the people as sovereign in both documents, could possibly believe that the document of 1787 breaks with that of 1776.

Framers versus Progressives

The battle today pits two very contrasting viewpoints about agency, freedoms, rights, power, and government. Here are the key points from the Declaration and the Constitution as written by the Framers, and the opposing school of thought by those labeling themselves Progressives.

The Framers	The Progressives
Man has natural rights to life, liberty, and the fruits of his labor. Rights do not come from man, and man does not have the prerogative to take them away.	Man has only those rights his society is willing to grant him.
The people are sovereign and governments derive their just powers from the consent of the governed.	Government is sovereign over the people. People as a whole cannot be trusted to become sufficiently informed to exercise sovereignty over the state.
The purpose of government is to protect the God-given inalienable rights of the people, as extended in the Preamble.	The purpose of government is to shape society and control the behavior of the people for the benefit of all.
Timeless principles and moral absolutes exist to guide the behavior of man.	There are no immutable principles. All guidelines must arise from the social context of the time.

The Framers	The Progressives
The Constitution is based on just principles that never go out of date. Society's circumstances may change, but human nature has remained remarkably constant over the centuries.	The Constitution is a living document, not a mechanistic one. It is an organism that evolves according to the changing needs of society as determined by those in the best position to judge.
Government must be limited. A society with too much government becomes tyrannical.	Government must expand as needed. A society without sufficient government becomes anarchic.
The Constitution is what the Constitution says it is.	The Constitution is what the Supreme Court says it is. Justices should utilize case studies from other nations in their rulings about the Constitution.
Laws, properly and constitutionally created by representative government, govern society. We are a nation of laws, not of men.	There will be circumstances where exemptions from the law, such as for Congress and its staff, must be granted to ensure efficient functioning of government.
Law is the great leveler. All citizens stand equal under the law; no one is above the law.	Law is a tool in the hands of experts to bring about the well being of society as a whole.

The Framers	The Progressives
Limited government honors the agency of man; ever-expanding government diminishes it.	Power concentrated in the hands of non-partisan experts is the most efficient model of government. Such concentration facilitates unity of purpose and action rather than gridlock and squabbling.
Three methods keep power in check and restrain leaders from abusing it: (1) separation of powers between the three branches of government; (2) division of powers between the states and the federal government; and (3) specific enumerated powers – all others revert to the states and/or the people.	Separation and division of powers impedes progress and prevents government from acting in unison. Experts from a mature society can accomplish more for the nation if freed from the checks and balances of power.
Legislation originates in Congress and is implemented by the executive.	Government policies should originate and be implemented by the same people, as in the British parliamentary system.
There shall be no aristocracy and government shall not grant titles. Circumstances of birth confer no right to rule.	There shall be no aristocracy by birth, but educational titles are useful in selecting administrative experts.

The Framers	The Progressives
The judicial branch should protect freedoms and render decisions based on the original intent of the Framers of the Constitution.	The judicial branch and elite law schools play a path-breaking role to discover new powers for the administrative state.
Maximum individual freedom is the best road to prosperity for all.	Maximum power centered in the administrative state is the best road to prosperity for all.

The Framers' principles focus on limiting power and maximizing freedoms of the individual, whereas living-constitution ideas center on increasing state power and controlling the individual.

If we have natural rights, then government cannot restrict them, only preserve them. If, however, our rights come from government, then under what regimen can government ever be constrained?

Charles C. W. Cooke uses the squabble over the bearing of arms to underscore who is on top and who is subordinate:

> It makes little philosophical sense for the elected representatives of a government that is subordinate to the people to be able to disarm those people. **An enlightened state may not remove from the people the basic rights that are recognized in the very document to which it owes its existence.** To ask, 'Why do you need an AR-15?' is to invert the relationship. A better question: 'Why don't you want me to have one?'[19] [Emphasis added]

Rights preceded government; government can only be their preserver.

* * *

The secular world would fob onto us their naïve view that old white men 200+ years ago could not possibly have foreseen the complexities of our technological age. The truth is, they did not need to see the details of our day; they knew the connection between emotions and behaviors, and the principles to hold those behaviors in check whatever the era.

More to the point, they were directed by God.

Chapter 17

Cherry Picking the Cotton-Pickin' Laws

"When the people fear the government, you have tyranny. When the government fears the people, you have freedom."

– Thomas Paine

The Constitution states that the executive "shall take Care that the Laws be faithfully executed..." Government's execution of the law today has all the faithfulness of a streetwalker and the uniformity of the Stanford marching band.

The first step to tyranny is unequal application of laws.

Catherine Engelbrecht, founder of a nonprofit election integrity organization, testified before Congress that she and her husband had never received visits or inquiries from government agencies for over 20 years – no interactions with government other than filing tax returns. Then immediately after applying for nonprofit (501-c-3) status, her personal business, her family, and the organization were investigated 15 times by the IRS, OSHA, the FBI, and even the Bureau of Alcohol, Tobacco, and Firearms. She testified that "these events were occurring while the IRS was subjecting me to multiple rounds of abusive inquiries, with requests to provide every Facebook and Twitter entry I'd ever posted, questions about my political aspirations, and demands to know the names of every group I'd ever made presentations to, the content of what I'd said, and where I intended to speak for the coming year."[1]

To reiterate, she was told to turn over *every* Twitter and Facebook posting, names of groups, content of speeches, and intended speeches. How can one not conclude that government agencies are being fundamentally transformed into partisan tools to monitor and harass political opponents?

Victor Davis Hanson observes, "It is no exaggeration to state that the IRS has now surrendered its reputation as an impartial agency and lost the public trust; it has degenerated into an extension of the White House."[2]

Tyranny in embryo.

Government by fiat

If you were president and wanted to rule by decree, what would you do first?

Having run that thought experiment a few times, one idea repeats: ignore the laws Congress passes if you don't agree with them. Paint the Constitution as an archaic and cumbersome structure that blocks you from accomplishing good things for the people. Then demonize opponents who dare to argue.

Congress is easily snubbed and at times appears toothless. It tends either to pass monstrous legislation (ObamaCare contains 363,000 words, more than 98% of all books ever written[3]) in which a variety of executive-power mischief can be hidden, or, as already noted, it passes a wish list (think Clean Water Act and Clean Air Act) and punts away its legislative authority to the tender mercies of unelected grandees. These functionaries – members of the executive branch, by the way – increasingly write directives that go far beyond "filling in the details" of what Congress passed. Congress allocates money by Continuing Resolutions rather than by tight budgeting, which allows each agency, rather than Congress, to decide how its funds are spent, sometimes going years without a formal budget.

All this is not in harmony with the Constitution.

As this book goes to press, Congress has taken few substantial steps against a president who has unilaterally modified an act of Congress in blatant violation of the first article of the Constitution. President Obama has changed the Affordable Care Act at least 38 times since its disastrous rollout. Note the clever formula: Change a good law and people will resist, but change a bad law and people will see it as a benevolent move. Presto, precedent is established in the public mind that it's okay for the president to modify the law without going through Congress. Concerns about arbitrary one-man rule weaken and authoritarian rule creeps closer.

In a December 2013 House Judiciary Committee hearing, George Washington University law professor Jonathan Turley testified: "The danger is quite severe. The problem with what the president is doing is that he's not simply posing a danger to the constitutional system. **He's become the very danger the Constitution was designed to avoid.** That is, the concentration of power in every single branch."[4] [Emphasis added]

Calling a sitting president "the very danger the Constitution was designed to avoid" is startling, especially because Mr. Turley has been an open supporter of President Obama.

He then explained that the checks-and-balances relationship between the three branches is delicate and "designed to prevent this type of concentration," and continued:

> There are two trends going on which should be of equal concern to all members of Congress. One is that we have had the radical expansion of president powers under both President Bush and President Obama. We have what

> many once called an imperial presidency model of largely unchecked authority. And with that trend we also have the continued rise of this fourth branch. We have agencies that are quite large that issue regulations. The Supreme Court said recently that agencies could actually define their own or interpret their own jurisdiction.[5]

A former Department of Justice lawyer, J. Christian Adams, says that America is "the first country ever founded for the principle that every individual has individual dignity, divinely inspired individual dignity, to be treated by their government as an individual, not differently than somebody whose brother is an earl." But, he continues, under the Obama Justice Department, "law is a tool to help those in power aid those they agree with. It is not a great leveler. It's no longer a means to make everybody equal and to create those fences that everybody must stay within. It's a way to punish your opponents and reward your [friends]."[6]

One columnist observed that Obama is rebalancing the checks-and-balances system toward a national-leader model that is alien to the American tradition. He quotes the president in Florida: "So where I can act on my own, I'm going to act on my own. I won't wait for Congress." And in Illinois: "We're going to do everything we can, wherever we can, with or without Congress." The columnist writes further, "Mr. Obama doesn't merely criticize Congress. He mocks it repeatedly. Washington 'ignored' problems. It 'made things worse.' It 'manufactures' crises and 'phony scandals.' He is persuading his audiences to set Congress aside and let him act."[7]

Judicial ability to restrain the executive is also weak because it can take years for a complaint to wend its way through the court system, even if one has standing. And what happens if a president simply ignores a judgment? When Chief Justice John Marshall ruled against Georgia in an Indian lands dispute in 1832, popular myth has it that President Andrew Jackson responded, "John Marshall has made his decision, now let him enforce it."[8] Even if he didn't say it, the sentiment has undoubtedly occurred to more than one president who disagreed with a SCOTUS decision. In the end, both Georgia and Jackson ignored the decision, and the court did nothing. Why couldn't such happen today? A highly visible snubbing of a court decision might trigger a contempt citation, but what if that, too, were ignored? Would the justices order the Army to haul their commander-in-chief into court? And would it be obeyed?

Such a president risks impeachment, of course, but recent history demonstrates that although the House may bring articles of impeachment, a Senate controlled by the president's party is highly unlikely to convict. Richard Nixon resigned from the presidency over Watergate because his Republican party controlled neither house of Congress and he could hear how that minuet was going to play out. Bill Clinton, on the other hand, was impeached by a Republican House, but the Democratic Senate refused to convict. Lesson: Don't sweat the threat if your party controls at least one of the two houses of the legislative branch, especially if it is the Senate where a 2/3 vote is required for conviction.

Warning signs of malfeasance in office are easy to spot; figuring out a solution is another matter. What enforcement mechanisms other than impeachment even exist? **Presidential vetoes can be overridden, but nothing in the Constitution can force him to act if he chooses not to.** The impeachment process can remove him but cannot make him act. Chances are by the time the other branches of government got their acts together and senatorial spines stiffened, a dictatorial executive would be difficult to dislodge short of millions marching on Washington.

Faithful execution of the law

Equally, if not more, problematic than ignoring checks and balances is a president who selects which laws to enforce and which not.

In the eyes of progressives, the only true sin in today's government-centric society is refusing to comply with a bureaucratic regulation. But these same people are silent if a federal agency refuses to obey the Constitution or the law. As House Speaker John Boehner said in February 2014, "There's widespread doubt about whether this administration can be trusted to enforce our laws...."[9] More writs of mandamus – rare direct judicial orders for government to follow the law – are being issued by the courts, which is evidence that more agencies, by themselves, are cherry-picking the laws they will obey and the ones they will disregard. Instances of this high-handed attitude are growing:

- The National Labor Relations Board continued to issue orders even after receiving a writ of mandamus from a federal court to cease because new board members were illegal recess appointments.[10]
- The Nuclear Regulatory Commission disregarded a law requiring an approve-disapprove decision of a Yucca Mountain nuclear waste storage facility within three years, a stalling tactic that has gone on since 1983, ignoring the D.C. Circuit Court of Appeals ruling that "the President may not decline to follow a statutory mandate or prohibition simply because of policy objections."[11]
- Health and Human Services (HHS) contraceptive mandates on Catholic Church employees ignore the Religious Freedom Restoration Act, which restricts government from forcing people to act contrary to their conscience or religious beliefs.
- When the Justice Department announces that it will not defend a federal law, or a state attorney general refuses to defend an initiative passed by the people, can one believe that those laws will be as uniformly enforced as any others, even if and after courts determine constitutionality?
- The U.S. Senate itself ignored the law when it refused to pass a budget for three years.
- In 2009, the administration ignored the rights of Chrysler's secured creditors in favor of its union supporters in violation of the standard rules of bankruptcy law.
- In 2014, the executive branch, without congressional approval, ignored immigration laws requiring deportation of illegal aliens

and, instead, offered de facto amnesty to certain categories of children. It didn't take long for people in Central America to figure out the formula: get children into America where they will gain citizenship and act as anchors for the later arrival of their parents. It triggered a flood of unattached children into our nation overwhelming border security.

- Congress does not exempt itself from all laws its passes, but does so in enough cases that there is clamor for a 28th Amendment stating that Congress shall make no law that applies to citizens that does not apply equally to the Senators and/or Representatives.

The phrase "be faithfully executed" is found in the Constitution; the current White House justification phrase "enforcement discretion" is not.

After selective *avoidance* comes selective *enforcement*, often exuberant as the Engelbrecht case shows. Such zealous enforcement can be driven by the need to justify one's job, but also occurs when public employees affiliate with the ideology that desires an all-encompassing administrative state, and hence are tempted to put opponents in their place:

- The Internal Revenue Service has treated organizations applying for tax-exempt status differently depending upon their political leanings, for example stalling Tea Party-affiliated groups for months and years in a process that normally takes less than 30 days. By contrast, applications from the liberal side of the ledger were not subjected to the same scrutiny and were, in fact, expedited.[12] Senator Mitch McConnell observed: "I don't believe that the president ever actually picked up a phone and told someone over at the IRS to slow-walk those applications or audit anybody. But the truth is, he didn't have to. The message was clear enough."[13]
- In another case, the IRS gave confidential tax information about the National Organization for Marriage to administration officials who gave it to NOM's opponents.[14] (The IRS got off with but a $50,000 settlement.) It has also targeted critics of

the administration for audits that are unusual if not retaliatory, such as Dr. Ben Carson after he spoke against Obama's policies at a national prayer breakfast in 2013, with the president in attendance.[15]

- The Department of Health and Human Services not only ignored the Religious Freedom Restoration Act as noted above, but seemed to delight in requiring Catholic nuns, such as the Colorado-based Little Sisters of the Poor, to buy insurance that covered contraception. (What's next – force the NFL to buy coverage for mammograms and Pap smears?) The government said it would accommodate religious exceptions if the nuns designated a third party – their insurer – to provide the coverage. The nuns saw that directing others to pay for their contraception insurance was but a gimmick that would still make them complicit in a matter they doctrinally oppose. It was "a raw assertion of state power directing the religious to follow orders."[16] The Little Sisters refused and the Supreme Court not only stayed the HHS order pending a full hearing, but ordered HHS not to try to force the nuns to sign the accommodation form. Unanimously … for now.
- OSHA, the Occupational Safety and Health Administration, does not have jurisdiction over farming operations with fewer than ten employees. So to extend its reach, it rewrote the definition of farming to re-categorize small family farms as commercial grain handlers knowing that almost every farm must have small on-farm storage facilities to facilitate an even flow of grain to market. It was then able to assess, for example, a $132,000 fine against a small Nebraska farmer who employs one non-family worker.[17]
- The Justice Department indicted an anti-Obama filmmaker for a $15,000 campaign-contribution violation (a pittance in the multi-billion-dollar campaign industry), but ignored investigating a high government official for the much more serious charge of lying to Congress under oath about National Security Agency citizen surveillance.[18]

- Government is an equal opportunity snoop. The Federal Communication Commission planned to study how television stations (and newspapers, over which the FCC has no authority) decide which stories to cover and which to ignore. For what reason would an agency study "perceived station bias" if not to police what news is fit to broadcast?[19] An uproar from press and voters alike caused them to back off, but the telling point is that these rule writers actually thought they were justified.

So what does all this have to do with the relocated war in heaven? Plenty. The more government regulations increase, the fewer the choices for the people. As choices decrease, so does agency, and therefore the more God's plan for us is frustrated.

When government believes it can pick and choose which laws to follow, which to bend, and which to ignore, we have lawlessness by definition – we have gangster government, we have a culture of intimidation. **The unequal and capricious application of the laws is a sure sign of a budding tyranny**, which in turn is a sure sign that agency will be violated. The growing list of such examples indicates not only an unhealthy concentration of power, but evidence that administrators have little fear their actions will be countermanded.

James Madison warned, "I believe there are more instances of the abridgement of the freedom of the people by gradual and silent encroachments of those in power than by violent and sudden usurpations."

* * *

So why haven't such encroachments on the Constitution triggered more outrage? Simple: The more immoral a society becomes, the less sensitive it is to mortal threats.

Chapter 18

About That Food Storage You Thought You Owned

"The art of government consists in taking as much money as possible from one class of citizen to give to the other."

– Voltaire

People will fight oppressive governments when they're hungry, but not when they're famished.

"A chicken in every pot" was a 1936 campaign slogan for President Franklin Roosevelt as he sought re-election in the middle of the Great Depression.[1] Sounded like a good idea to one Roscoe Filburn, an Ohio farmer, who also wanted to improve his family's meals. So he raised chickens and fed them the extra wheat he grew on his 23-acre farm.

Well, the same government that wanted a chicken in every pot wanted fewer chickens in Filburn's pots. He was restricted to growing wheat on only 11 acres, and none for his private use. To drive up prices, you see.

When the government found out that he was growing extra wheat, they fined him 49 cents for every bushel over his allotment although none of the extra wheat was ever shipped to market. His own wheat on his own land for his own chickens, and no intent to sell it. Didn't matter; he was interfering with interstate commerce. It was a product, ruled the Supreme Court in 1942, that he otherwise would have had to buy in the marketplace, and hence it impacted trade.[2]

What a stretch.

But stretch, ignore, expand, redefine, extend, invent are part of the repertoire of those who change laws and powers for personal gain.

Return of the unelected sovereigns

The historical infringer on freedom – the sovereign ruler – had its modern incarnation when Woodrow Wilson thought that major problems were under control and that mankind had moved beyond splitting themselves into squabbling factions. He felt the time had arrived that self-interests could be subjugated to more noble drives, that a new form of government comprised of non-partisan experts – dispassionate and selfless – could run an efficient administrative state.

Non-partisan experts? No self-interests? Reliably impartial?

Wishful thinking. The self-interests of the Wilsonian administrator continue well beyond putting rice and beans on the table. In fact, there are no limits to self-interest when comforts and luxuries entice. As for impartiality, no man lives free of influence from others no matter his intelligence or skills. Neutrality is elusive. Give him the title of expert and he is even more likely to fall prey to power and act with an eye toward how his decisions might affect the fortunes of his family and friends. Neutral application of laws and regulations? In your dreams.

But Wilson's fiction held and with Franklin Roosevelt, Lyndon Johnson, and Richard Nixon picking up the banner, government grew and Congress has had increasing difficulty exercising effective oversight. There are about 2.7 million unelected federal employees overseen by 535 elected Senators and Representatives with fewer than 25,000 staffers.[3] Do the math. Who's going to win that Super Bowl?

The unelected rule-writers sense they are safe – *de facto* immune. When a congressional committee convenes a hearing, civil servants cannot seem to remember simple facts or who in their ranks is doing what. That's what Congress earned for itself when, in the late 1960s and early 70's, it chose to become part of the administrative state, "fundamentally altering the separation of power and the federal system,"[4] giving up law-making authority and taking on the task of oversight. Failure on both counts. Danger of becoming insignificant.

There is no action that enterprising administrators cannot find mentioned somewhere in the almost million and a half pages of the Federal Register that, with a creative stretch, cannot be said to serve as authority for whatever the state wants done.

The pen and the phone

Now picture what an ambitious president can do backed by hundreds of thousands of these unelected sovereigns who, because of their claimed intelligence and expertise, love to boss people around. He merely signals which laws he favors and which he opposes. No need for direct orders. The minions of the administrative state, upwards of 90% of whom share the president's political ideology,[5] get the hint and act. Selective enforcement again.

So, once checks and balances have been shelved, and once faithful execution of the law is but a people's unfilled wish, **the final step for an aspiring sovereign to rule by decree is simply to … rule by decree**. Clothe whims in executive orders. The law becomes whatever the president says it is. And if the populace raises eyebrows, the president falls back on election victory – "I won" – as the supposed argument-ending authority.

The "above it all" attitude is no respecter of persons or parties. President Richard Nixon in a David Frost interview in 1977 said, "Well, when the president does it, that means it is not illegal."[6] Unbelievable gall. Though some defended him by saying it was spoken in the context of national security, where the president as commander-in-chief does have more latitude, such a mindset is still flat out wrong.

If a president arbitrarily makes up the rules as he goes along, which Obama is doing, Congress is isolated and the Constitution ignored. And We the People cease to be sovereign.

In a recent article in the Harvard Journal of Law and Public Policy, Boston College law professor Gary Lawson bluntly declared, "The modern administrative state is not only merely unconstitutional; it is *anti*-constitutional. The Constitution was designed specifically to prevent the emergence of the kinds of institutions that characterize the modern administrative state. The founding generation would have been dumbstruck by the governmental edifice that has arisen from its handiwork."[7] [Emphasis in original]

The increasing number of violations of the Constitution in recent months by that edifice cannot be chalked up to random happenings. The pattern of avoidance and distortion suggests an underlying strategy to bring about a law-unto-himself leader – imperial power.

- As already mentioned, President Obama, CEO of the Good Intentions Paving Co.,[8] has unilaterally altered the Affordable Care Act. He delayed the employer mandate, exempted Congress and staff contrary to the language in the law, delayed implementation of exchanges for small business, directed Congress to continue paying health benefits that should have ceased, required officials to accept an applicant's word about his income (and hence eligibility) without verifying it, rescinded insurance cancellations (albeit a popular move), and altered rules, among other imperial waivers – all in opposition to constitutional principles.[9] One's signature legislation does not grant the namesake cheerleader the authority to disregard Congress. Adjustments to legislation are still the job of Congress, not the president.
- Obama made recess appointments to the National Labor Relations Board when the Senate in fact was not in recess, thus staking the claim that the executive has the power to determine when the Senate is or isn't in session – an attempt to make Congress subservient to the President. Fortunately, the Supreme Court overturned this violation of constitution rules – *unanimously*. But the attitude remains.

- Obama directed the Immigration and Naturalization Service – by email – to cease deportation proceedings involving 11 million illegal immigrants. The amnesty program, known as the DREAM Act, had been rejected by Congress, but Obama decided to move forward with it anyway. Everyone sympathizes with the plight of children of illegal immigrants, but to solve it by going around Congress only entrenches the practice of one-man rule. Charles Krauthammer pointed out this parallel: If a Republican president wanted to eliminate, say, the capital gains tax, and when Congress refused he instructed the IRS not to collect the capital gains tax, he would be impeached. But this has been the pattern with Obama and the DREAM Act.[10]

  As of this writing, thousands of teens and children from Central America have flooded through our porous borders because the president has refused to follow the law.

Beyond the above examples, the attitude of end runs around Congress is unsettling: "We're not just going to be waiting for legislation in order to make sure that we're providing Americans the kind of help they need. I've got a pen and I've got a phone."[11] And the next day Obama said, "I can use that pen to sign executive orders and take executive actions … that move the ball forward. … When I can act on my own without Congress, I'm going to do so."[12]

Remember the Barack Obama of another time, before he became president?

> The biggest problem that we're facing right now has to do with George Bush trying to bring more power into the executive branch and not go through Congress at all. That's what I intend to reverse when I'm President of the United States of America.[13]

One observer summed it up: "This is a might-makes-right presidency, and if Barack Obama has been from time to time muddled and contradictory, he has been clear on the point that **he has no intention of being limited by something so trivial as the law.**"[14] [Emphasis added]

The untouchable agency

In a blatant shifting of powers to the administrative state, the staffers who wrote the ObamaCare law insulated a particularly onerous panel – the Independent Payment Advisory Board (IPAB), aka death panel – from almost all accountability, and appear at this writing to be getting away with it. David Rivkin and Elizabeth Foley note these features:[15]

- The ObamaCare law stipulates that there "shall be no administrative or judicial review" of the board's decisions.
- Panel members will be presidentially nominated and Senate-confirmed, but after that can only be fired for "neglect of duty or malfeasance in office."
- Congress can overrule IPAB's decisions only after restricted debate, short deadlines, multiple process steps, and a super-majority vote.
- Congress can kill the board *only* if it *introduces* a resolution between January 1 and February 1, 2017, and then *passes* that resolution by a three-fifths supermajority vote by August 15 of that year. (Reminds one of the joke that government granted an Indian tribe all land beyond a certain river until the sun no longer shines, the wind no longer blows, or Saturday night, whichever comes first.)

Other analysts of the law note that "IPAB will have the power to ration care even for those who are not enrolled in government programs."[16]

Congress, in short, has abdicated its oversight responsibilities, has transferred its powers to an unelected board, and absolved the board of any accountability to Congress or to the president. This board will have the authority to deny medical procedures, deny payments, require providers to expand services without additional payment, require gynecologists to make abortion services available regardless of the doctor's beliefs, and require drug companies to set aside a percentage of revenues to fund prescription drug affordability.

Rivkin and Foley conclude that the IPAB is not just another agency, but "a new beast that **exercises both executive and legislative power but can't be controlled by either branch**. Seniors and providers hit hardest by the board's decisions will have nowhere to turn for relief – not Congress, not the president, not the courts. ... In the 225 years of constitutional history, there has been no government entity that violated the separation-of-powers principle like the Independent Payment Advisory Board does."[17]

And there is nothing we can do about it after 2017. Ever.

The symbols of today's dictator are no longer sword and mace, but pen and phone.

Penumbras and emanations

The opportunity for personal agendas broadened considerably when the Supreme Court discovered penumbras. By analogy, if the Constitution is the sun, then penumbras are those areas of partial eclipse, of partial light.

Penumbra doctrine theorizes that there are implied rights and powers that emanate from the Constitution – that surrounding that document are additional powers and rights beyond what the Founding Fathers actually wrote.[18] For example, the Supreme Court held in one famous case (*Griswold v. Connecticut*), that privacy is an implied right emanating from the Bill of Rights. Few would argue that we do not have a right of privacy, per se, and there may be other cases where a right should be extended by implication. But a penumbra means there is less light on the matter, as in that partial eclipse, and that's the rub. Less light means more shadows, more shadows spawn more interpretations, and more interpretations mean more opportunity to inject personal whims into the law.

Those who manufacture penumbras will, of course, always clothe them in comforting language and a veneer of constitutionalism. Which is why one-time Supreme Court nominee Professor Robert H.

Bork cautioned, "A legitimate Court must be controlled by principles exterior to the will of the justices. ... The judge must stick close to the text and the history [of the Constitution], and their fair implications, and not construct new rights."

In a previous book, I described a classic *Peanuts* cartoon in which Lucy asks Charlie Brown and Linus what they see as they look at cloud formations. Linus sees a map of British Honduras, a profile of Thomas Eakins, and an impression of the stoning of Stephen, with the Apostle Paul standing to the side. Charlie Brown sees a duckie and a horsie.

So it is with penumbra doctrine. Those in the lesser light of penumbras will see different emanations, which in turn invite mischief as judges discover penumbras to justify a pre-determined desired outcome. **Judges will see what they want to see and courts will find powers that the Founding Fathers never intended.**

If not checked, it means capricious government by Rorschach inkblot interpretations.

Expansion of powers

James Madison wrote in *Federalist 51*, "If men were angels, no government would be necessary. If angels were to govern men, neither external nor internal controls on government would be necessary." Since neither is the case, we must have government and we must have controls on government. The question is where to draw the lines.

Those who would fundamentally transform America from its original Constitution-based structure charge that those who favor minimal government want no government at all. That is silly, of course, but such demonizing introduces the concept of anarchy into the debate, which scares people into wanting more government so those nasty anarchists don't get their way. No surprise that these accusers are the same people who look to government as daddy – there to provide, decide, and kiss everything better.

Note the expansion of powers in these examples:

- Commerce Clause. Roscoe Filburn's losing case solidified the idea "that growing and consuming wheat entirely on your own farm still counted as interstate commerce that could be regulated by the federal government under the Commerce Clause."[19] Supporters of price supports and acreage quotas talk a good game and no one argues that agriculture is not due a certain amount of protection. What is disconcerting is how elastic the Commerce Clause has become, and the mischief that can be done in its name.

  Fast forward to 2005. Now instead of wheat and chicken, it's marijuana. Drawing on the Filburn case, the Supreme Court in *Gonzales v Raich* held that "medical marijuana cultivated and consumed entirely within the state of California" still counted as interstate commerce, which led Justice Clarence Thomas to remark, "If Congress can regulate this under the Commerce Clause, then it can regulate virtually anything – and the Federal Government is no longer one of limited and enumerated powers."[20]

  Roscoe is still with us. His wheat and chickens are considered part of our permanent law and were a *key precedent case* cited in defense of Obamacare's individual mandate.[21]

- Establishment Clause. "Congress shall make no law respecting the establishment of religion" is a restraint on Congress, not the granting of a right to an individual. Yet, the clause has evolved into just that – a dissenter's right to block public displays of religious symbols (think Christmas) if such makes one feel offended or uncomfortable.[22]

- General Welfare Clause. Mentioned as both a goal in the preamble and a power of Congress, the "general Welfare" clause has been turned into a rubber pretzel. It has been distorted more than any other to justify almost anything that activists of one stripe or another desire to impose on the citizenry for the benefit of those whose votes they seek. Food, clothing, housing, education, and now medical care. If the Founding Fathers had intended the phrase "promote the general welfare" to mean taking care of everyone's needs, why did they waste words on the rest of the

Constitution? Why not a one-phrase document: Government shall provide for the general welfare of its citizens. Period (as the saying goes). Obviously, that could not possibly have been what our Founders had in mind as the whole Constitution takes great pains to detail what the federal government may and may not do, leaving all other powers to the several states or the people, as confirmed by the Tenth Amendment.

- Necessary and Proper Clause. The Constitution empowers Congress "To make all Laws which shall be necessary and proper for carrying into Execution the foregoing Powers," meaning the 18 enumerated powers[23] specifically vested in the legislative branch by the document itself. The "necessary and proper" clause is an *incidental* power necessary to implement those principal powers; it is not a principal power in itself. Yet it is cited as justification for agendas one faction or another believes *necessary* to bring about the proper society they would mold America into – a "pretext of [Congress] executing its powers ... for the accomplishment of goals not entrusted to the government," in Chief Justice John Marshall's famous words.[24]

Such is the expansion of governmental powers by creative interpretations of constitution clauses. Any defender of the original intent of the Constitution who opposes such enlargement often finds himself branded an enemy to that very document.

Powers are also being expanded by bureaucratic fiat without any felt need to appeal to the Constitution. Civil asset forfeiture, for example, was originally designed to bank down drug use by depriving drug lords of their plunder. It has expanded such that government now seizes property merely on the *suspicion* of wrongdoing without ever bringing charges, let alone proving them in a court of law. And because police departments get to keep the goodies, guess who is motivated to do what?

Another example is the Economic Stabilization Act of 1970. Before Richard Nixon met his Waterloogate fate, he used the emergency powers of this act to declare in non-emergency times, "I am today ordering a freeze on all prices and wages throughout the United

States."[25] Breathtaking chutzpah. And the two czardoms he created to run the economy – the Pay Board and the Price Commission – were of a league with Obamacare's IPAB death panel noted above.

About that food storage of yours

Given government's generous interpretation of the commerce clause to the detriment of private property, two executive orders (EOs), one from President Clinton in 1994 and another from President Obama in 2012, have caught the attention of many Americans.

Though both orders address national defense preparedness, under Obama's Executive Order 13603, the Secretary of Agriculture is authorized to allocate food resources "as deemed necessary or appropriate to promote the national defense ... **under both emergency and non-emergency conditions**." [Emphasis added] Similar authorizations are given to cabinet heads for energy, health resources, water, and civil transportation, with whatever resources that are left – "all other materials, services, and facilities" – going to the Secretary of Commerce.[26]

Authorized to allocate food resources? Even under non-emergency conditions? Given Obama's numerous attempts to work around constitutional restrictions, can one be faulted for wanting a reassuring explanation for what it means for one's own private property?

No sooner were such questions raised than supporters of the president pounced on these concerns and labeled them as silly right-wing hysteria. Websites such as Snopes soon did their investigations and advanced three counterarguments:

- It is false to assume that these two executive orders give President Obama unprecedented new powers to appropriate national resources.
- Obama's EO is just a housekeeping tidy-up of Clinton's EO because of structural Cabinet changes.
- Both orders draw their authority from and are fully compliant with the Defense Production Act (DPA) of 1950, as amended.[27]

Let's examine them. First, the Defense Production Act itself is constitutionally suspect. Nowhere in the Constitution is Congress granted authority over all American resources and the fruits of its citizens' labor, let alone the right to delegate that authority to the executive branch. The Fourth Amendment preserves the right of the people to be secure in their persons, houses, papers, and effects – effects commonly understood as belongings. That cannot be overridden by Congress or by the president.

But for the sake of this discussion, let's assume that act is settled law. How well do the two executive orders conform to it?

- The two EOs address the allocation of food resources and define it in detail. No reference to food resources can be found in the 1950 DPA. In fact, the word "food" does not appear anywhere in its 21,418 words.
- The DPA distinguishes between industrial facilities and private facilities such as homes and churches. The two EOs do not.
- The tone of the DPA is industrial – the machinery to produce defense materials. Broader resources, especially food, are the emphasis in the two EOs.
- Nowhere do the orders differentiate between government and privately owned property. And nowhere is the word "appropriate" defined.
- The two EOs address the "full spectrum of emergencies." That phrase does not appear in the 1950 Act. Nor anything similar to it. That is a significant broadening of scope.
- Clinton's EO doesn't mention "non-emergency conditions." Obama's does. That is more than minor tidying.

Think about it. Can anything exist that is neither emergency nor non-emergency? **What product could an agile mind not construe to be part of defense preparations, and therefore under the control of government?** What is to stop the president from claiming that "allocation of resources" also means "collection of resources?"

To put it another way: If the commandeering of foodstuffs, whether publicly or privately owned, were ever declared necessary, do you think government agencies would *not* point to Executive Order 13603 as their authority?

Supporters want to make it appear that these executive orders are merely logical extensions of the authority granted in 1950. I believe the facts say otherwise. They are a glaring expansion of power. The significant addition of food allocation amounts to whole-cloth legislation forbidden by the Constitution.

At the very least, these are troublesome edicts housing ambiguous concepts, ill-defined directives, and enticing loopholes. Given President Obama's less-than-stellar track record regarding the Constitution, it is not unreasonable to wonder if government might some day appropriate private food storage or the Church's massive welfare system. Remember, too, that under the *Filburn* ruling, there isn't anything – your garden vegetables, the fruit from your trees – that the government can't consider to be part of interstate commerce and thus regulate. And if regulate, penalize. And if penalize, confiscate.

As Paul Begala, an advisor to Bill Clinton, infamously remarked, "Stroke of the pen, law of the land, kinda cool."

* * *

Once laws are selectively enforced, executive orders are common, and new powers invented, what will stop tyranny?

Chapter 19

The Cancerous Administrative State

"Nothing is so permanent as
a temporary government program."

– Milton Friedman

The difference between the human body and government? The body knows when to stop growing, at least vertically.

Ask victims of heart attacks when it happened and all but a few will give you place, date, and time. Ask the same question of someone with cancer and they will not be nearly that precise.

Both begin slowly – occluded blood vessels, abnormal cell division – but one leads to sudden destruction and the other to a gradual demise.

Threats to our Constitution and a limited-power government are more like cancer than a heart attack.

Thomas Jefferson warned that **"even under the best forms of government, those entrusted with power have, in time, and by slow operations, perverted it into tyranny."**[1]

This chapter looks at three slow cancer-like operations – one on the Constitution itself, one on government as it tries to control people's behavior, and one on the power to make laws.

Cancer on the Constitution

The attempt to plant malignant cells on the Constitution began with Woodrow Wilson, as we have discussed. Public appearance of the cancer came some 25 years later in President Franklin Roosevelt's 1944 State of the Union address in which he proposed a Second Bill of Rights including:

- The right to a useful and remunerative job;
- The right to earn enough to provide adequate food and clothing;
- The right of every family to a decent home;
- The right to adequate medical care; and
- The right to a good education.

Job, food, clothing, home, medical care, and a good education. What's not to like?

It is difficult to believe that leaders such as Wilson and Roosevelt were ignorant of basic human behavior. How can any leader not understand that if a person's wants are satisfied by government, that person will not work? I believe that they do, in fact, understand. But they don't care. Rather, they exploit it because they know that **the more people depend on government to provide for their wants, the more they will vote to keep that government in power**. A malignant tumor on an otherwise productive society if there ever was one.

Further, equating this list with the original Bill of Rights is deception of the highest cheek. It not only implies that the original ten aren't sufficient, but clothes the proposed rights with a dignity they do not deserve (remember Alinsky's moral garments). The reason: there's an unbridgeable difference between a Bill of Rights and a Bill of Wants – they're totally different animals.

Rights come from God and do not cost our fellow citizens a dime. Wants may also be God-given for His plan for our progress (how lazy would we be if we didn't know hunger and cold?), but they can only be filled through effort. These "rights" will cost someone something. If a person has a right to a job, food, clothing, and a home, who has the duty to supply them? Given human nature to want free gifts, the cost would be unbelievably huge.

We do not have a God-given right to the labors of others; we have a God-given responsibility to work for what we get. For those who cannot, we have a God-given commandment to assist them, but none of God's commandments are forced on anyone – only punishment or lack of blessings for failure to do so.

Still being pushed today by those who believe wealth is a self-existing commodity, Roosevelt's Bill of Rights also masks the origin of our natural rights. The state does not give us the freedoms in the Bill of Rights, but of necessity would be the enforcing taxing and distribution mechanism if a Second Bill of Rights were ever included in the Constitution. It's not hard to imagine that in time people would confuse which rights belong to which list, and would come to believe that we get all our rights from government. By any definition, that would severely weaken the Constitution.

Roosevelt had to know he had virtually no chance of seeing the Second Bill of Rights formally adopted. His real plan had to be to **provide a guiding template** for government activists. He and his followers would have preferred the belief be anchored in our country's foundational scripture, but have settled for it becoming an article of faith in the secular religion of government.

Cancer on government

The Lord told Joseph in Liberty Jail that "it is the nature and disposition of almost all men, as soon as they get a little authority, as they suppose, they will immediately begin to exercise unrighteous dominion."[2] This is troubling enough on a personal level, but what happens when these modern-day Pharisees band together to exercise dominion?

Satan can never rescind our God-given agency. But he can get governments to overwhelm people with so many stifling rules and regulations that agency and the freedom to learn from the bumps of life are effectively taken from them. People become sheeple, and control is ceded to the ambitious intellectual nobility squirreled away in sprawling bureaucracies.

We have the best form of earthly government and yet are suffering the slow operations that rob us of our freedoms one little regulation at a time. So many laws have been enacted, so many pettifogging rules and regulations written, that power in America today resides overwhelmingly in the executive branch, its 15 cabinet-level departments, over 450 major agencies, and numberless offices, institutes, bureaus, and centers under them.[3]

As of 2013, there were 1,430,000 pages of regulations in the Federal Register. Stacked up, it would weigh seven tons and measure 476 feet, **nearly as tall as the Washington Monument**, which it will surpass in 2016 as rule-writers churn out 60,000 additional pages of regulations each year.[4]

The Jewish people of the Savior's time were lucky – they only had 613 rules they had to follow. And yet still chafed under tyrannical Pharisees.

Obesity isn't limited to people, and government grows for at least three reasons:

> NO NATURAL LIMITING MECHANISMS. The marker of success in business is profit. If a business does not offer a product or service that people are willing to buy, it will fail. The success markers for government, on the other hand, are size of budget and number of employees, and there are no natural limiting mechanisms. If government services were dependent upon free-will purchases, would a majority commission

the writing of more regulations telling us what we can and cannot do? Would we hire more compliance officers? Hardly. Only services that protect us against foreign enemies, maintain domestic tranquility, and help us adjudicate our differences would be freely purchased.

As the tumor grows, it is almost superfluous to note that recipients of government jobs do not view kindly the political party that favors chemo.

PROCESS IS MORE IMPORTANT THAN SOLUTIONS. If government solves a problem, public employee jobs could be lost, which triggers two reactions in a bureaucracy. First, burrow deeper into Americans' daily lives to find, or manufacture, problems that justify the agency's existence. Second, subject the problem to a process rather than a solution. As one columnist observed, "...politicians require a steady stream of crises from which they can purport to save us" – the saving, of course, coming in the form of handing over more money, power, and freedom to the state.[5] Another observer concluded that bureaucracies never want to solve problems, but to *manage* them; their success is, perversely but directly, a function of inefficiency.[6]

Thomas Sowell put it, "You will never understand bureaucracies until you understand that for bureaucrats procedure is everything and outcomes are nothing."[7]

The bureaucratic mindset: convene conferences, study it, complicate it, stretch it out, then write rules, dream up acronyms, monitor, regulate, and administer, but for heaven sakes don't solve the hummer or we'll all be peddling apples and pencils.

PERVERSE INCENTIVES. As I mentioned, public employees gain status by the number of people under them. Thus are fiefdoms built as career public servants search for more

> things to regulate so more people are hired so their status goes up and their own position becomes more secure. All of which leads to more intrusion into people's private lives. Is it really government's role to monitor our weight and dictate what we eat?

Unless a sovereign people clearly draws red lines circumscribing permissible action, government will grow until it collapses of its own weight, and perhaps the republic with it. **It will never halt on its own**. And if things collapse, will people recognize the causes?

Unfortunately, such growth abets corruption, makes it difficult to terminate unproductive employees (a member of my local school board estimates it takes $300,000 to fire a public school teacher), insulates agencies that forget who their masters are (note the slogans, symbols, flags and even songs of the us-versus-them agency cultures), fosters a "circle the wagons" mentality when an agency comes under fire, and uses taxpayer money to sell itself to taxpayers. Government is not too big? Then why, when Washington is hit with a snowstorm, does it tell "non-essential federal workers" to stay home?

No aspect of life today exists that one or more government agencies have not claimed to be within their purview. **No human activity exists that the state has not, in one way or another, placed under its umbrella** to monitor, administer, and if necessary bend to its will. (Even bovine activity is open game as the White House is fretting about how to control cow flatulence, believe it or not.[8])

Senate Minority Leader Mitch McConnell: "Over the past several decades, the same public employees who've arrogated vast powers to themselves have conspired with their patrons in Congress to expand those powers even more, and to endlessly increase the budgets that finance them."[9]

Bureaucratic growth is a malignant tumor that stifles dissent, initiative, and agency, and squeezes life from the body politic. The growth-intrusion-control pattern in America's government is alarming.

Cancer on legislative powers

If I give you permission to drive my car, may you give that permission to others to drive my car? If I allow you to pick apples from my apple tree, does this mean you have the authority to tell your friend he may also pick apples from my apple tree?

No. Such authority is not transferrable.

So it is with the legislative power in the Constitution. Once past the preamble, the *very first sentence* in the whole Constitution addresses power. It states:

> All legislative Powers herein granted shall be vested in a Congress of the United States, which shall consist of a Senate and House of Representatives.

Think of that. The very first topic the Founders addressed was who has the power to make laws. There is no ambiguity at all in that sentence: ***All*** **legislative powers herein granted shall be vested** .... Anything confusing about that? All authority to make laws belongs *only* to Congress, there can be no sub-delegation (it is neither mentioned nor implied), and those powers are *restricted* to what is *explicitly* written in the Constitution.

A priesthood holder, to draw a parallel, may hold the priesthood, but he did not create it. The same with Congress. It holds the power to legislate, **but it did not create that power**. The people did. Therefore, it has no right to pass that authority or power on to any other body unless the people so grant in the founding document. Which they have not done.

Look, we all know that laws must necessarily be properly applied and regulated. Regulatory agencies fill that need. They write rules to fill in the logical details of a congressional statute. Think of your home and your local building codes as an example. The code writers may specify 2x4s or 3x6s, specifications for weight bearing columns, thickness of the dry wall, etc. Those are obviously regulatory details that need not concern the city council. But is it a regulatory matter to specify where your home may be located? Is it regulatory to specify the property tax rate? No, those powers are legislative and belong to the city council. And shouldn't the financing of that home be neither regulatory nor legislative, but left to you and your bank to work out?

So it is with Congress, bureaucracies, and us. The problem is that over time, **boundaries have become fuzzy and regulatory practices have gradually morphed into administrative laws** – statutes in all but name – when agencies find it easier to state a rule and execute it through intimidation than go back to Congress. At what point the switchover happens is a matter of definition and argument. But, to paraphrase an apt simile, if it looks like legislation, waddles like legislation, and quacks like legislation … it is legislation.

The hide-behind excuse from Woodrow Wilson's ideological descendants is that administrative law is necessary because of the demands of a modern and more complex society – needs that the old Constitution could not have envisioned. In actuality, today's administrative laws and executive orders are not modern but are ancient. Close cousins to the extralegal decrees and proclamations of English kings in the Middle Ages, they tempt tyrants in embryo to exercise absolute prerogative power, as we are seeing. The administrative state is a step backward, not forward.

Columbia Law School professor Philip Hamburger in his book *Is Administrative Law Unlawful?* elaborates:

> Most profoundly, the English defeated absolute prerogative power by developing ideas of constitutional law. The English constitution … made clear that there could be no extralegal or absolute power.
>
> Americans reinforced this rejection of absolutism. Americans knew the English experience with absolute power, and they feared any recurrence of it in America. They therefore framed the U.S. Constitution to bar any version of this power.[10]

He quotes John Locke's irrefutable argument:

> The legislative cannot transfer the power of making laws to any other hands. For it being a delegated power from the people, they, who have it, cannot pass it to others.[11]

So why do administrative rules today have the power of law?

> [A]dministrative governance is a sort of power that has long been understood to lack legal obligation. It is difficult to understand how laws made without representation and adjudication made without independent judges and juries, have the obligation of law; instead they apparently rest *merely on government coercion.*[12] [Emphasis added]

In short, forces inimical to the Constitution have resurrected the abusive practices of old English kings and deposited them in the executive branch of the U.S. government – and are enforcing them through intimidation and coercion.

In summary, let's connect the dots. The Constitution grants no legislative power to the executive. It grants no legislative power to the judiciary. None whatsoever. All legislative power belongs to Congress. Extralegal administrative law is, therefore, but a sneaky way around the principle of separation of powers – **an undemocratic imperial parasite inside a representative democracy host**. When a fourth branch of government arises with legislative, executive, and judicial powers combined, the painstakingly built structure of our founding document is so weakened that the whole Constitution, how shall I put it, hangs by a thread.

Hanging by a thread

On October 30, 2008, Barack Obama declared, "We are five days away from fundamentally transforming the United States of America." Twelve weeks later in his inaugural address he stated, "Starting today, we must pick ourselves up, dust ourselves off and begin again the work of remaking America."

Dismissed at the time as the exuberance of victory, is there any doubt today of his intention to bring about the decline of America so America can be remade? Any doubt that he intends to build a new form of government by tearing down the old one? Anyone still believe that the president and his allies are faithfully executing the laws and honoring the Constitution?

What does it mean when we say the Constitution will hang by a thread, as Joseph Smith phrased it? It simply means that a new form of government is threatening to replace the government the Founders established.

So how do we preserve it? By reinstating the separation of powers throughout government structures.

First, agencies in the executive branch are responsible for law enforcement; they should not be allowed to determine the guilt or innocence of those they are prosecuting. All citizens charged with a crime or misdemeanor must be given their day in a **court of the judicial branch, and not by a make-believe court composed of employees of the executive branch** usurping the powers of Article 3 of the Constitution. There should be no such thing as administrative judges.

Second, and this is tougher, Congress must review every rule written by any and every agency in the executive branch and determine whether it is regulatory or legislative in nature. If legislative, it must be deliberated afresh by the branch having the authority under Article 1 and either eliminated or instituted officially by this proper legislative body. To those who say there are too many rules for Congress to pay attention to, I say you have just made my point. There are too many rules. **But if a rule is important enough that people must obey it, their elected representatives must read and properly affirm it.**

Third, we must defeat at the ballot box those who would govern us with swarms of powerful and unelected administrators. **We must elect**

those who embrace the Constitution and truly take their oath of office seriously. Yes, this is an idealistic goal and we have fallen short time and again of achieving it. But coming events may well help us.

* * *

I wonder what the Founders are thinking tonight?

SECTION V

THE WAR TO DESTROY AMERICA

"I believe in America. I am grateful for the Constitution under which this nation lives and moves and has its being. I am profoundly grateful that somehow for more than two centuries of time we have existed as a nation and grown to become the strongest and most free in the entire world. I am grateful for those men whom the God in Heaven raised up and inspired and who pledged their lives, their fortunes, and their sacred honor to establish this nation and its government. I believe in America – one nation under God, indivisible, with liberty and justice for all."

– Gordon B. Hinckley

Chapter 20

Just One of the Bunch?

"The happy union of these states is a wonder; their Constitution a miracle; their example the hope of liberty throughout the world."

– James Madison

America is a crucial target for Satan because it is undeniable evidence of what people who are agents unto themselves – not subjects of king, czar, or tyrant – can accomplish. It stands in defiant contrast to the utter emptiness of Satan's plan. If Satan is to persuade additional millions to his miserable side, he must destroy America.

One way is by mocking, belittling, and attempting to subject America to supranational organizations and their philosophies.

It is one thing when Russian President Vladimir Putin, referring to America, says it is "extremely dangerous to encourage people to see themselves as exceptional,"[1] but what does it signify when America's own leader, when asked whether he thinks his country is exceptional, gives this ringing endorsement, "I believe in American exceptionalism, just as I suspect that the Brits believe in British exceptionalism and the Greeks believe in Greek exceptionalism."[2]

"Proud of America" is not a phrase that leaps to mind when one hears such equivocation. Someone who truly believed in America and its destined role in the world would not have answered that question that way.

If everyone is exceptional, then no one is.

America did not happen because of a tax on tea

America was part of the Father's plan even before it was formed and isolated by protective oceans. It was the land of the Garden of Eden, Adam and Eve its first citizens, and will host the New Jerusalem to which the lost ten tribes will return. It will facilitate the spread of the gospel. In the center of this favored land, the Savior will come to His temple and from His thrones here and in Jerusalem govern the earth during the Millennium.

This promised land was foreordained to be a choice and precious land of liberty without kings,[3] a beacon of freedom to the world. Nephi prophesied "that the Lord God will raise up a mighty nation among the Gentiles..." and that "the Lord God will proceed to make bare his arm in the eyes of all the nations..."[4] America is that nation and through it the Lord will show His power.

Only a free country could become the base of operations for the re-established original Christian church. No other country in the early 1800s would have fit the requirements. At the end of the Napoleonic Wars and the Congress of Vienna in 1815, all the major European nation-states – Austria, Prussia, Russia, Great Britain, and France – were monarchies, and religious freedom was anything but assured. Less than a hundred years after the First Vision, however, all those kingdoms had crumbled.

Does something about a stone cut out of the mountain without hands and breaking kingdoms come to mind?

A punching bag for the elite

America has always had its critics, but when have our own leaders so criticized and apologized for it as now? Cultural elites and politicians in high offices mock America. They sneeringly call it belligerent, selfish, oppressive, colonial, enslaving, dictatorial, inciter of wars, the world's bully, the source of all the world's problems and … arrogant.

- Bill Ayers, presidential advisor: "The United States is the most violent country that has ever been created."[5]
- Samantha Power, then U.S. Ambassador to the United Nations, likens America's sins to those of the Nazis.[6]
- Former House Speaker Nancy Pelosi dilutes a valued tradition by combining it with a partisan political accomplishment: "Next week, when we celebrate Independence Day, we'll also be observing health independence."[7]
- The president obsequiously bows to foreign potentates, but is noticeably cold toward leaders in his own country if they're from the opposite party.
- First Lady Michelle Obama says her husband's election was the "first time in my adult lifetime I am really proud of my country."[8]
- And at the 70th anniversary of the D-Day landings, the president, who rarely indulges an unplanned move, is seen casually chewing gum like a teenager at a ceremony honoring Americans who fought for our freedom. Pure disrespect.

Then we have many university professors who, over the last 50 years, have been complicit in fostering anti-Americanism. Ask yourself which two nations intellectuals hate the most. It's not even close: they hate America and Israel. Why? Might it have something to do with these two nations being destined to play major roles in the events prior to the Millennium? Promised lands, promised people, covenant people. The America God envisions is competition to intellectual elites. So they attack it.

Dennis Prager notes, "Nowhere were Stalin and Mao as venerated as they were at the most anti-religious and secular institutions in Western society, the universities. Nowhere in the West today is anti-Americanism and Israel-hatred as widespread as it is at universities."[9]

Of course we have made mistakes, but they are minor compared to what we have accomplished. America has fed more people and freed more people than all other nations combined. How many French, Dutch, Italians, Belgians, Japanese, Koreans and Brits are buried on our soil after defending us against our enemies? Not many. But how many Americans now rest in graves throughout the world? (If you want a sobering affirmation of this, walk around the American Cemetery at Omaha Beach in Normandy.) **Without a world-power *Pax Americana*, how many nations would be free today?** And yet some of our own leaders accuse us of being the bad guys.

Unexceptional, that's what you are

Nephi saw this promised land in a vision[10] – that its discoverer was wrought upon by the Spirit of God to go "forth upon the many waters," that other Gentiles went forth "out of captivity" (economic, political, and religious varieties), that "many multitudes" came to this land of promise, and that they prospered because of the Spirit of God, which is also the spirit of freedom.[11]

America was destined by God to become the model for nations to emulate. Top banana, not one of the bunch. By a 59-27 margin, likely U.S. voters think America is more exceptional than other nations.[12] Unfortunately, a fourth of Americans apologize: Let's not be exceptional or someone might be offended.

Ancient Israel was another God-chosen nation that winced about being exceptional. God wanted them to stand out, but the Israelites wanted to blend in. Other nations had kings, so they clamored for one even though Samuel told them that a king would take their sons to be his soldiers and farmers; their daughters to cook and bake for him; their best fields and vineyards for the benefit of his inner circle; and even take a tenth (we should be so lucky) of their seed and sheep, and in general turn Israel into his servants.[13] Despite Samuel's best efforts, they rejected his counsel and followed the world. Israel could have been evidence of the blessings God gives to those who follow Him. Nothing doing: "…we will have a king over us; That we also may be like all the nations…"[14]

America also blends with the world if we allow glorified diversity, perpetuation of hyphenated groups for political power, and muted red-white-and-blue patriotism to overshadow our unique founding idea. We are different by definition. Most nations are collections of people who share a *characteristic* – ethnicity, language, religion, culture, heritage, politics – whereas Americans are Americans not because of any one characteristic, but because we subscribe to an *idea* – the idea of freedom and sovereignty of the people.

You could move to France and be a resident, but you will never become French. You could move to Germany, but never become German. Same with immigrating to Denmark, Norway, China, Kenya, Japan, and many such nations. But if one moves to America, he or she, assuming immigration procedures are met, can not only become a resident of America, but can become an American by swearing allegiance to the values that formed this nation.

So I say to immigrants: Be proud of your ancestors. Pass down customs and costumes to your children. Keep your wienerschnitzels, sushi, and tamales. But **leave your flags in your old country** and become an unhyphenated American in *the* exceptional nation.

SCRAMBLED ALLEGIANCES

Men are willing to die for only three things: family, faith, and freedom. All three block tyrants.

We are *born* with a natural allegiance to our families. We *develop* a spiritual allegiance to our faith. We *pledge* an allegiance to our country, which acts (or should) as a protector of our freedom.

It appears to be Satan's strategy to scramble these allegiances.

Country becomes government.
Religion becomes a hobby
Family becomes whatever

The goal is to so weaken family and faith that allegiance to government is all that's left. Disparage and squash all associations that compete with the state. No buffering groups providing assistance, support, encouragement, solace, guidance, education – and surely none capable of energizing and channeling deep passions. Funnel all yearnings for togetherness into government-led togetherness. Redefine success – that only through government can one be successful. Then subject the nation to international tribunals.

PEACHY TITLES AND THE THREAT OF TRANSNATIONAL LAW

The brilliance of the Constitution is that the people grant government its just powers. But not a few in high places today claim that the Founding Fathers created government and government created rights. That stands the truth on its head.

If we are to look to government for our rights, who or what does government look to for legitimacy? If people entertain the notion that government derives its power from something other than the consent of the governed, what is that something – reason, tradition, brute power, perhaps the supposedly more advanced ideas from other lands? If the latter, Europe is held as the gold standard in such thinking – refined, sophisticated, intellectual, advanced, and modern. In fact, the thinking goes, why not subject our nation to such governments that have these better ideas?

That's what is being proposed in elite international circles. It's called transnational law.

International law defines the relationships between countries. Transnational law, in contrast, inserts itself into the relationship between a nation's government and its people. **It defines what laws a nation must follow regarding its own citizens** – all in the name of universal justice for all peoples of the earth. Usurped sovereignty masquerading as benefit.

In a Wall Street Journal interview, former U.S. Senator Jon Kyl warned that if the U.S. were to ratify an international treaty such as the

U.N. Convention on the Elimination of all Forms of Discrimination Against Women, for example, we would find it to "have a lot of loose language that in the hands of the wrong people can demand far more than was ever intended by the American people."[15]

Beware the mischief hiding behind a peachy title.

In practice, on matters related in any way to such treaties, the U.S. would become subject to oversight by an external body based in Geneva, and unelected bureaucrats and self-appointed busybodies from other countries – beyond the reach of American citizens – could download into American law their creative diktats. It is not a theoretical threat as the European Union proves, says Mr. Kyl: "What they have now is a situation where their sovereignty has largely been supplanted by others who are not accountable to voters in individual European countries."[16] If the model were applied here, it would be **open warfare on the idea of America**.

Justice Stephen J. Markman of the Michigan Supreme Court adds that transnationalism would legitimize reliance by American judges upon foreign law in giving meaning to the United States Constitution, bind us to international treaties not ratified or even enacted into law by Congress, render our conduct subject to review of international tribunals, expose American soldiers and leaders to sanctions for war crimes if we use force to defend liberty abroad, and replace the judgments of American officials with those of multinational panels of bureaucrats and judges.[17]

Senator Kyl again: "Once you have ceded authority to an external body to make decisions, our theory of government – accountability in officials, consent of the governed – is very difficult to uphold. … When your society is regulated to that extent by someone who has no accountability to voters, something is very, very wrong."[18]

* * *

Precisely as Satan would have it.

Chapter 21

My Country, 'Tis of Me

"We the people are the rightful masters of both Congress and the courts, not to overthrow the Constitution but to overthrow the men who pervert the Constitution."

– Abraham Lincoln

Hooray for America. The judicial branch wants to legislate, the legislative branch passes wish lists, unelected officials really run the country, and the self-absorbed executive thinks its all about him and wants to be a messiah.

Our Founders would not find this amusing.

My family and I once visited Beijing and did the usual tourist gig of filing past Mao Zedong's embalmed body. Guards cautioned us not to even whisper – reverence, silence, as if we were in the presence of deity, which, of course, they so thought. As I watched the adoring faces of the pilgrims in line (some even wept), I could only think, "They're worshipping the guy who killed 75 million people." I got the same impression from another deified stiff a few years later when I "narrowly looked upon" (love that Isaiah phrase) Lenin's formaldehyde-buttressed remains in Red Square.

Top dog, vast power, adoration even after death. How did they do it? And what are the warning signs for us?

The need to feel superior

Lucifer likely appealed to two types of people in our pre-earthly existence: the prideful who believed they would have more power as his lieutenants, and the lazy who wanted a passing grade without taking the test. His recruiting arguments up there may have unfolded like this:

> Power: You deserve better than what God has planned. You are intelligent and talented. I will give you more power than the Father will.
>
> Guarantee: It's not fair. Look around. Some of our brothers and sisters you see will not make it back. That's not right. We're all children of Father and we all deserve to return and live in heaven forever. I will guarantee it.
>
> Discrimination: The Father's plan is discriminatory. He has favorites. He speaks of His noble and great ones, His elect, His covenant people, and He has already ordained some to be His leaders on earth. You're not one of them, so come join us.
>
> Hate: Followers of the Father hate you. You must hate in return. We will have revenge.

Down here, Satan in his suave and charming ways whispers the same formula to would-be tyrants seeking power: Find marginalized or discontented groups, commiserate with them, identify villains, fan hatred, and whip it into a crisis (never let one go to waste, as they say).

Satan especially targets those who, as my good friend Glen Greener describes them, have a need to feel superior. They are plentiful and easily manipulated. It is not happenstance that in the Book of Mormon "lifted up" occurs in the context of pride 22 times, and "puffed up" another five times. First pride, then power, wealth, class distinctions, and finally persecution:

> "Now those who were in favor of kings were those of high birth, and they sought to be kings; and they were supported by those who sought power and authority over the people."[1]
>
> "...there began to be among them those who were lifted up in pride ...and they began to be divided into classes..."[2]
>
> "...and they persecute the meek and the poor in heart, because in their pride they are puffed up."[3]
>
> "...and some were lifted up unto pride and boastings because of their exceedingly great riches, yea, even unto great persecutions...."[4]

President Ezra Taft Benson said that pride includes arrogance, conceit, and self-centeredness, but the core element is enmity – hatred. He then gave bottom line of Satan's plan: "It is the power by which Satan wishes to reign over us."[5]

Exaggerating differences between people, **Satan fans prideful hate at the top and envious hate at the bottom** to produce us-versus-them mentalities and class warfare. To the upper ranks, lower classes are looked down on as ignorant hicks living in fly-over country who don't even know how to use the Internet. To the lower ranks, the rich are greedy and the powerful are uncaring snobs who do sneaky things when no one's looking.

There are no humble villains

Watch out for these types of people:

- Those who promise rewards without effort
- Those who say all will be well if they are put in charge
- Those who promise to give followers power and authority over others

- Those who puff up their audiences by saying they deserve better
- Those who can lie with eloquence and charm
- Those who are prideful and brag about their abilities

In addition, watch for those who **change their persona**, beginning oft-times with their names. A coarse Georgian seminarian surnamed Dzhugashvili, for example, changed his name to exude strength: Stalin, man of steel.

Others changed their names to denote crispness or purpose:

- Adolf Hitler's father changed the family name and perhaps altered history. It wouldn't do, you see, to command followers to cock their arms 135 degrees and yell, "Heil Schicklgruber." Hard to goose-step if hysterical laughter turns your knees to rubber.
- In a similar vein, Doroteo Arango became Pancho Villa, Lev Bronstein became Leon Trotsky, Ernesto Lynch became Che Guevara, Malcom Little became Malcom X, and Goyaale ("the one who yawns") became Geronimo, for obvious reasons. (And one Marion Morrison in the non-villain category took on the much more masculine name of John Wayne.)

Beware of an **overemphasized image of caring** for people. That the Lord uses the term "unfeigned love" in D&C 121 implies there must be feigned love, and related feigned caring. Hugo Chavez, "a skilled orator with keen Machiavellian instincts," used temporary handouts from the country's oil wealth to show poor Venezuelans he cared about them, but in reality left them worse off than when he took office. Inflation over the last 10 years of his rule was over 1200% for food.[6] And many are the Cubans who still think Fidel Castro has their best interests at heart.

Above all, watch for **narcissism**, a sure sign of the difference between righteous and unrighteous leaders. Constant references to self and excessive use of first-person pronouns are telltale signals.

- Hitler in the rubble of Berlin is quoted as saying, "The German people don't deserve me. They have let me down."[7]
- Hermann Goering to Karl Doenitz in Landau prison at the end of WWII: "You watch, Doenitz. Fifty years from now there will be statues of me all over Germany."[8]
- Nicolae Ceausescu, Romanian dictator and inventor of false prizes for his wife, decreed that his many homes had to be kept warm 24/7 in case he happened to drop by. This in a country where people were freezing in the dark.
- In Saddam Hussein's Iraq, no one was allowed to throw away newspapers because his picture was in virtually every issue and was not allowed to touch the ground.

Has the tyrant ever existed who did not consider himself a god?

Narcissism and force together produce a cult of the personality and unthinking hero worship. But if the tyranny eventually leaves followers in rubble, as it assuredly will, the tyrant will tell them how good they have it. "We Have Nothing to Envy in the World" is a song North Korean children are taught to sing, and a former high-ranking communist party official in Boris Yeltsin's hometown told me that she grew up feeling genuinely sorry for American children who did not live in a Marxist society. Is it hard to shake? By a 45-35 margin, Russians in 2011 still had a positive view of Stalin's role in the life of their country.[9]

The above were players in the last 100 years and we haven't even included Pol Pot, Idi Amin, the Kims, Ho Chi Minh, Tojo, Mussolini, Kaiser Bill, Mugabe, among others. We could go on and on with Gengis Khan, Ivan the Terrible, Vlad the Impaler, Henry VIII, Roman Caesars and Asian warlord monsters of yester-centuries. The building doesn't exist that could house a Tyrants Hall of Fame museum.

It is difficult to imagine they once chose to follow the Father's plan.

Creeping royalism

No dictator achieves power by himself. He must have allies who propel him to the top, and they will do so only if there's something in it for them. In the days of Captain Moroni versus Amalickiah: "And they had been led by the flatteries of Amalickiah, that if they would support him and establish him to be their king that he would make them rulers over the people."[10]

And again a few years later when Gadianton came on the scene: "… if they would place him in the judgment-seat he would grant unto those who belonged to his band that they should be placed in power and authority among the people…."[11]

Satan hasn't given up on the idea of divine right of kings, its distortion of agency, and its obvious slap at the Father. He knows as did the brother of Jared: "Surely this thing leadeth into captivity."[12] But before there can be a king, there must be an aristocracy in waiting.

Any signs of creeping royalism in America? Well, in addition to worship of the intellect discussed earlier, try these three:

> Self-worshiping office holders. Being elected to high office is heady stuff. Titles, recognition, power. Those we elect should enjoy our support and a proper amount of deference, but their temptation is to picture themselves several notches above the rest of us. Once having drunk the water of Washington, Sacramento, Albany, or Austin, it's difficult for our political royalty to remember their true place in society is only one notch above the rest of us – and answerable.
>
> Celebrity worship. How do societies treat royalty? By paying attention and buying whatever they're selling. More than DVDs, CDs, movie tickets, rock concert tickets, ballgame tickets, and associated paraphernalia, too many buy their lifestyles. How often we see little girls in front of a TV saying, "I'm her!" or boys acting out the male characters they see. (I have a brother-in-law who as a little boy was so taken

> with Superman that he jumped off the garage roof wearing a cape. Not much of a hero worshiper since.) So sad that the celebrity lifestyles have more in common with alley cats than decent citizens.
>
> Windsor worship.
>
> I wonder what the king is doing tonight?
> What merriment is the king pursuing tonight?
>
> Why do Americans care what the House of Windsor is doing? When a new heir to the English throne was born, you might well have wondered if you had been transplanted to that island nation given all the media attention … here … in America. Princess Diana has been gone for years, and yet she's still the subject of stories … here … in America. And isn't it a tad much that American reporters refer to them as "*the* royal family?" They're surely not *my* royal family.
>
> I recognize the agency of residents of the land of my forefathers to choose their government and aristocracy systems as they will, but is America's royalty fixation healthy? Why the aristocracy addiction? Why the fascination with a system where you are a subject instead of a citizen?

Perhaps the inordinate attention we pay to officeholders, inane celebrities, high intellect, and royalty is nothing to worry about, but what if it presages a clamoring for a king, as the relatively enlightened Israelites did many centuries ago? Mosiah explained the risk:

> Therefore, if it were possible that you could have just men to be your kings, who would establish the laws of God, and judge this people according to his commandments, … then it would be expedient that ye should always have kings to rule over you.[13]

But he cautioned: "…because all men are not just it is not expedient that ye should have a king or kings to rule over you." He told of king

Noah and his priests who "were lifted up in the pride of their hearts,"[14] assessed themselves better than others, and laid a 20% tax on the people to support their opulent sloth. Should such a king be enthroned, Mosiah continued,"...ye cannot dethrone an iniquitous king save it be through much contention, and the shedding of much blood."

Again, the predecessor to a king is an aristocracy – being distinguished by ranks. How often we hear of special perks for those in power. How often we discover government officials who have failed for years to pay income taxes. How often we read of celebrities pulled over for speeding who indignantly hiss, "Don't you know who I am?" What's the use of being better than others, they seem to be thinking, if you have to live by the same rules as the great unwashed?

Aristocratic thinking is a sure sign Satan has been at work.

Is this the king they've been waiting for?

"It's good to be the king," said a Mel Brooks character in an old movie. Many are the reasons: massive power, first dibs on the fruits of peasant labor, fancy clothes, adulation and even worship by the masses. We know that America will never be ruled by a king as long as we keep God's commandments. Are we measuring up, or do the following postures hint of scepter and crown soon to come?

- Narcissism permeates every speech that President Obama gives. For example, in a July 2014 address in Austin, Texas, about unilateral executive action to achieve his goals, he used a first-person singular pronoun – I, me, my, mine – 199 times in 40 minutes, or about once every 12 seconds. By comparison, Abraham Lincoln did not even once refer to himself in the Gettysburg Address.[15]
- August 14, 2013: In looking to unilaterally impose a $5 a year tax on all cellphone users, President Obama told his staff: "We are here to do big things – and we can do this without Congress."[16] Perhaps he should read Article I, Section 7 of the Constitution: "All Bills for raising Revenue shall originate in the House of Representatives."

- February 10, 2014: To French President Francoise Hollande: "That's the good thing about being president, I can do whatever I want." Perhaps a light-hearted quip as they broke protocol, but given his pronouncements on other matters, one wonders. As the saying goes, "A joke is truth wrapped in a smile." Obama also joked in 2009 about using the IRS to audit his political enemies.
- April 4, 2013: While calling for Congress to limit access to guns, President Obama revealed his feelings: "I am constrained, as [other elected officials] are constrained, by a system our Founders put in place."[17] When a president implies that his ideas are better than the Second Amendment, one cannot lightly dismiss fears that he will try to work his way around it.
- On numerous occasions, the same theme: "We can't wait for a dysfunctional Congress to do its job" … "Where Congress isn't acting, I act on my own" … "Wherever and whenever I can take steps without legislation…." … "That's what I'm going to do with or without Congress" … "We can't wait for Congress to solve it."[18]
- June 27, 2014 in Minneapolis, the same tirade: "I'm not going to let gridlock and inaction and willful indifference and greed threaten the hard work of families like yours. … And so we can't afford to wait for Congress right now. And that's why I'm going ahead and moving ahead without them wherever I can."[19] Would-be potentates hate deliberative bodies that slow them down. Thus do they demonize inaction by coupling it with greed and framing it as the *enemy* of hard-working families while calculated, slow-moving legislation is precisely what the Constitution requires of our representatives to *protect* those same hard-working families.
- May 6, 2013, Ohio State University commencement address: "I think it's fair to say our democracy isn't working as well as we know it can. It could do better."[20] In other words, he could accomplish more good things if he weren't restrained.
- Same address: "And I think of what your generation's traits … might mean for a democracy that must adapt more quickly

to keep up with the speed of technological and demographic, even wrenching economic change." The implicit point: The Constitution isn't nimble enough to keep up with technology.

- Same address: "Unfortunately, you've grown up hearing voices that incessantly warn of government as nothing more than some separate, sinister entity that's at the root of all our problems; some of these same voices are also doing their best to gum up the works. They'll warn that tyranny is always lurking just around the corner. You should reject these voices."

When those in power say, "Don't worry about X lurking around the corner," you can be fairly sure that X is lurking around the corner.

We can also compare today with a previous situation on this soil. Thomas Jefferson listed 26 specific grievances against King George III in the Declaration of independence. Five are hauntingly familiar today:

1. "He has erected a multitude of New Offices and sent forth swarms of Officers to harass our people and eat out their substance." A most accurate description of today's explosive growth of government agencies and functionaries.

2. "He has called together legislative bodies at places unusual, uncomfortable, and distant … for the sole purpose of fatiguing them into compliance with his measures." As we will see in Chapter 24, government prosecutors intimidate, badger, and exhaust.

3. "… his invasions on the rights of the people." The larger the government, the smaller the people.

4. "For imposing Taxes on us without our Consent." If Congress sub-delegates legislative power to unelected bureaucrats, and the bureaucracy imposes fees, that is taxation without representation, without accountability, without answerability. Only elected representatives are vested with legislative power to tax. No

accountability exists with unelected and faceless bureaucrats who impose penalties and fees hiding under an assumed blanket grant of power from Congress.

5. "… for altering fundamentally the Forms of our Governments…." If our Founding Fathers returned today, they would be appalled at the size, let alone the questionable legality, of what has become the fourth branch of government – the administrative state.

Also appropriate to today, the Declaration charges that a "Prince whose character is thus marked by every act which may define a Tyrant, is unfit to be the ruler of a free people." List the characteristics of a tyrant, match them against various politicians and decide for yourselves which ones are unfit to lead a free people.

Given the ambitions of the man currently in the White House, a fawning government aristocracy, and rampant immoral behavior among our people, how sure can we be that "Yes, your majesty" will remain a foreign phrase?

* * *

Two types of leaders fundamentally transform the societies they lead – great statesmen and great tyrants.

Chapter 22

The New Plague of Locusts

"[A] man's support for absolute government is in direct proportion to the contempt he feels for his country."

– Alexis de Tocqueville

A Department of Agriculture bureaucrat, the yarn goes, was especially glum one morning. When asked the problem, he replied, "My farmer died."

The ratio of bureaucrats to workers may not be 1:1 as yet, but past a certain point one wonders, "How big is government going to get?"

Toward the end of Willie Sutton's infamous career, someone asked him why he robbed banks. His "duh" answer: "Because that's where the money is." Same reason the ambitious flock to Washington – that's where the power is. If you don't achieve fame in L.A., you park cars and pump gas, as the old song goes. But in Washington …

Put a hundred down and buy a car
In a week, maybe two, they'll make you a czar

Grow, baby, grow

President Obama has appointed more than 30 czars – drug czar, health reform czar, TARP czar, salary czar, car czar, even a Guantanomo-closing czar – unelected special aides with considerable authority and influence over public policy, and virtually no check-and-balance mechanisms such as senate confirmation hearings. With increased government control over more facets of life in America comes more opportunities to wield power … and to abuse it.

Count the many staffers, name them one by one.

We have already noted the snowballing growth of federal regulations, but government grows and smothers freedoms at the state and local levels as well. Our Founding Fathers visualized part-time legislatures composed of citizen-legislators whose main occupations lay elsewhere. The professional, full-time legislator was to be a rarity.[1] Today, however, according to the National Conference of State Legislatures, ten of the most populous states have full-time legislatures in which legislative salaries are sufficiently high that members need no outside income, 23 have hybrids in which legislators receive most of their income, and only 17 conform to the original ideal of a part-time legislature.[2] Total it up and we have over 7000 state representatives and senators to go along with 535 counterparts in Congress, most of whom seek to move up, establish a reputation, or at least be re-elected.

The bragging rights in this game are the number of bills introduced and the number of bills passed. Think what that means. If the average state or federal legislator introduced but ten new bills per year (some states have limits ranging from five to fifteen such), we could be saddled with as many as 70,000 new laws. Of course, not all become laws. Estimates of the number of state laws passed in 2011, for example, range from 14,227 actual laws signed by a governor upwards to 40,000 including resolutions (which often lack the significance of statutes). At the same time, Congress passed 80 bills which spawned somewhere between 3000 and 4000 regulations.[3] Where does it end?

The significance of these numbers is that **more and more legislators and their staffs are digging for problems they can address (but never solve) to justify and protect their careers**. Are there really that many problems in citizens' daily activities requiring intervention by powerful governments? Add state and federal laws and regulations together and we have, as one columnist put it, "a mob of powerful people looking to turn their utopian ideals into citizen requirements with compliance backed by weapons and prisons."[4]

Even if we grant that an all-powerful government could indeed solve all of humanity's problems, would we learn the lessons God sent us to learn? Would such an arrangement provide rich experiences, stand us in good stead in eternity?

No. As government expands, individual initiative recedes and …

- We lose a sense of personal responsibility: "Someone else will take care of the problem; I don't have to be involved."
- We fall into a culture of nanny-state dependency.
- We lose sight of the Founders' original intent.
- We fail to appreciate the great gift of agency.
- The chance of power being wielded by unelected string pullers increases.

Government grows for a variety of reasons including what I call the Heisenberg Uncertainty Principle applied to human behavior. Heisenberg's rule says that in quantum physics the act of observing something changes it. In legislation, **the fallacy is that a new law or regulation can be introduced and it will only affect people in the precise way it was intended – that nothing else will change**. Surprise. When unexpected changes occur, which they almost always will because human behavior is a dynamic system not static, then, well, more regulations have to be written. Is there no end?

Equality of outcomes as the engine of bureaucracy

Before people will sit still for government growth, they must buy into a rationale. That rationale is equality. Not equality of opportunity, mind you, but rather equality of outcome as the desired state of society. But our varied choices and uneven effort make equality of outcome impossible. The stage is thus set for mischief.

Power seekers for millennia have exploited inequality – especially income and wealth – to stir up envy, jealousy, and hate, and channel those passions into political support. All the wealthy – whether the easily caricatured lazy rich who inherit wealth without work, or the ambitious whose toil yields great rewards – are lumped together and it doesn't take a statistics professor to figure out that those at the top end will always be outnumbered by those below them. And will be demonized as exploiters of the poor, while the real exploiters pull the strings.

Hammer on the evils of inequality long enough and people will be persuaded that government must be the equalizer to stamp out all unfairness. That in turn requires, well, lots of government employees who write lots of rules – rules that smother, rob us of agency, and destroy freedom.

The current political fad is to brand inequality of income as unfair and equality of outcome as a right. In the heat of this argument, the real danger is overlooked. If everyone received equal income, it would not be long before some people through creative efforts – buying, selling, saving – would have more wealth. **Equality of income leads to an unstable state that cannot be sustained without force**, which proponents are only too willing to employ to preserve their power. That inevitable force is a de facto threat to freedom, which leads to this beautiful observation from Milton Friedman:

> A society that puts equality – in the sense of equality of outcome – ahead of freedom will end up with neither equality nor freedom. The use of force to achieve equality will destroy

> freedom, and the force, introduced for good purposes, will end up in the hands of people who use it to promote their own interests.
>
> On the other hand, a society that puts freedom first will as a happy by-product, end up with both greater freedom and greater equality. Though a by-product of freedom, greater equality is not an accident. A free society releases the energies and abilities of people to pursue their own objectives. It prevents some people from arbitrarily suppressing others. It does not prevent some people from achieving positions of privilege, but so long as freedom is maintained, it prevents those positions of privilege from becoming institutionalized; they are subject to continued attack from other able, ambitious people. Freedom means diversity but also mobility. It preserves the opportunity for today's disadvantaged to become tomorrow's privileged and, in the process, enables almost everyone, from top to bottom, to enjoy a fuller and richer life.[5]

Failure to recognize this connection means that the siren song of a fix-everything bureaucracy still wafts on the air.

A government-centric society

There can be no argument that the Founding Fathers envisioned a responsible populace and a federal government with limited and enumerated powers, and that activities beyond those expressly granted are the purview of the states and the people, as per the Tenth Amendment. Our government-centric society today, however, sees government not only as the country's most important institution, but the administrative state through which all individual ambitions can be realized, the solver of all problems, provider for all needs, caretaker of everyone, and, if it were possible, the tucker-inner at night.

Once that viewpoint is adopted, people seeking unrighteous gain will vote themselves goodies out of the public treasury, as Tocqueville feared, and a modern prophet warned, "An unvirtuous citizenry tend to elect representatives who will pander to their covetous lustings."[6]

Our government today increasingly postures itself as the cause or facilitator of everything that is good for the individual. It is touted as the prime entity of the people, the engine of society, the indispensable ingredient for progress, and that individuals could not have built what they built had it not been for government (some actually equate the American dream with American government). And citizens become "nothing but materials for legislators to exercise their wisdom upon."[7]

Now, no one doubts that a society's infrastructure is necessary to smooth commerce, but did roads trigger the discovery of polio vaccine? Did bureaucracies invent the light bulb? Will more people dependent upon government bring about a cure for cancer? Does anyone really believe that progress would halt if government funds were no longer available?

Insidiously, government uses taxpayer money and its borrowing power to become, in the words of George Will, ever bigger, more expansive, more intrusive, and more coercive.[8] **Only counterbalancing private associations can check the growth of state power**, yet even sturdy groups of yesteryear are succumbing to the enticements of government largesse. Freedoms do not exist because of government, but corrupt and smothering governments can snuff them out.

In an amicus brief in a recent Supreme Court case, The Becket Fund for Religious Liberty observed: "The expansion of the modern regulatory state has increasingly led to financial involvement of the government with private organizations — including churches, religious universities, and religious charities — in ways that potentially give the government power over those organizations. Tax exemptions, which have been treated by this Court as tantamount to the provision of funds, are a prominent example...."[9]

In time, government goodies such as tax exemptions become thinly disguised bribes that require organizations, in the words of Chief

Justice John Roberts, to pledge allegiance to government policies.[10] **Using taxpayer money to expand state control is the leveraged buyout maneuver of the 21st century.**

Enter the cheerleaders: We need to get things done; we need to work together; we need to get behind the president, and so on into the night.

The grip government can hold on people became even more apparent to my wife Jan and me a few years ago when we traveled to Tomsk, a city of 700,000 in western Siberia, where she conducted a women's workshop and explained how Americans work together to improve their communities. After teaching principles of voluntary organizations, she divided the audience into teams, told them to choose an activity that would benefit their community, and decide the first steps to accomplish it. An hour later they gave their reports.

> "We want to help children and their education, and the first thing we will do is apply to the government for money," said the first team leader. Whoa.
>
> Next up: "We want to promote music and so we need to ask the government for some money."

Same with neighborhood beautification, assisting the unemployed, cutting crime, caring for the sick: find government money. Lesson lost. Right over their heads.

These women – above average in education and social standing – had become so steeped in viewing government as the prime moving force in their Soviet society that even after democracy (sort of), a free market (sort of), and a multi-party system (sort of) were introduced, the Russian tradition of a centralized strong-figure government continued to dominate. People in Russia believe that without government help, things won't get done. (Funny, but even *with* it, things *still* don't get done.) Under Vladimir Putin, paternal government has returned in force to Russia.

The danger is that America is going down the same path – enticed by the idea that government is the be-all solve-all entity when citizens should instead be looking to themselves.

The permanent ruling class

Nothing more effectively circumvents the Constitution's genius for handling power – separate it, divide it, and enumerate it – than giving it to unelected, sporadically accountable, and massively self-interested officials. The regulation writers today make laws that not long ago were the purview of congress, and they complicate life in the process.[11]

In a 2005 study, New York University professor Paul Light found an average of 18 layers of bureaucracy between the cabinet secretary and the person being regulated – "between, say, the secretary of agriculture and the forest ranger…" – up from "only" seven layers in 1960. "Accountability has been shredded, and you can't tell who makes the decision, where the information gets stuck, or who is responsible for doing the job well."[12]

When accountability is shredded, goodbye justice.

Columnist John Fund adds that "the biggest problem with our bureaucracy is not its complexity. It is its ability to sidestep democratic procedures and make decisions on its own. Congress has increasingly delegated authority to agencies run by unelected functionaries who have incredible discretion in implementing laws that in turn can be incredibly vague." He then cites the new Consumer Financial Protection Bureau given the mandate from Congress to ensure that "all consumers have access to makers for consumer financial products and services … [that are] fair, transparent and competitive" and concludes: "Whoever interprets those high-sounding phrases is making law, not following it. That's why it's all the more important to both shrink the power of bureaucrats and make them as accountable as possible."[13]

Here is what has evolved. Congress either passes an idealized goal such as the Clean Water Act, the Clean Air Act, etc., or a humongous plan running into thousands of pages that few have read, and then grants authority to the permanent ruling class – aka the partisan bureaucracy – to implement it:

- Agencies write the actual do's and don'ts that people must follow – that's legislative power.
- Agencies judge who is or isn't in compliance – that's judicial power.
- Agencies enforce compliance with armed agents if necessary – that's executive power.

In 2012, federal agencies conducted ten times the number of trials and similar actions than were held in all federal courts,[14] bought billions of bullets (not even counting the Defense Department),[15] and wrote more actual do's and don'ts than all state legislatures and Congress put together.[16] And spent the fines and fees, thank you very much.

Because all three powers can be found in every administrative agency, the ingenious separation of powers is blurred and a critical constitutional principle is dismantled.

God's principle of agency requires that every action have a consequence and every actor be accountable. But try to find the person who actually wrote the regulation or gave the order to use the police powers of the state to enforce compliance. Even the oversight committees in Congress find it exasperatingly maddening to find out who gave whom what directions. And that assumes Congress still has power to hold agencies accountable. A scary portent for the future, as explained earlier, is the Independent Payment Advisory Board of the ObamaCare legislation whose decisions are not subject to administrative or judicial review and can only be overruled by a super majority vote of Congress under a Rube Goldberg contraption of processes between January 1 and August 15 of 2017.[17]

You can't make this stuff up.

Swarms of locusts

Saddling Americans with mentors, minders, busybodies, and snoops – thousands of little tyrants, in John Yoo's memorable phrase – was not what the Founders had in mind. In fact, such rampant power over the people was a point of complaint against King George III sufficient to be listed in the Declaration of Independence:

> He has erected a Multitude of new Offices, and sent hither Swarms of Officers to harass our People, and eat out their Substance.

Who can say this is not happening today? Unless we the people act decisively to protect our sovereignty[18] from bureaucratic usurpers, these swarms of officers, the nonsense will only get worse for at least six reasons:

> Deference to experts. Too many buy the argument that today's rapid pace and complexities require experts to create, monitor, and enforce myriad regulations to keep society humming, never mind Tocqueville's observation that complicated rules reduce a nation to a flock of timid animals. [19]

> Power-accountability disconnect. Power coupled with loose accountability attracts those who have a desire to feel superior and lord it over others, all while out of the spotlight. Above-average remuneration only sweetens the desire to join the game.

> Mission creep. As government payrolls increase, public employees scramble to justify their existence, which spawns increased ideas for projects, which stimulates hiring to insulate the previously hired from the pink slip. Growth spawns more growth.

> Growth decreases accountability. As government grows, there is less oversight by elected representatives. So many overseen by so few.

> Growth diminishes sovereignty. Increased government activity leads to more string-pulling intrusion into private lives. People become subjects of government control instead of controllers over government. Sovereignty is reversed.

> Satan loves centralized power. He would prefer power be concentrated in one man, be it a king (known at times as the Sovereign) or even an elected president, because singular power is easier to manipulate than dispersed power. But even the power of thousands of bureaucrats is easier to influence than power broadly dispersed among 320 million citizens, especially if centrally located (think cultural mind-set and the contagion factor). That is why the core idea of America – sovereignty of the people – blocks Satan's goals.

Burgeoning bureaucracies and their badge-heavy officers feasting at the public trough have been a bane to societies throughout history. Mormon pointed out three large professions – merchants, lawyers, and officers (obviously government officials) – among the Nephites just prior to the Savior's coming who boasted of their exceedingly great riches and who persecuted lesser ranks.[20] It is becoming that way with us today where, according to a 2009 study by the Bureau of Economic Analysis, **federal employee compensation is double that of private sector workers.**[21] With so much power in the hands of ambitious, unelected, and lightly accountable people, corruption and abuse of power (think fancy retreats to Las Vegas for the General Services Administration, 80% of Veterans Affairs executives receiving large bonuses, and too many IRS offenses to list here) should not be a surprise.

C.S. Lewis' take on the matter: "Of all tyrannies, a tyranny sincerely exercised for the good of its victims may be the most oppressive. It would be better to live under robber barons than under omnipotent moral busybodies. ...[Those] who torment us for our own good [classify us] with infants, imbeciles, and domestic animals."[22]

Peter was even more blunt: "But let none of you suffer as a murderer, or as a thief, or as an evildoer, or as a busybody in other men's matters."[23] Stellar company for busybodies.

Although the Constitution is clear on the point, the actionable sovereignty of the people is never safe. Unfair elections, withheld information, organizational complexity, ambiguity of responsibility, bureaucratic red tape, difficulty petitioning government, inaccessible officials, deification of the elected, and unaccountability of rule-making agencies are well-known methods by which a power elite attempts to rule those who hired them.

If we can protect our sovereignty against power abusers in our midst, God's intended blessings are ours.

Otherwise, it's serf city here we come.

* * *

Where are those seagulls when you need them?

Chapter 23

Your Friendly Speech Control SWAT Team

"Whoever would overthrow the Liberty of a Nation must begin by subduing Freedom of Speech."

– Cato

The ends of all speech are education and persuasion. Control the flow of information and control which viewpoints can be expressed, and you control society.

A cattle-grazing dispute in Nevada came to a head in the spring of 2014 when the Bureau of Land Management, backed by court orders, began rounding up cattle that the agency said were grazing illegally. Protestors gathered and a video of the clash with federal agents made nationwide news. The BLM then called off the operation and the dispute, as of this writing, is back in the courts.

The rancher's legal case is weak to non-existent. But more important than who is right, and immensely more disturbing than protestors being attacked by dogs and tasers, is that federal agents arrived with professionally printed signs and orange webbed fencing, cordoned off a small piece of land, called it a "First Amendment Area", and told citizens that it was the only place where they could speak about the dispute.[1]

That is ominous.

What were these government heavies thinking – that the only place people could exercise their right of free speech about the issue is a small parking-lot size piece of public land and nowhere else? Did they really believe that government has the power to demarcate where the First Amendment applies and, by implication, *where it does not?*

Yes they apparently did ... and no doubt still do. Unbelievable audacity.

If this anti-constitutional mindset is allowed to spread and harden, what happens when the dispute is not about cattle grazing but about people preaching? It's not a stretch to imagine quick-to-be-offended groups enlisting state power to prevent offensive words such as "Jesus" and "sin" from reaching their tender sensitive ears.

If allowed to stand, what is to prevent governments from dividing their cities, states, or even the whole nation into First Amendment zones – little islands of free speech surrounded by oceans of limitations? Free speech archipelagos.

Given everything happening in society that we once thought implausible if not impossible, you could wonder whether orange webbed fencing and restriction signs – physically or figuratively – might soon surround your neighborhood church, temple, synagogue, or mosque.

Far fetched? You'd better hope so.

Repentance and hate speech

As government grows and more rules are written, the focus is shifting from what a person can and cannot *do*, to what he can or cannot *say*. This is critical because if the rule writers prevail, the ammunition we use in this relocated war – words – will dry up.

Pause a moment to consider the action verbs in the scriptures that describe what prophets and other emissaries of the Savior do:

teach, preach, explain, persuade, exhort, admonish, command, and stir people to repentance, among many others. Almost every act of a prophet revolves around words. Here is Jarom, for example:

> "... for they did prick their hearts with the word, continually stirring them up unto repentance."[2]

To prick hearts with words and stir people to repentance is no tiptoe through the marigolds. To stir up means to prod the recall of stupid acts, memories the listener would prefer remain buried. Some will humbly own up to the deeds and seek to change. Others will be offended and retaliate, which is why prophets through the ages have been beaten, spit upon, imprisoned, cast out, stoned, burned, and decapitated.

Prophets do not call us to repentance because they hate us; they do so because they love us. (A foreign idea for many.)

Enter now the bureaucratic grandee who believes his job is to maintain calm (there's that lulling again) and prevent discomfort. He believes he must curb offensive speech – the pricking of hearts being precisely that – and **use the taxing and policing powers** of his government to do so. If Satan, through these rule writers, can stop the words, phrases, and sermons that prick hearts, he stops repentance. If he stops repentance, he stops the Father's plan.

Here's Satan's anti-repentance logic chain:

- Repentance requires a change of heart
- A person can't change until he knows what he's doing wrong
- He can't know what he's doing wrong until someone points it out
- Stop that someone from pointing out wrongs and you stop repentance
- Stop repentance and you stop mercy, justice, agency, and progress

And here's his method:

- Sensitize people to differences of opinions
- Inflate differences into arguments
- Inflate arguments into hate
- Equate disapproval of beliefs with hate of the person
- Establish a victim-sensitive mentality in society
- Label sermons against sin as hateful, and sinners as victims
- Pass laws to prohibit hate speech

Of course people desire peace and quiet. Opposing something called hate speech seems consistent with that desire. They don't realize that **a measure of discomfort must be inserted into people's lives** – no pearl without a gritty grain of sand – to set them on the road to change. Otherwise they remain comfortable in their sins and will never enjoy the balm of the Atonement until they look past the false labeling Satan applies to religious sermons.

What about other topics over the pulpit? Let's say that two candidates for public office take opposite positions on abortion or same-sex marriage or government spending, and voters are very aware of their stands. Now comes a Sunday morning when a preacher delivers an emotional sermon on the issue leaving no doubt where he stands. Everyone knows it is a de-facto endorsement of one candidate and a rejection of the other although no names are mentioned. Has he violated the law under the Johnson Gag Order described in Chapter 8? The administrative state will say yes.

Imagine. A land founded on religious freedom tells religions they cannot have a voice in the public square or the pulpit in the most significant of political events: electing our representatives.

The free speech restrictions on religion may in fact tighten. If government can tell the clergy that they cannot voice their opinions about public issues that might have a thread of connection to an election, what sermons on what issues can it not make subject to its control? How long will it be before words and phrases from the *Proclamation on the Family* are considered hate speech?

Controlling political speech

Stifling religious speech is an obvious objective of evil forces, but limiting political speech can be just as damaging because religious freedom rests on the Constitution which can be weakened by inhibiting vigorous debate.

Watch for eager and broad political correctness (tyranny with manners). Racial and ethnic slurs have no place in civil discourse, but that category of smears has been conveniently expanded to cover viewpoints that once were merely the back and forth of political discussion. A Harvard columnist, for example, lumps racism, sexism, and heterosexism together as -isms to oppose, which means that speech favoring natural marriage is equivalent to uttering the N-word – deception by equivalence. She asks, "[Why] should we put up with research that counters our goals simply in the name of 'academic freedom'?" and proposes that academic freedom be replaced with academic justice.[3] Guess which organizations will be on the chopping block for heterosexist oppression, aka natural marriage?

In time, PC bullying becomes creeping speech control of a formal nature. One of the most threatening in recent months was a trial-balloon regulation proposed by the IRS. Withdrawn for now because of the uproar, this rule would have required that any communication, public or private, by non-profit organizations be considered "candidate-related political activity" if it expressed a view that could be identified with any candidate or candidates of a political party. And thereby fall under government campaign rules and be subject to penalties.

Well, under that definition, is there any issue that *cannot* be associated with one party or the other, and thus with one or more candidates? Under this controlling structure, if a non-profit organization expresses an opinion about taxes, education, crime, land use, the environment, or anything else, the IRS (prosecutor and judge in one package) could rule that it is connected to a candidate who may have expressed a similar view, thus causing it to fall under IRS rules for non-profits, and its tax-exempt status would be pulled.[4] Thereby chilling political speech in general.

Note these additional chills:

- Those who disagree with the theory of man-made global warming are castigated as climate deniers, an allusion to Holocaust deniers, and a professor at Rochester Institute of Technology wants people jailed if they disagree with the "settled science" of global warming.[5]
- The Girl Scouts want to ban the word "bossy." The irony escapes them, of course.
- Non-profit organizations with a 501-c-4 tax exemption cannot spend more than 49% of their funds on political issues. Now the IRS, again, wants to expand this rule to not only limit money, but also no more 49% of the time the organization spends on public issues. Byzantine rules for one purpose: advantageous control. And you thought keeping a time card was laborious.

Such encroachments on our freedom of speech run counter to the ten Bill of Rights. Look at the direction of the action verbs and constraints in this signal document:

I: Shall make no law … prohibiting … abridging…

II: Shall not be infringed …

III: No soldier shall … be quartered…

IV: Shall not be violated… no warrants shall issue …

V: No person shall be held … nor shall any person be subject … nor shall be compelled … nor be deprived of … nor shall private property be taken …

VI: Accused shall enjoy …

VII: Right of trial by jury shall be preserved …

VIII: Shall not be required … imposed … inflicted

IX: Shall not be construed to deny or disparage …

X: Powers not delegated … are reserved to the states … or to the people

The Bill of Rights does not tell the *people* what they can and cannot do; it tells *Congress* what it shall and shall not do. We could easily rename it the Bill of Congressional Restrictions.

So why are all of these action verbs targeted on Congress? Because our Founding Fathers understood human nature and knew the time would come when power-seeking men would abuse the powers of government to their own advantage. They would attempt to silence dissent. Which is precisely what is happening today and why speech control is blatantly in violation not only of the First Amendment, but contrary to the concepts throughout our great Constitution.

Speech on the chopping block

Censorship is a most effective tool. It reduces information, limits choices, damages agency. It can destroy the nation because America without free speech is no longer America.

Those who a few years ago agitated for free speech now clamber for clampdowns. Once worried about their right to speak, they now worry that others may say things they don't want to hear, so they seek to muzzle religion-informed speech and increasingly censor political speech.

They are making headway as evidenced by an April 2014 Rasmussen survey that found that 55% of Americans believe the government should be "allowed to review political ads and candidates' campaign comments for their accuracy and punish those that it decides are making false statements about other candidates."[6] And only 31% disagreed – a 5:3 majority for the speech control that could bring America to its knees.

While the idea may sound good on the surface (who could possibly be against punishing false statements?), government as censor would be a disaster. Can we really trust a government agency to decide what is false, judge impartially, and not abuse its powers? Such thinking smacks of the Wilsonian notion that government experts stand apart from the tiffs of daily life and will act in a neutral and unbiased manner. This is simply not the case. The agency in charge, part of the secular state religion and knowing the favored fads, will be a walking conflict of interest. It is difficult to see how their edicts will not skew in favor of those in power.

The camel's nose under the tent is that if government is empowered to control speech in political campaigns, then why not extend that power to other arenas? Why not deploy government monitors to make sure no untruthful speech of any kind reaches our ears? Why not sanitize all social discourse and punish offenders? Why not enforce it with ruinous fines? With police power?

While truth in all speech is the ultimate goal (and the reason we need to be guided by gospel principles), **the Founders did not establish a Bureau of Accuracy as part of the First Amendment**. Freedom of speech must include both the truthful and the untruthful, and people must be left to sort it out as they will. Anything contrary foils both agency and democracy.

Goofy political correctness

The Supreme Court's ruling in *Citizens United* reaffirmed the right of all Americans, whether as individuals or as a group, to free speech. Opponents to this affirmation of freedom have threatened a forceful response. Under their vision, organizations the administration in power favors will get a bye while the speech of less well-connected groups will be under the microscope. Viewpoints contradicting those in power will be defined as hate speech and silenced.

All of this is the *macro* threat – statements judged unworthy of utterance even though they may be built with everyday words. Potentially as stifling is the *micro* threat – individual words judged offensive that must, the reasoning goes, be outlawed.

Few dispute that there must be limits if speech causes true harm, such as yelling "Fire" in a crowded theater when there isn't one. And out of respect and civility, no decent person should use ethnic slurs or aspersions on one's parentage. But how many words and phrases will be branded as politically incorrect, and candidates for censorship, before the silliness ends?

> A broken home is now a dysfunctional family. Global warming is now climate change. The 9/11 terrorists were misguided criminals, thugs are troubled youth, and murderers are merely insane. The term illegal aliens is racist and even illegal immigrants is a no-no; illegal must be replaced with undocumented. Garbage men are sanitation engineers, housewives are domestic engineers, a ghetto is an economically disadvantaged area, to fail is to achieve (!) a deficiency, and don't even think about saying "man up" on certain university campuses. Some even view the word illegal as a slur. As for losers, well, there can't be any; every child must be a winner because all kids are above average.

Most such changes are harmless except they make us overly sensitive and judgmental. The problem is they tend to come from one side of society only and establish that segment as the arbiter of proper language. With time, an approved way of thinking deferential to that side of society sets in. Thus, a person of faith who uses such common words as husband and wife, old, lazy, pet owner, bald, jungle, secretary, swamp, handicapped, short, tall, crazy, vagrant, and even unemployed is berated while a non-believer can use God's name in vain and mouth the filthiest of words on TV and receives not so much as a tut-tut. (Maybe because "tut-tut" is politically incorrect.)

Then there's the downright goofy. The city department of education in New York suggests words like dinosaurs, birthdays, and Halloween be avoided because they might offend various religious groups. City workers in Seattle have been told not to use the terms citizen and brown bag[7] and I have already mentioned the movement to eliminate the term bossy. It gets better: Columbus Day has been changed to Explorer's Day because Columbus was supposedly the beginning of ethnic cleansing of native Americans, holding down the fort is offensive to Indians because they were the ones against whom the fort was being held down, and the peanut butter sandwich was deemed insensitive to other cultures by a Portland grade-school principal.[8]

Watch out for bossy cavalry sentinels brown-bagging peanut butter sandwiches on Halloween.

Where to draw the line? A list of forbidden words will always favor those in power. And if you're on the wrong side of that list, you're hateful (an indiscriminately applied word if there ever was one). More to the point, just the threat of being hauled before a Human Rights Commission (as author Mark Steyn was in Canada[9]) or some equally noble-sounding tribunal freezes robust and lively debate.

Pity our society if we allow the state to use its police powers to define and prevent offensive speech. Those quick to yell for new laws don't realize that there isn't enough parchment in the world to write all the regulations that will govern man in all possible actions, let alone speech and thought. Yet there are busybodies who are only too happy to try.

America can survive the rough and tumble of free and open speech. Whether it can survive censorship is another matter.

Militarized agencies

I cannot guess the probability that America might be taken over by an incarnation of Gadianton robbers, but the story must be in the Book of Mormon for a purpose. Not long before the coming of Christ, Zarahemla was in a state of awful wickedness. The Gadianton robbers[10] ...

- Filled the judgment seats (the executive branch of the day)
- Had usurped power and authority
- Ignored the commandments of God
- Did not do justice to the children of men

- Condemned the righteous for being righteous
- Let the guilty and wicked go unpunished because of their money
- Ruled according to their wills (no more laws of Mosiah)
- Used their positions to get gain and glory
- Used their positions to more easily commit adultery, steal, and kill

Mormon notes it all happened "in the space of not many years."[11]

Maybe we will escape the full parallel of the Gadianton happenings in Nephite times, but wrestling against "the rulers of the darkness of this world" and "spiritual wickedness in high places"[12] was the lot of Paul and early Christians as well, and one cannot deny that not a few of the above nine characteristics are happening today even if no covenant alliance between perpetrators has been uncovered. Mormon states clearly that Satan tempted the Nephites "to seek for power, and *authority*, and riches, and the vain things of the world."[13] If he did it before Christ's birth, why not before His Second Coming?

Many are the ways to abuse executive power, but two disturbing trends demand closer vigilance. I am especially concerned about expansion of government power through real and manufactured crises, and the militarization of federal agencies and local police.

Executive orders multiply during crises not least because there are no firm guidelines as to their use and people in various stages of panic will demand that government "do something." The pressure to act can sometimes accomplish good things: Harry Truman racially integrated the military, Abraham Lincoln issued the Emancipation Proclamation, John Kennedy created the Peace Corps, and Thomas Jefferson used an executive order for the Louisiana Purchase.[14] But even a good outcome weakens legislative processes and emboldens misuse.

So it was in the Great Depression. Franklin Roosevelt used the crisis to lead (some say rule) by decree. With only sporadic pushback, Congress rubber-stamped laws FDR wrote in the White House, thus concentrating power that didn't abate when it was over.

Then when World War II broke out, accustomed and excessive deference to the president led to the most shameful executive order in our history, to date. Assuming more than generally acceptable discretionary power, Franklin Roosevelt, the closest thing to a king America has had until now, sent thousands of Japanese-Americans into internment camps by executive order in 1942. They were freed when World War II ended, but what would have happened had the war with Japan dribbled down to an uneasy standoff between two exhausted nations? How long would Americans of Japanese ancestry have languished in those camps? Under the guise of military necessity, what powers would President Roosevelt not have arrogated to himself?

Relying on the Supreme Court to spot flawed executive orders is not good enough. Initially approving Roosevelt's move in the *Korematsu* case, the court eventually righted the wrong but it took more than 40 years.[15] Whistles must be blown earlier than that.

Which brings us to a related development – the militarization of federal agencies and America's local police forces. Several have traced the origin of this phenomenon to the Racketeer Influenced and Corrupt Organizations Act of 1970 (RICO) that prosecutes racketeering and provides for the confiscation of ill-gotten gains, to be kept by the confiscators. Writing in *The New Yorker*, one reporter asked:

> Does it make sense that civil-forfeiture laws, which allow police to confiscate and keep property that is allegedly tied to criminal activity, are often enforced at gunpoint against, say, nonviolent partygoers? What, fundamentally, are SWAT teams for? When does it make sense to use machine guns, armored vehicles, and flash-bang grenades on a crowd of people or on a family, and how are these warfare-inspired approaches to law enforcement changing America?[16]

Judging by articles, columns, and blogs on the issue, the left and the right agree quite often on this worry, how intensely depending on which party controls the White House. Though domestic police power is reserved to the states and local jurisdictions, this line of separation has been blurred over the years, witness that over 40 federal agencies now have armed divisions.[17] Logical for the FBI or Bureau of Prisons, but why the Federal Reserve Board and, until recently, the Library of Congress (now under the protection of the Capitol Police)? Even granting that the books and documents in the Library of Congress are of immense value, once armed agents are deployed, the government-growth truism kicks in and **there is nothing to stop that armed division from expanding**. (When the librarian says "Shhhh," she really means "Shhhh.") Under such reasoning, what activity, substance, or purview cannot be considered valuable enough to require armed enforcement – the environment, grazing land, energy, agriculture, commerce, trade? What is to stop the militarization of any and all federal agencies?

What is further unsettling is that the Department of Homeland Security is buying 1.6 billion bullets, about 20% of them hollow point,[18] that SWAT teams differ from military units only by the color of their uniform, and that police through federal grants and RICO gains have purchased substantial stocks of military equipment.[19] Even the Post Office and the Social Security Administration have purchased large amounts of ammunition.[20]

Who is protecting whom from whom?

Against all enemies, foreign and domestic

As more federal agencies are militarized and others beef up their weaponry, the other pincer is the attempt to disarm the people.

When flatterer extraordinaire Amalickiah fought to become king, Captain Moroni rent his coat and raised the title of liberty.[21] Did the people rally to his banner but then lament that they didn't have swords? ("Sorry, Cap'n, would sure like to help but the government took our swords away. Got any spare cimeters?") No, they had their weapons because past wickedness prepared them to be armed. Maybe the king-men agitated for sword control (for others, of course), but fortunately sword rights prevailed.

As for our day, the Constitution did not affirm the right to own and bear arms so that people could hunt ducks. Nor was it ratified for individual self defense, useful as that is. **The right to bear arms was put in the Constitution so people could, if necessary, defend it against tyrants who usurp and destroy.**

The possibility the people may have to rise up with arms to dislodge tyranny is not an unusual scenario. Consider these quotes from three different centuries:[22]

> Thomas Jefferson, 1787: "What country can preserve its liberties if its rulers are not warned from time to time that their people preserve the spirit of resistance? Let them take arms."

> George Mason, Constitutional Convention delegate, 1787: "To disarm the people – that was the best and most effectual way to enslave them."

> Supreme Court Justice Joseph Story, 1833: "The militia is the natural defense of a free country against sudden foreign invasions, domestic insurrections, and domestic usurpation of power by rulers. The right of the citizens to keep and bear arms … offers a strong moral check against the usurpation and arbitrary power of rulers."

> Senator Hubert Humphrey, 1959: "Certainly one of the chief guarantees of freedom under any government, no matter how popular and respected, is the right of citizens to keep and bear arms. … The right of citizens to bear arms is just one guarantee against arbitrary government, one more safeguard, against the tyranny which now appears remote in America but which historically has proven to be always possible."

The Oath of Allegiance taken by immigrants desiring to be citizens contains the phrase "defend the Constitution … against all enemies, foreign and domestic…"[23], a phrase that **would not make sense if enemies of the Constitution could only come from abroad**.

And could defending against such enemies always be accomplished with words only? While James Madison in Federalist 46 and Alexander Hamilton in Federalist 29 focused on the relationship between state and local militias on the one hand and a standing federal army on the other, it was a given that their reasoning assumed an armed citizenry that "forms a barrier against the enterprises of ambition…."[24]

Adolf Hitler's main fear: "The most foolish mistake we could possibly make would be to allow the subject races to possess arms. History shows that all conquerors who have allowed their subject races to carry arms have prepared their own downfall by so doing."[25]

* * *

Speech control is for speech therapists.

Chapter 24

Power Corrupts and Profligacy Corrupts Absolutely

"Alexander Hamilton started the U.S. Treasury with nothing – and that was the closest our country has ever been to being even."

– Will Rogers

More than one resident of Washington environs has told me that Washington has power and wants money, whereas New York has money and wants power. Given the history of money and power, this alliance between America's two de-facto capitals is not reassuring.

On June 20, 1941, Adolf Hitler attacked the Soviet Union. By September, his armies were at the gates of Leningrad and had cut off the last road leading to it. No more supplies for the beleaguered city.

As war came to their doorstep, people in Leningrad still casually dined in downtown restaurants though they could hear German artillery in the suburbs! They refused to believe what was about to happen. Denial of the first order. Within 30 days of their blissful evenings out, they were peeling wallpaper off their walls to get at the potato-based paste and stave off starvation. They later boiled leather briefcases to make soup and were even reduced to digging up dirt under a bombed-out Badayev sugar warehouse to find a few calories of the melted commodity it once housed.[1]

They refused to see what was coming. They paid the price – over one million civilians died in the 28-month siege, the costliest in history.

Inoculation by conspiracy theories

We do not hear an enemy's artillery on our borders, but we are coming under siege of a different sort, the siege of intrusive government.

Some pooh-pooh it as the upshot of a deranged imagination, while others feel all too well the reality. So how does Satan immunize that first group of our fellow citizens from figuring out the dangers he and his useful idiots have unleashed on America?

He does it by distracting us with **false conspiracies that mask his true one** – by mocking the very activity he is doing and demonizing those who dare blow the whistle (a type of inoculation known as projection). I became aware of this tactic in a class on propaganda techniques at the height of the Cold War. The professor said that if we wanted to know what the Soviet Union was up to, we should listen carefully to what they accuse us of doing. Even the devil needs a devil.

Here's Satan's process:

- He stimulates imaginations to go bananas so that crazy conspiracies are entertained, such as the doozy that destruction of the World Trade Center towers on 9/11 was an inside U.S. government job.
- He creates conspiracy theories of every hue and fear, whether on the right or the left: the New World Order, Judeo-Masonic conspiracies (the whack-a-mole *Protocols of the Elders of Zion* pops up every couple of decades), the Illuminati, the vast right-wing conspiracy, the Clinton body count, the Rothschild banking conspiracy, Da Vinci Code-type religion conspiracies, the Koch

brothers, George Soros, terrorist conspiracies, assassination conspiracies, suppressed technology conspiracies (oil companies killed the inventor of a more efficient carburetor), things the ubiquitous "they" don't want you to know, and so ad nauseam on.[2] Proliferate and give them visibility.

- He encourages arguments as to whether a theory is plausible or preposterous. He doesn't care how people decide; he just wants the idea of conspiracies to be on their minds.
- He includes his own actions in the conspiracies people decide are ludicrous.
- He mocks all conspiracies – especially where Satan is claimed to be behind them. Ridicule as conspiracy nuts those who believe that he is actually doing what he is doing.
- He continues until Pavlovian conditioning kicks in – that the word conspiracy invokes images of foaming-at-the-mouth crazies with more time than brains.

Thus, in a world full of conspiracy theories, those who warn that Satan is orchestrating significant dangers to America are demonized as scaremongers, cranks, and mentally off balance. And ignored.

Prosecutorial extortion

So now, in a world seemingly awash with conspiracies and villains, it's easy to tempt the ambitious to overuse their proper powers and advance intrusive government.

The most frequently trod path to election to state and federal office is through a district attorney's office. America wants crime fighters, and prosecuting attorneys deliver. Most of the time. Most of it honestly.

But there is a dark underbelly.

The problem is when a U.S. or district attorney faced with flimsy evidence of a crime nonetheless pursues a case for career-building reasons. Or when an agency pursues a case hoping for a money settlement that it can direct to causes it favors. **Prosecutorial discretion becomes prosecutorial extortion when it forces compliance by intimidation.**

Fighting a government agency in court can be made so expensive that the defendant caves to a plea bargain instead of having his case decided by a fair judge or jury. Stephanos Bibas, a professor of law and criminology at the University of Pennsylvania, explains the intimidation game of behavior control:

> Federal prosecutors can also hold the threat of criminal enforcement in reserve, using it to coerce civil settlements and consent decrees *even where proof of wrongdoing is shaky.* Indeed, prosecutors of white-collar crimes often enter into deferred-prosecution agreements, in which businesses are not prosecuted in exchange for paying fines, firing employees, or making other internal changes *not provided for by law or regulation.* That allows regulatory agencies to flex their muscles and read laws expansively – for example reading the Clean Water Act to cover all kinds of building in wetlands. Any criminal conviction amounts to the death penalty for a legitimate business (as it was for Big Five accounting firm Arthur Andersen, even after its conviction was reversed on appeal). Thus, few businesses dare to fight federal power grabs, and regulators can push the envelope of their power.
>
> Federal regulators can afford to use criminal prosecutions sparingly so long as the loaded gun of criminal penalties lies in full view on the negotiating table. A corollary is that defendants are *prosecuted* not for being the worst of the worst, but *for refusing to play ball.*[3] [Emphasis added]

The threat of criminal prosecution is but one more bullying way to get people to do what the state wants them to do without all that messy checks-and-balances stuff. And in the process weaken citizens' respect for our justice system.

(By the way, the tactic is not new. Nephi, son of Helaman, was offered a plea bargain: money if he would name his supposed confederate in the murder of the chief judge, death if he would not. Nephi told them to buzz off as he knew their true intent was to discredit him as a prophet.[4])

Numerous are the stories of bogus felonies, creative indictments, and selective prosecution, often nakedly partisan. The recipe is simple:

> 1. Find a supposed violation of law or regulations, or at least the pretext of one. With thousands of laws on the books, the average citizen commits three felonies a day without even knowing it, according to Harvey Silverglate, author of a book with that title.[5] Opportunities for zealous prosecution – often a stepping-stone to elected office for the victorious prosecutor – are plentiful.
>
> 2. From the gaggle of supposed violators, select a target who has few resources to defend himself in court.
>
> 3. Freeze the indicted person's bank accounts, especially in high-visibility cases, so he cannot hire quality legal counsel and mount a strong defense. Goodbye to the principle of innocent until proven guilty.
>
> 4. Withhold evidence that might show the defendant is innocent.[6]
>
> 5. Offer a plea bargain, especially if the case is weak.
>
> 6. Cultivate publicity as a signal to innocent and guilty alike not to resist government edicts, whether constitutionally justified or not.

In short, **intimidate, badger, and exhaust.** Add an enemies list to the recipe, and political opponents bake in jail.

A variation of this abuse is the "funnel money to your friends" scheme. In 2012, the Environment and Natural Resource Division of the Justice Department charged the Gibson Guitar Corporation with illegally importing wood from Madagascar for its guitar fingerboards.

The company decided to settle rather than incur substantial legal expenses. As part of the settlement, it was required to pay $50,000 (20% of the fine) to a *private charity*[7] – a private enterprise, by the way, that was not injured by Gibson's actions and was totally irrelevant to the case. Money was funneled to a cause **favored by ideologically driven government lawyers** instead of to the general fund where all fines and penalties should be paid.

Potentially even more destructive is the capricious tool called civil forfeiture to cow Americans into bowing before government. Under present laws, federal and state agencies – the IRS, FBI, local police, prosecutors – **can seize personal property if they merely *suspect* wrongdoing. Merely suspect!!** No charges, no trial, no evidence, no conviction, only suspicion that the property seized *might* be associated with a crime.

This is Wild West stuff – shoot first and ask questions later. Supermarket chains are rarely questioned about the cash they deposit in banks, but watch out if you own a small mom-and-pop grocery store. Or gas station. Or any other small business making, of necessity, frequent cash deposits. George Will says the civil forfeiture law "is an incentive for perverse behavior: Predatory government agencies get to pocket the proceeds from property they seize from Americans without even charging them with, let alone convicting them of, crimes. Criminals are treated better than this because they lose the fruits of their criminality only after being convicted."[8]

When assets can be seized on the *mere suspicion* of criminal activity, what's to keep the IRS from intimidating anyone given the many regulations on the books and easy-to-find violations?

Even the Environmental Protection Agency is getting in on the plunder. It now claims it has the "authority to bypass the courts and unilaterally garnish paychecks" if it, alone, determines that someone has violated one of their rules. Huge per-day penalties. No judicial review because it was not a "significant regulatory action," they said.

And if the person challenges it, he has to travel to where they are. All part of the pressure to settle on their terms.[9]

Crony capitalism and corruption

Those who seek control over people and things inordinately focus on money. They don't like the freedom aspect of our market system, based as it is on bedrock principles of agency and choice, and disparagingly call it capitalism, implying the worship of money – a system where possessors of capital supposedly run the show. It especially became a pejorative in the writings of Karl Marx, even without prefacing it with the word *greedy*. Thus when people cheat the financial system, or government spends more than it takes in, it is somehow the fault of capitalism – an unfair attack on the second best economic system ever developed for the benefit of mankind.

The cases of sweetheart deals between business and government have become so prevalent that the pattern has earned its own name – crony capitalism. This is fortunate in a quirky way because it implies there must be at least two types of capitalism and that capitalism as a whole is not always tarred with the sins of thieves. But unfortunately it is, as a form of corruption, a definite threat to America.

Corruption begins with little favors from someone in power or someone with money. Perhaps it's actionable information shared with a moneyed friend, or a campaign donation traded for a vote, wink-wink of course. In time such practices become regularized and deepen as special interests receive something that others do not, which is why they're called special. The activity at some point goes underground and becomes a secret – a secret deal, a secret understanding, a secret … alliance, shall we say? Maybe even with promises to protect one another in their nefarious doings.

Can it really be that bad? Well, those who have seen our day have warned us that such corruption can happen here. On the same land where it has happened before.[10]

'Til debt do we part

If a zealous prosecutor is a shark, debt is a termite – not as flashy as extortion, but more destructive.

People argue whether John Adams said, "There are two ways to conquer and enslave a nation: one is by sword, the other is by debt." If he did, it sounds like him. If he didn't, he should have because that is how the Lord's prophets have preached, Adams himself one of the great and noble ones from whose ranks prophets and founders were called to their mortal missions. Elder Joseph B. Wirthlin called debt a form of bondage, a financial termite[11] and J. Reuben Clark Jr. warned of interest on debt: "... it yields neither to entreaties, demands, or orders; and whenever you get in its way or cross its course or fail to meet its demands, it crushes you."[12]

We weakly protest exploding government spending, but do not face up to its power to crush us. Certain circles would rather fan hysteria about climate change, nee global warming. But it is a piker compared to the national debt, and there is no contest which one is more imminent.

Our Federal Reserve and its counterparts in Europe, Japan, and China "have printed an astounding $10 trillion since 2007, tripling the size of their combined balance sheets."[13] **The U.S. government spends $120,000 per second, $52,000 of which is borrowed,**[14] **and yet complains that it doesn't have enough.** Our difficult-to-fathom national debt has arisen from unwise spending policies and entitlement programs to buy vote loyalty, and few are the leaders on either side of the aisle determined to roll it back though they all cluck about how unsustainable it is. Too many are only concerned that wealth be more equitably distributed, it being a magically appearing commodity, you know.

Because of the myopic belief that we can borrow our way into prosperity, I fear two nation-splitting clashes in the not-too-distant future:

Private sector vs. public sector. Businesses without chummy government connections will grow increasingly resentful of the controls, backed by taxing and policing powers, that government elites wield over them. Individuals in the private arena will become embittered when they compare their station in life with the privileged upstream position those on the government payroll occupy, especially when work-reward ratios are examined.

Young vs. old. It doesn't take a genius to see generational resentment building. The day will come when a youthful agitator will thunder, "Why should we pay for meals someone in Toledo ate before we were born? Or their housing subsidies? Or their health care? Or the trillions of dollars of debt we've been saddled with?" And we in the older generations will not have calming answers.

When this maelstrom happens, many will be the excuses and many fingers will affix blame. But one thing remains: Satan approves of economic chaos whatever its causal agents.

The leaf is wet

The time has come to **face the reality of government corruption**. A time to finally recognize, paraphrasing Jefferson's warning in Chapter 19, that those entrusted with power are by slow operations perverting government into tyranny.

One cannot determine the exact moment corruption becomes tyranny any more than one can specify the moment the overnight dew made a leaf wet. But by slow operations – abuse of power, trading favors for votes, bribery with tax exemptions, excessive rules and regulations, ignoring the Constitution, unbridled bureaucratic overreach, viewpoint discrimination, misuse of resources, favoritism, crony capitalism, scratch-my-back tradeoffs – the case-after-case evidence piles up until one must finally say, "Yup, that leaf is wet."

We are on the cusp of the tyrannization of the government of the United States of America. The cases of corruption – dishonest or fraudulent conduct by those in power for the benefit of themselves or special interest groups – are too numerous to think otherwise.

When government spends more than it takes in and refuses year after year to balance its budget, that is corruption.

When government fobs off its debt to generations yet unborn (talk about visiting the iniquities of the fathers upon the children), that is corruption.

When government intentionally diminishes the purchasing power of its currency, that is corruption.

When anyone can vote without verification of identity and eligibility, that is corruption.

When the philosophy of prosecutors is that a defendant is guilty until proven innocent, that is corruption.

When an arm of government seizes property on the mere suspicion of wrongdoing, that is corruption.

When that same arm of government spends the seized assets even before the party is charged, let alone proven guilty, that is corruption.

When that same arm of government refuses to return those assets when a party is acquitted, that is corruption.

When an agency targets individuals or small companies for securities violations with the goal of squeezing a settlement, knowing that the party does not have the resources for a lengthy court battle, that is corruption.

When a zealous prosecutor knows he has a weak case, but files charges anyway to bolster his credentials as a crime fighter as a path to higher office, that is corruption.

When an agency stalls and stretches out legal proceedings to delay a defendant's day in court and wear down his resistance, that is corruption.

When government fines an organization and money paid in settlement is funneled to favored causes instead of into the general fund, that is corruption.

When an agency requires a state to flush billions of gallons of water down a river for the comfort of fish while people are suffering one of the worst droughts in history, that is both stupidity and corruption.

When an agency funds research into hypotheses it favors but not to those testing opposing theories, that is corruption.

When a government agency selectively holds tax-exempt status over someone's head, not to prevent a bad behavior but to compel a behavior favored by a particular political ideology, that is corruption.

When the government requires a person to violate sincerely held religious beliefs and thus appear to approve something he or she disapproves, that is corruption.

When political beliefs are protected while religious beliefs are not, that is corruption.

When an agency compels mandatory sensitivity training on a topic in vogue, that is corruption.

When an agency ignores congressional requests for documents Congress is legally entitled to, that is corruption.

When an agency conveniently loses email correspondence and other documents it is required to archive and is under congressional subpoena to produce, that is corruption.

When some people get prime seats at state functions as an honor or recognition for service, or simple kindness, that is not corruption. A quid pro quo for such perks is.

When an agency either selectively enforces or selectively ignores the law, that is corruption.

When the Justice Department chooses not to investigate allegations against favored constituencies, but enthusiastically investigates similar allegations against opposite constituencies, that is corruption.

When the IRS shares confidential tax returns with another agency or with a favored constituency, information that by law shall not be shared, that is corruption.

When an agency stonewalls congressional investigations into possible wrongdoing, that is corruption.

When the judicial branch entertains fad legal theories instead of following the law as written, that is corruption.

When the judiciary manufactures new laws or rights from emanations and penumbras, that is corruption.

When the legislative branch relinquishes legislative power to unelected bureaucrats, that is corruption.

When Congress exempts itself from the laws it passes, that is corruption.

When the president refuses to follow immigration and deportation laws resulting in a destabilizing flood of illegal immigrants across our southern border, that is corruption.

When the president freezes all wages and prices contrary to the conditions established by Congress, that is corruption.

When the president presumes to control all of the nation's resources, whether privately or publicly owned, that is corruption.

When the executive attempts to bypass Congress and write and enforce new laws through executive decrees, that is corruption.

When the president unilaterally changes a law, that is corruption.

When a president ignores checks and balances and governs by decree, that is corruption.

When the president exceeds his authority, regardless of whether to do good or evil, that is corruption.

When the executive refuses to faithfully execute the law as required by the Constitution, that is not only corruption, it is a high crime and misdemeanor – a violation of his oath.[15]

How can one deny it? The government of the United States of America, as currently constituted, is riddled with corruption as never before in our history.

* * *

If our Founding Fathers were to read the above litany of offenses against the system they established, on which side of the ledger in the battle between good and evil would they place the leaders of our nation?

Chapter 25

America: Great Promise, Terrible Curse

"For behold, this is a land which is choice above all other lands; wherefore he that doth possess it shall serve God or shall be swept off; for it is the everlasting decree of God."

– Ether 2:10

"And only a few years have passed away, and they were a civil and a delightsome people."[1]

I was a missionary in Germany when the Berlin Wall went up and it was the best day of tracting I had in my whole mission. Nothing like a potential war to give people religion. (The flurry lasted only about 48 hours, however.) But it was five months after the Wall came *down* that I experienced in ways never before how much America really meant to me.

In those crumbling days of the Soviet Union, I was part of the first civilian delegation to be allowed to visit the till-then closed city of Sverdlovsk, Russia (later Yekaterinburg, its original name) – Boris Yeltsin's home town, the place where the U-2 spy plane was shot down in May of 1960, and scene of the slaughter of Czar Nicholas II and his family in 1918 – to teach budding democrats about political campaigns and how democracy works.

Before we got into the mechanics of campaigns, the leader of our delegation asked me to give an introductory lecture on the philosophical roots of the American experiment to establish the people as sovereign. You will believe me when I tell you it was one of the great thrills of my life to stand at the lectern of a steeply banked snake-pit lecture hall and tell 200 Russians, who had never before even seen a live American, the story of Washington, Jefferson, Madison, Franklin and all those who pledged their lives, fortunes, and sacred honor to declare our independence and then establish the Constitution and launch America 11 years later.

All while a painting of Karl Marx glowered from a side wall and a huge bust of Lenin looked over my shoulder.

An experience I will always treasure.

So now, as we finish this next-to-last chapter, here, in addition to the previously discussed tactics Satan is using to try to destabilize America, are four final actions Satan would have us embrace:

Ignore prophecies
Kindle pride
Glorify sin
Reject the Great Promise

Ignore the prophecies

Not every natural upheaval is a message from God, but at times He uses such phenomena to warn His children to change their behavior. He sent fire to consume Sodom and Gomorrah. He sent plagues of frogs and locusts to drive a message into pharaoh's thick skull, and then sent winds to sucker the Egyptian army into driving their chariots onto newly appearing dry ground that only minutes before was the Red Sea, and then to calm those winds – the loudest sound of "Oh, oh" ever recorded. And of course there was the Great Flood.

Knowing that God has promised to visit the wicked with even greater calamities in the last days, **Satan redirects attention to a different framework so people will fail to recognize God's message**. That framework is environmental stewardship.

Of course God expects us to be good stewards and take care of the earth, and most people, religious or not, do so. But true-believer greenies take it to extremes and exaggerate man's role as a causal agent in nature's events. As they do, a use-resources-wisely environmentalist (which most of us are) may become a lock-it-up environmentalist and then an extreme environmentalist who sees man's failure to be green enough as the reason for all natural disasters. The message changes as needed to keep it on the public's radar: First it was global warming (that fizzled when the average temperature has remained flat for 15 years), then climate change (so when does the climate not change?), and now it's climate disruption.

It is also tied to power. Those seeking to control the lives of others conveniently use computer-model predictions of doom (almost all of which fail the test of being able to predict in reverse the weather that actually happened) to justify their power grab.[2]

Extreme environmentalism thus inoculates mankind so when God's promised cataclysms happen – earthquakes, tempests, hailstorms, seas heaving their bounds – people will chalk them up to man's polluting the air, fouling the water, burning fossil fuels, pumping CO2 into the atmosphere, destroying the ozone layer, and unwise use of resources. Thus desensitized, they will not recognize these events as the God-sent consequences of sexual immorality, pornography, class warfare, financial dishonesty, false gods, exploiting the laborer, and other failures to keep the commandments.

(Ever wonder if the scolds of Noah's day said as the rains began, "I told you guys not to burn so much wood"?)

The secular religion points to poor stewardship, not immorality, as the great sin. Belief that immorality will bring destruction by natural events and wickedness is mocked as a superstition of the ignorant.

Kindle pride

There is proud and there is pride.

We should be proud of our nation, our religion, scriptures, and other sacred things in the proper sense of being respectful and deferential to the truths they contain or upon which they are based. We can also be proud of the accomplishments of others, if honestly attained.

But pride is cloth of a different weave. It is the puffed-up narcissism that puts down others. It is the arrogance of always being right. It is the self-worship that indulges the lusts of the world. It is the vain imaginations symbolized by the large and spacious building in Lehi's and Nephi's visions.[3]

It is the destroyer of nations.

The Nephite pride cycle is illustrative:

> 1. Righteousness → 2. prosperity → 3. pride → 4. wickedness → 5. destruction and suffering → 6. humility and repentance → and back to righteousness.

Sometimes it takes but a few years to circle the track. I submit that the US of A today is fully immersed in Stage 3, a near majority wallows in Stage 4, and Stage 5 is closer than we think.

No better exposition on the dangers of pride has been given than President Ezra Taft Benson's April 1989 conference address. Ponder these excerpts:

> The Doctrine and Covenants tells us that the Book of Mormon is the "record of a fallen people." Why did they fall? This is one of the major messages of the Book of Mormon. Mormon gives the answer in the closing chapters of the book in these words: "Behold, the pride of this nation, or the people of the Nephites, hath proven their destruction." And then, lest we miss that momentous Book of Mormon message from that fallen people, the Lord warns us in the

> Doctrine and Covenants, "Beware of pride lest ye become as the Nephites of old."[4]
>
> It was pride that felled Lucifer....
>
> There is no such thing as righteous pride – it is always considered a sin.
>
> The central feature of pride is enmity – [hatred] toward God and ... our fellowmen. ... We are tempted daily to elevate ourselves above others and diminish them.
>
> Pride is essentially competitive in nature. We pit our will against God's.
>
> The proud make every man their adversary by pitting their intellects, opinions, works, wealth, talents, or any other worldly measuring device against others. In the words of C. S. Lewis: "Pride gets no pleasure out of having something, only out of having more of it than the next man. ... It is the comparison that makes you proud: the pleasure of being above the rest. Once the element of competition has gone, pride has gone."
>
> Pride is a damning sin in the true sense of that word. It limits or stops progression. The proud are not easily taught. They won't change their minds to accept truths, because to do so implies they have been wrong.

President Benson continued with warnings against pride-related actions such as contention, selfishness, disobedience, envy, etc., and then gave a most telling observation for our topic here:

> Pride results in secret combinations which are built up to get power, gain, and glory of the world. This fruit of the sin of pride, namely secret combinations, brought down both the Jaredite and the Nephite civilizations and has been and **will yet be the cause of the fall of many nations**. [Emphasis added]

Can't happen here? That's what the people of Zarahemla thought when Nephi, son of Helaman, warned them of pending destruction if they did not repent:

> Why do you suffer this man to revile against us? For behold he doth condemn all this people, even unto destruction; yea, and also that these our great cities shall be taken from us, that we shall have no place in them. And now we know that this is impossible, for behold, we are powerful, and our cities great, therefore our enemies can have no power over us.[5]

Every destruction in Nephite and Jaredite histories has been triggered by an eloquent power-seeker flattering the people and kindling pride. Substitute New York, Washington, or San Francisco wherever Zarahemla appears in the scriptures for a useful perspective.

Glorify sin

We have experienced a deep cultural shift within the last few years. Whereas the power of public opinion once guarded a modicum of decency in movies and media, today cuss bombs, nudity, and how-to-sin scenes abound. We shrug.

It begins with small things that coarsen: a me-first mentality, lack of politeness, diminished respect for another's race or ethnicity, diminished civility in public policy debates, such as constant interruptions (hello, talk-show hosts) and using harsh terms to describe opponents.

Then come lies: twist the facts, convolute the meaning of words, and masquerade improprieties as noble.

Then wink at sin (everybody's doing it), trivialize it (no big deal; try it, you'll like it), and in time nonchalantly dismiss it (there's no such thing as sin; no consequences).

And finally glorify all that is gross, filthy, and putrid. Rub it in. Browbeat us into silence by political correctness. A most disgusting example was, as described by those who sat through it, a film of nothing-left-to-imagination lesbian sex scenes that received a standing ovation from the glamorous and a Cannes International Film Festival award, and saw top American moviemakers tripping over tongues to heap praise upon it.

Elder Boyd K. Packer tells us the evils of this world will not abate this side of the Second Coming:

> The world is spiraling downward at an ever-quickening pace. I am sorry to tell you that it will not get better. … I know of nothing in the history of the Church or in the history of the world to compare with our present circumstances. Nothing happened in Sodom and Gomorrah which exceeds in wickedness and depravity that which surrounds us now. Words of profanity, vulgarity and blasphemy are heard everywhere. Unspeakable wickedness and perversion were once hidden in dark places; now they are in the open, even accorded legal protection. At Sodom and Gomorrah these things were localized. Now they are spread across the world, and they are among us.[6]

And the cognoscenti are worried about carbon dioxide polluting the planet!

Where are the brave souls who will say, "Now wait just a cotton-pickin' minute"? Where are the outspoken like Mahatma Gandhi who said, "I will not let anyone walk through my mind with their dirty feet"?

How did we get into this pickle? Easy. **The world has rejected absolutes – good and evil, right and wrong.** They say that we who talk of good and evil are simplistic and unsophisticated, while I maintain one must be gullible and naïve not to so believe. Remember, as noted in Chapter 5, Satan's finest trick is to convince us that he doesn't exist. If people buy that, the corollary is easy to accept: there is no evil. And if no evil, then whatever a person does is no sin. And if no sin, then no consequences, no justice, no agency. Satan's top strategies are all too successful.

Reading Isaiah, one wonders how people could be so dumb as to mistake darkness for light and light for darkness.[7] It is easy if they reject absolutes and see the world in shades of nice or not nice, or good and not-so-good. Call it the pastel-ization of America. People lose sight of light and dark incrementally: black becomes grey and then purple, and white becomes yellow and then pink. In a world of pastels, it's easy to mistake light purple for dark pink. Rationalization is easy, situational ethics reigns, and sins are frequent.

Power seekers love a pastel point of view because people are malleable without anchors. They can be more easily persuaded and molded by string pullers. Agency is undermined, state power is advanced, America is weakened.

Frederic Bastiat cautioned:

> When misguided public opinion honors what is despicable and despises what is honorable, punishes virtue and rewards vice, encourages what is harmful and discourages what is useful, applauds falsehood and smothers truth under indifference or insult, a nation turns its back on progress and can be restored only by the terrible lessons of catastrophe.[8]

Reject the Great Promise

If there is one action that deserves the Number One slot – the one thing that will do more to destroy America than anything else – it is not worshipping Jesus Christ as the God of the land.

The great promise, as early immigrants seeking religious freedom seemed to understand intuitively even before the Book of Mormon was published, was that the land would be free of kings if its people followed a simple formula found in Ether:

> Behold, this is a choice land, and whatsoever nation shall possess it shall be free from bondage, and from captivity, and from all other nations under heaven, *if they will but serve the God of the land, who is Jesus Christ....*[9] [Emphasis added]

The idea that Jesus Christ is the God of the land brings hoots of derision from the non-religious, sometimes even from self-identified Christians. "What about Jews, Muslims, Buddhists?" they ask. The answer was given by Mosiah to his people just prior to the introduction of the rule of judges. It centers on the majority – the voice of the people (I call it the Pollster's Passage):

> Now it is not common that the voice of the people desireth anything contrary to that which is right; but it is common for the lesser part of the people to desire that which is not right; therefore this shall ye observe and make it your law – to do your business by the voice of the people.[10]

In other words, it is common that a minority will choose iniquity, but that does not negate the blessings of God *if the majority does what is right.*

Then comes the kicker if the minority becomes the majority:

> And if the time comes that the voice of the people doth choose iniquity, then is the time that the judgments of God will come upon you; yea, then is the time he will *visit you with great destruction* even as he has *hitherto* visited this land.[11]

And when was the "hitherto"? It was when the people of Jared and his brother were guided to this "land of promise, which was choice above all other lands, which the Lord God had *preserved for a righteous people.*" They were told that "whoso should possess this land of promise, from that time *henceforth and forever*, should *serve him*, the true and only God, or they should be swept off when the fullness of his wrath should come upon them."[12] [Emphases added]

And what happened to them? They failed the test and were swept off.

Is there a message here?

Now imagine a modern people given this choice land and the same deal: Keep God's commandments and prosper, or turn immoral and get booted out. Not very complex, is it?

Imagine that in this land which cannot belong to an unrighteous people ...

- 48% of women ages 15-44 cohabited with a partner as a first union compared to 34% in 1995[13]
- 55 million abortions, as previously noted, have been performed in the last 40 years[14]
- 48% of first births happen outside of wedlock[15]
- 22% of men 25-44 have had 15 or more sexual partners[16]
- 78% of 15-44 year olds say it is okay for an unmarried female to have a child[17]

Imagine further that a sizeable and growing number believe that good and evil are subjective opinions, gender is a social construct, male and female distinction is not important, marriage is merely a piece of paper invented by religions to keep women down, and that fathers aren't necessary.[18]

As this immorality and muddled thinking proceed, picture yourself on the other side of the veil defending this nation. **What arguments could you possibly employ to acquit them?** How would you explain why destroying angels should not be unleashed? How would you excuse the corruption and obvious "spiritual wickedness in high places"?

Please explain why this people should not be "destroyed from off the face of the land."[19]

* * *

Fortunately, prophets have testified of America's resilience. Nephi: "And this land shall be a land of liberty unto the Gentiles, and there shall be no kings upon the land, who shall raise up unto the Gentiles."[20] And President Harold B. Lee stated:

> [America] is the greatest country in all the world. This is the favored land. This is the land of our forefathers. It is the nation that will stand despite whatever trials or crises it may yet have to pass through.[21]

This nation, but not necessarily all segments of the population, will survive. But how many freedoms will be curtailed along the way? How many tyrants will misuse power? How many will fudge on their oath to "preserve, protect and defend the Constitution of the United States?"

How battered and bruised will it – and we – be before the Savior ushers in the Millennium?

SECTION VI

THE WORK TO PRESERVE

"Even this nation will be on the very verge of crumbling to pieces and tumbling to the ground, and when the Constitution is upon the brink of ruin, this people shall be the staff upon which the nation shall lean, and they shall bear the Constitution away from the very verge of destruction."

– Joseph Smith

Chapter 26

Stand Up, Say Something, and Don't Sit Down

"The best lack all conviction, while the worst are full of passionate intensity."

– W. B. Yeats

The world is run by those who show up, such as the senior citizen who walks into the fire station every Tuesday and asks, "Got anything I can vote on today?"

Of the five battlefields examined in this book, the battle for the Constitution will be the most critical in the immediate years ahead because a failure on this front will destroy America and disrupt preparations for the Second Coming more than any other setback.

The Prophet Joseph frequently spoke of the Constitution, its sacred principles, its guarantees of religious freedom, its protections, its genius, and its benefits for all mankind. On several occasions he warned of a coming crisis when the Constitution would hang by a thread. In one version he said that "this people, the sons of Zion, would rise up and save the Constitution and bear it off triumphantly." In another, that "this people the Latter-day Saints will step forth and save it." Orson Hyde recalls a more conditional prophecy that "the time would come when the Constitution and the country would be in danger of an overthrow; and said he, If the Constitution be saved at all, it will be by the Elders of this church."[1]

At a minimum, Joseph knew that members of the restored Church must and will be involved.

Now, when Satan battles against the individual, Christ's teachings, and the family, we know what to do. We have thousands of years of experience on these battlefronts and the doctrines of the Church are replete with the principles and the do's and don'ts we must follow.

What is less clear is what we must do to preserve the Constitution and thus protect America, a battle that has been with us for only a couple of centuries. Let's face the facts. When, as prophesied, the Constitution is on the verge of destruction and the nation teeters, it will not be easy to dislodge those who have usurped power. But change the arrangement we must, for **the only way to preserve the Constitution is to demand that government obey it**.

We cannot persuasively warn of the consequences of overbearing government **unless we are familiar** with the Constitution and its underlying principles. We must know the stories of how it was inspired and crafted, debated and drafted. We must be familiar with the arguments the Founders themselves used to secure its ratification. Given how the war on the Constitution and America may well play out, here are the points, not exhaustive, I feel will be most useful.

THE DECLARATION OF INDEPENDENCE: FIVE KEY POINTS

We are well familiar with the happenings leading up to July 4, 1776 when the Declaration was signed. As a general overview, consider it our national statement of beliefs:

1. Our rights come from our Creator. They are not given to man by any other man or group of men.

2. Among these rights are life, liberty, and pursuit of happiness. God gave us life. God gave us agency. God allows us to decide our own course.

3. Governments get their power from the consent of the governed.

4. Should government become destructive of these natural rights, the people have the right to alter it or abolish it, but not for light and transient reasons.

5. When it is apparent that abuses by government are by design intended to subject the people to despotism, the people have the right and duty to throw off that government.

A similar declaration of our beliefs as a Church "regarding government and laws in general" is found in D&C 134, verse two being appropriate in this context: "We believe that no government can exist in peace, except such laws are framed and held inviolate as will secure to each individual the free exercise of conscience, the right and control or property, and the protection of life."

The Constitution: Ten key points

It has been said that if the Declaration of Independence is a statement of beliefs, then the Constitution is an owner's manual. It was hammered out during the sweltering Philadelphia summer of 1787 and submitted to the states for ratification on September 17th. It was ratified by the required nine states by June 1788. It was formally put into operation one year after it was first submitted to the states, eleven states having then ratified it. The final two states ratified it the following spring.[2]

1. The people are sovereign. That means that we the people retain all power over government.

2. The people ordained the Constitution and the Constitution created government. Government did not create the Constitution.

3. Government did not and cannot give people their natural rights. It can only defend and preserve those rights for their benefit.

4. The Constitution was written to control how power is to be employed in a society. Its checks and balances prevent tyranny by separating power between the three branches of government, dividing it between federal government and the states, and restricting the federal government to 18 enumerated powers.

5. All legislative power is vested in Congress. It cannot be delegated to any other body. Executive departments cannot legislate.

6. All bills for raising revenue shall originate in the House of Representatives. As with its general legislative powers, this power also cannot be delegated.

7. The president shall take care that the laws be faithfully executed. That means equal and uniform application and no favoritism. He is not allowed to change any law on his own.

8. The president shall be the commander-in-chief of the armed forces and has the chief responsibility to protect the country.

9. The Constitution provides for an energetic and independent presidency for national security and a legislative branch more focused on domestic issues. It did not intend the presidency to dominate domestic matters and be timid on foreign affairs.

10. All officers in the executive, legislative, and judicial branches must swear an oath to preserve, protect and defend the Constitution.

The Bill of Rights: Nine key points

A group known as the Anti-Federalists feared a too-strong federal government, felt the new Constitution did not go far enough to protect individual rights, and held up ratification. Those favoring the

Constitution, the Federalists, promised that upon ratification, the newly formed Congress would take up specific amendments guaranteeing those rights. In 1789 when the First Congress convened, James Madison, with inspiration from Thomas Jefferson, drafted ten amendments and, as promised, steered them through Congress. The requisite majority of states ratified them by December, 1791 and the Bill of Rights became part of the Constitution.[3]

1. The Bill of Rights does not tell the *people* what they can and cannot do; it tells *Congress* what it shall and shall not do. We could easily rename it the Bill of Congressional Restrictions.

2. Freedom of religion is the first freedom mentioned because it is the keystone freedom upon which all others depend. (I)

3. Religious freedom is more comprehensive than freedom of worship. (I)

4. Freedom of speech is the second freedom mentioned followed by press, assembly, and the right to petition government. They are mentioned together because they are interdependent and mutually supportive. (I)

5. The right to keep and bear arms is a preservation of the right of individuals, not of an army, which right the army already holds. It is a check against tyranny. (II)

6. Our homes and personal effects are off limits to search and seizure without a specific probable-cause search warrant properly issued. (IV)

7. Anyone accused of a crime shall enjoy the right to a speedy and public trial by an impartial jury. (VI)

8. The rights of the people are not restricted to only those mentioned in the Constitution. (IX)

9. All powers not delegated to the federal government are reserved to the states or the people. (X)

THE FEDERALIST PAPERS: SIXTEEN USEFUL QUOTES

The Federalist Papers were a collection of arguments to answer objections to the new Constitution, what we would call public outreach and persuasion today. The first Federalist appeared 40 days after the Constitution was signed; the last one was published ten months later in August 1788.

If you are inclined to read the original arguments for ratification of the Constitution with a special eye on today's problems, friends more knowledgeable than I suggest the following Federalist papers:

#51: Checks and Balances
#47: Distribution of Power
#41: Powers Conferred by the Constitution
#45: Dangers of Powers
#70: The Executive
#39: Republican Principles
#49: Guarding Against Encroachments
#29: The Militia
#10: Safeguard Against Factions and Insurrection

If, however, you would be satisfied having a familiarity with a few of the most profound statements in the 85 papers, here are my favorites:

1. "Enlightened statesmen will not always be at the helm." (Madison, #10)

2. "[A]ccumulation of all powers, legislative, executive, and judiciary in the same hands ... may justly be pronounced the very definition of tyranny." (Madison, #47)

3. "If men were angels, no government would be necessary. If angels were to govern men, neither external nor internal controls on government would be necessary. In framing a government which is to be administered by men over men, the great difficulty lies in this: you must first enable the government to control

the governed; and in the next place oblige it to control itself." (Madison, #51)

4. "The fabric of American empire ought to rest on the solid bases of THE CONSENT OF THE PEOPLE. The streams of national power ought to flow from that pure, original fountain of all legitimate authority." (Hamilton, #22; his emphasis)

5. "It will be of little avail to the people that the laws are made by men of their own choice if the laws be so voluminous that they cannot be read, or so incoherent that they cannot be understood." (Madison, #62)

6. [W]hatever fine declarations may be inserted in any constitution respecting it, must altogether depend on public opinion, and on the general spirit of the people and of the government." (Hamilton, #84)

7. "The house of representatives .. can make no law which will not have its full operation on themselves and their friends, as well as the great mass of society. This has always been deemed one of the strongest bonds by which human policy can connect the rulers and the people together … but without which every government degenerates into tyranny." (Madison, #57)

8. "It will not be denied that power is of an encroaching nature and that it ought to be effectually restrained from passing the limits assigned to it." (Madison, #48)

9. "An elective despotism was not the government we fought for; but one in which the powers of government should be so divided and balanced among the several bodies of magistracy so that no one could transcend their legal limits without being effectually checked and restrained by the others." (Madison, #58)

10. "We have heard of the impious doctrine in the old world, that the people were made for kings, not kings for the people. Is the same doctrine to be revived in the new, in another shape…?" (Madison, #45)

11. "The powers delegated by the proposed Constitution to the federal government are few and defined. Those that are to remain in the State governments are numerous and indefinite." (Madison, #45)

12. "The Constitution preserves the advantage of being armed which Americans possess over the people of almost every other nation where the governments are afraid to trust the people with arms." (Madison, #46)

13. "Those politicians and statesmen who have been the most celebrated for the soundness of their principles and for the justice of their views, have declared in favor of a single Executive and a numerous legislature. They have … considered energy as the most necessary qualification of the former, and … the latter as best adapted to deliberation and wisdom…." (Hamilton, #70) (The context is "[d]ecision, activity, secrecy, and dispatch" in the executive for the security of the nation, and a calmer tempo in Congress for domestic issues.)

14. "The danger from legislative usurpations, which, by assembling all power in the same hands, must lead to the same tyranny as is threatened by executive usurpations." (Madison, #48)

15. "A nation, despicable by its weakness, forfeits even the privilege of being neutral." (Hamilton, #11) (Does the world view our present foreign policy as robust?)

16. "[The] danger will be evidently greater where the whole legislative trust is lodged in the hands of one body of men…" (Madison, #63) (Could he have been warning about an unelected fourth branch of government?)

Ask probing questions

To identify threats to the Constitution, ask these twelve questions of those who would be our leaders:

1. Do they recognize the people as sovereign and their rights as God-given?

2. Do they respect individual agency? Do they want people to make their own decisions or do they empower those who want to make decisions for us?

3. Do they actively preserve, protect, and defend the Constitution? Do they speak well of it?

4. Do they see America as grounded in the foundation of the Constitution, or do they seek to fundamentally transform it?

5. Do they live by the Constitution's checks on power, or just give it lip service?

6. Do they seek to restrict an armed citizenry?

7. Do they minimize freedom of religion by relabeling it as freedom of worship?

8. Do they faithfully and uniformly execute the laws?

9. Do they promote American values to the world?

10. Do they recognize America as an exceptional nation?

11. Do they express love for our country?

12. Do their plans advance or hinder the cause of the Gospel of Jesus Christ?

Run through the questions again and ask yourself how President Barack Obama would answer them.

His answers should not surprise you. His formative years were spent in Indonesia where he was politically socialized under the tutelage of relatives and friends who divided the world into oppressor nations and victim nations. He has accepted that mindset, America being an oppressor. He does not have a deep appreciation for America in his bones; it is a barely hidden hostility. Hence his vow to fundamentally transform it. Under his leadership, America has declined on virtually every measure.

At the beginning of this book I said that if you didn't believe Satan is a real being, this would not be the book for you. So now I ask, has Satan played a role in the actions of the Obama administration or has he been a passive and uninterested observer on the sidelines?

The staff the nation shall lean upon

Let's return to Joseph's prophecy and ask why the nation will lean upon this people – "the Latter-day Saints", "the sons of Zion", "the Elders of this church" – to save the Constitution? What do we, a mere two percent of the American population, have that other religions do not? Why are we destined to bear off the Constitution triumphantly?

Because of five unique characteristics that no other religion or volunteer organization can match:

1. We revere the Constitution. No other religion of size has as part of its canonized doctrine – as canonized *scripture* – that the U.S. Constitution was established by God. We cannot stand idly by when man attacks it.

2. We are vertical. We are a top-down religion for doctrine and broad Church policies, but with substantial member latitude to do many things of our own free will to bring about righteousness.

3. We are geographic. Because we are organized by geographic units, we know our leaders and they know us. When there is an emergency, we can mobilize hundreds or even thousands of people within a matter of minutes or hours.

4. We are unpaid. If just five leaders in a ward or branch were paid the salary of the average American pastor, we would shovel out $3.5 billion dollars a year. This money goes instead to more important goals than feeding preachers.

5. We are consecrated. We commit to follow Jesus Christ when we are baptized and as we progress we make solemn covenants of honesty, morality, and service. No other church can point to such general membership commitment.

A time to act

Edmund Burke: "The only thing necessary for the triumph of evil is for good men to do nothing."

If we are the staff upon which the nation shall lean, what we are we doing right now? Must we wait until events overwhelm us? The threats are obvious and in the spirit of being "anxiously engaged in a good cause, and [doing] many things of [our] own free will,"[4] there is much we can do to roll back the encroachments on the Constitution.

First, we must discuss political issues in church *circles* if religion is to have a voice in the public *square*. Together with allies in other faiths, we must speak up and publicize our concerns. While our legal experts must do the heavy lifting in the judicial arena, the hot glare of publicity in the court of public opinion can work where courtroom maneuvers fall short.

Our arguments and explanations will convince many of the threat we face. But given our adversaries' blatant acts, those who work for America's decline will not likely be dissuaded by reasoned debate. So the next step is to **build a public presence** through a variety of actions. These may include canvassing, collecting petition signatures, information meetings, lobbying, expanded use of social media, paid media, cultivating mass media attention, vote-oriented campaigns, rallies, vigils, and demonstrations.

I have seen the impact numerous times. The lower house of a Midwestern state legislature, for example, once passed a bill by a comfortable margin and sent it to the upper house. The senate didn't even deign to vote on it. Why? Because busloads of protesters showed up. Their presence even had original supporters apologizing for the votes they had cast. Court-watchers have always said that judges read newspapers. Well, legislators look out their windows.

Legislators, administrators, and bureaucrats who would change our government from what God intended **will one day have to look out their windows and see a sea of faces**. Our faces. People willing to be counted. Polite and civil, to be sure, but firm and determined with placards that state such truths as: "We don't need your permission to exercise our rights." "Obey the Constitution." "The people are sovereign, not the government."

Thirty or forty people making their displeasure known in front of hundreds of local federal buildings across the nation once a week at noon for one hour, or a candlelight vigil at night, may well be more effective than a one-time million-man march on Washington.

Finally, if the above steps are not successful and the administrative state continues to issue unconstitutional edicts, active refusal to obey will be our only option. Accepting one-man-rule decrees will only lead to more of them. Failure to resist unconstitutional orders dooms our agency to destruction.

Elder Neal A. Maxwell gave us this hope:

> There will also be times, happily, when a minor defeat seems probable, that others will step forward, having been rallied to righteousness by what we do. We will know the joy, on occasion, of having awakened a slumbering majority of the decent people of all races and creeds – a majority which was, till then, unconscious of itself.[5]

President Ezra Taft Benson told us our responsibility:

> I have faith that the Constitution will be saved as prophesied by Joseph Smith, but it will not be saved in Washington. It will be saved by citizens of this nation who love and cherish freedom. It will be saved by enlightened members of this Church, men and women who will subscribe to it and abide

> the principles of the Constitution. I revere the Constitution of the United States as a sacred document. To me the words are akin to the revelations of God, for God has placed His stamp of approval upon the Constitution of this land. I testify that the God of heaven sent some of his choicest spirits to lay the foundation of this government and he has sent other choice spirits, even you who hear my words this day, to preserve it. We, the blessed beneficiaries, face difficult days in this beloved land – a land which is choice above all other lands. It may also cost us blood before we are through. It is my conviction, however, that when the Lord comes, the stars and stripes will be floating on the breeze over this people. May it be so. And may God give us the faith and the courage exhibited by those patriots who pledged their lives and fortunes that we might be free.[6]

Similarly, Samuel Adams told us: "If ever the time should come, when vain and aspiring men shall possess the highest seats in government, our country will stand in need of its experienced patriots to prevent its ruin."[7]

And from Ronald Reagan two centuries later: "Freedom is a fragile thing and is never more than one generation away from extinction. It is not ours by inheritance; it must be fought for and defended constantly by each generation, for it comes only once to a people. Those who have known freedom and then lost it have never known it again."[8]

Just as the original Church was re-established after the dark night of apostasy, original government must be re-established to save us from the evil night of tyranny.

* * *

Our unfolding constitutional crisis may well be the event the Lord will use to bring His latter-day work out of obscurity.

Epilogue

For thousands of years, the war that began in heaven has continued. Satan has roamed the world seeking to destroy everything and make everyone as miserable as he is.

It will have an end.

But until it does, all five battlefields will require our vigilance, counteraction, and perhaps sacrifice.

What are we ready to put on the line to preserve what God has ordained?

Thomas Jefferson's final sentence in the Declaration of Independence reads,

> "And for the support of this Declaration, with a firm Reliance on the Protection of divine Providence, we mutually pledge to each other our Lives, our Fortunes, and our sacred Honor."

Are we more privileged than they?

* * *

ACKNOWLEDGEMENTS

To my talented and loving eternal companion, Jan, for her edits, wise suggestions, and website development.

To my daughter Stephanie Smith for graphic design of the dust jacket and layout of the manuscript while being just a little busy raising five children.

To my daughters Kristen Lawrence and Lindsey Miller for their timely suggestions and encouragement.

To Maurine and Scot Proctor for serializing excerpts in Meridian Magazine and for their supportive comments.

To my good friends whose contributions were so varied they defy a single metric, I list them in alphabetical order: Colleen Arrington, Larry Eastland, David Frey, Glen Greener, Steve Hanson, Bruce Hughes, Ralph Johnson, Marilyn Middleton, Craig Nelson, Peter Rancie, Bud Scruggs, and Brian Thomassen.

To good people who stand up and defend our God-given agency, rights, and institutions.

And to those who will do so in the future.

* * *

Notes

Introduction

[1] "Echo From a Past Leak Probe", Wall Street Journal, August 7, 2013, A4, regarding a story on June 7, 1942 that was headlined "U.S. Navy Knew in Advance All About Jap Fleet."

[2] D&C 76:25

[3] 2 Timothy 3:7

Chapter 1: Nice Try, Pinocchio

[1] Job 38:7

[2] Abraham 3:27-28

[3] Ibid

[4] D&C 29:36

[5] Moses 4:4

[6] Moses 4:3

[7] Ibid

[8] Isaiah 14:12-14

[9] Moses 4:2

[10] Matthew 8:29

[11] Joseph Fielding Smith, ed., Teachings of the Prophet Joseph Smith, 181

Chapter 2: Alone on the Seas of Life

[1] L.A. Times, June 12, 2010, A-1, 9.

[2] http://en.wikipedia.org/wiki/List_of_terms_used_for_Germans

[3] Isaiah 29:21

[4] Elder David A. Bednar, "We Believe in Being Chaste," April 2013 General Conference

[5] D&C 123:7 and 45:26

[6] Elder James E. Faust, Voice of the Spirit.^ http://speeches.byu.edu/?act=viewitem&id=771

[7] Ibid.

Chapter 3: Calling Shots and Pulling Strings

[1] Alma 42:13

[2] Alma 42:20-22

[3] Alma 42:25 Brigham Young put it this way: The volition of [man] is free; this is a law of their existence, and the Lord cannot violate his own law; were he to do that, he would cease to be God.

[4] Moroni 7:17

[5] Some theologians contend that the "third part" constitutes a numerically undetermined segment and not a percentage. I don't know the answer, but if the phrase does not refer to a percentage or size of the segment, then who constitutes the other two parts of the hosts of heaven?

[6] 2 Nephi 28:8

[7] Mormon 8:31

[8] Alma 30:17

[9] Alma 1:4

[10] Helaman 5:10

[11] An insightful discourse on this was given by Dr. Robert Matthews, former dean of Religious Education at BYU: Why a Savior is Necessary, and Why Only Jesus Christ, December 4, 1984: http://speeches.byu.edu/?act=viewitem&id=932

[12] http://publications.maxwellinstitute.byu.edu/periodicals/jbms/

[13] 2 Nephi 2:13, 14, 26, and 16.

[14] http://www.lds.org/general-conference/1995/10/acting-for-ourselves-and-not-being-acted-upon?lang=eng

[15] See Alma chapters 59 and 60

[16] Alma 61:9, 19

[17] 3 Nephi 11:29

[18] Dallin H. Oaks, Same-Gender Attraction, Ensign, October 1995

Chapter 4: You Work; I'll Eat

[1] Dinesh D'Souza, Oregon State University debate, October 8, 2012: https://www.youtube.com/watch?v=rEM4NKXK-iA

[2] Frederic Bastiat, The Law, Foundation for Economic Education, Irvington-on-Hudson, New York, 5-9

[3] Ibid, 16

[4] Wall Street Journal, August 15, 2013, A4

[5] D&C 42:42

[6] http://en.wikiquote.org/wiki/Benjamin_Franklin

[7] Oops. It already happened during the Democratic National Convention in September 2012

[8] Bastiat, 19-20

Chapter 5: Lull, Flatter, Rage: The Secrets of Nephite Villains

[1] Paul Johnson, Modern Times, Harper & Row, 1983, 1

[2] 2 Nephi 28:21

[3] Hugh W. Nibley, Neal A. Maxwell Institute, Lecture 81: 3 Nephi 3-5. See: http://maxwellinstitute.byu.edu/publications/books/?bookid=118&chapid=1401

[4] Mosiah 27:8

[5] Jacob 7:4

[6] Helaman 2:4

[7] Mosiah 27:8

[8] Alma 30:31, 53

[9] Isaiah 30:10

[10] 2 Nephi 28:22

[11] 2 Nephi 2:11

[12] Moses 1:12

[13] Moses 1:19-22

[14] Helaman 16:22

[15] 3 Nephi 11:29

[16] 2 Nephi 28:20

[17] D&C 122:1

[18] 3 Nephi 6:15

[19] Jacob 7:7

[20] Alma 2:5

[21] Alma 11:20

[22] Alma 1:7-12

[23] Alma 62:40

[24] 3 Nephi 3:2-10

Chapter 6: The Epitome of Sibling Rivalry

[1] http://www.forbes.com/sites/realspin/2013/03/26/fau-college-student-who-didnt-want-to-stomp-on-jesus-runs-afoul-of-speech-code/

[2] https://www.lds.org/topics/print/satan

[3] Matthew 4:3-10

[4] Ante-Nicene Fathers, Origen Against Celsus, Volume IV, p 410, Hendrickson Publishers, Peabody, Massachusetts.

[5] Ibid.

[6] Ante-Nicene Fathers, Origen Against Celsus, Volume IV, p 399, Hendrickson Publishers, Peabody, Massachusetts.

[7] Matthew 28:11-15

[8] http://www.forbes.com/sites/realspin/2013/03/26/fau-college-student-who-didnt-want-to-stomp-on-jesus-runs-afoul-of-speech-code/

[9] I won't even print the link to the Wikipedia article about this because of its offensive juxtaposition of two words, but you can find all you care to know about this stupidity by googling crucifix and urine.

[10] http://www.ibtimes.co.uk/articles/500845/20130822/ecce-homo-spain-painting-christ-monkey-cecilia.htm

[11] Congressman Tom McClintock, California Drains Reservoirs in the Middle of a Drought. Wall Street Journal, May 24-25, 2014, A11.

[12] Boyd K. Packer, "Finding Ourselves in Lehi's Dream", BYU devotional address, January 16, 2007

[13] Ibid.

[14] Neal A. Maxwell, "Meeting the Challenges of Today," BYU Devotional, October 10, 1978

[15] Psalms 2:2-4

Chapter 7: Secular Religion and Its Three-Pound God

[1] 2 Nephi 4:34

[2] https://www.lds.org/general-conference/2013/10/lamentations-of-jeremiah-beware-of-bondage?lang=eng&query=intellectual

[3] http://speeches.byu.edu/?act=viewitem&id=578

[4] James E. Faust, Voice of the Spirit. Ibid.

[5] 2 Nephi 9:28

[6] Ronald M. Hartwell in "The Politicization of Society," Wall Street Journal, August 21, 2013, A 11

[7] Wall Street Journal, 23 August 2013, A11

[8] http://www.kairosjournal.org/document.aspx?DocumentID=6022&QuadrantID=3&CategoryID=6&TopicID=23&L=1

[9] Human Life Review, Summer 1978, 58

[10] Neal A. Maxwell, Ibid.

[11] Alma 46:5

[12] John 15:5

[13] Jonah Goldberg, "Gods of the Godless," National Review, April 8, 2013, 10

[14] 1 Nephi 13 and 14

[15] 1 Nephi 22:23

[16] Stephen E. Robinson, Nephi's "Great and Abominable Church," Journal of Book of Mormon Studies: Volume 7, Issue 1, Pages 32-39, 70; Maxwell Institute, 1998

Chapter 8: The Miter and the Gavel

[1] http://www.firebuilders.org/JAmCEC.htm

[2] http://www.loc.gov/loc/lcib/9806/danpre.html

[3] Neal A. Maxwell, "Meeting the Challenges of Today," BYU Devotional, October 10, 1978

[4] 3 Nephi 6:12-13

[5] M. J. Sobran, Human Life Review, Summer 1978, pp. 51-52

[6] https://myaccount.nytimes.com/auth/login?URI=http://takingnote.blogs.nytimes.com/2013/07/12/an-unholy-religious-exemption/&OQ=Q5fQ72Q3dQ30

[7] Deseret News, September 26, 2013) http://www.deseretnews.com/top/1863/5/Faith-based-adoption-agencies-Adoption-abortion-and-the-pledge-Controversial-religious-liberty.html

[8] http://rxethics.org/Quinn%20Edited%20PDF.pdf

[9] http://www.lowellsun.com/breakingnews/ci_24013489/high-court-hears-under-god-case

[10] Deseret News, Ibid.

[11] http://www.townhallmail.com/bqdkpntjkkcypjkjyjpftysqqzyqqjztbbfnmpccbjpdqd_bzgpbcpzfgf.html

[12] George Washington's Farewell Address, September 17, 1796

[13] Catholic New World, November, 2012

[14] http://www.latimes.com/opinion/editorials/la-ed-prayer-20130819,0,3445882.story

[15] http://www.law.cornell.edu/supremecourt/text/12-696

[16] Sec. 2-552 (b) "Prior Discriminatory Acts" and Section 7 in https://webapps1.sanantonio.gov/rfcadocs/R_10799_20130905091047.pdf

[17] http://radio.foxnews.com/toddstarnes/top-stories/san-antonio-passes-non-discrimination-law-christians-fear-reprisals.html

http://www.kens5.com/news/SA-City-Council-adds-protection-for-LGBT-community-in-non-discrimination-ordinance-222526651.html

http://www.christianitytoday.com/gleanings/2013/september/san-antonio-city-council-bans-lgbt-bias-in-word-and-deed.html

[18] http://www.gallup.com/poll/1597/confidence-institutions.aspx

[19] http://www.christianpost.com/news/military-chaplains-banned-from-using-jesus-name-reciting-bible-lawsuit-filed-in-calif-108734/

[20] http://townhall.com/columnists/toddstarnes/2014/03/12/air-force-academy-removes-bible-verse-from-cadets-whiteboard-n1807834/page/full

[21] http://townhall.com/columnists/toddstarnes/2013/05/03/air-force-officer-told-to-remove-bible-from-desk-n1586385/page/full

[22] http://www.military.com/daily-news/2012/06/14/dod-yanks-consent-for-military-seals-on-bibles.html

[23] http://speeches.byu.edu/?act=viewitem&id=909

Chapter 9: Send in the Clowns

[1] http://en.wikipedia.org/wiki/Sabbatai_Zevi

[2] http://en.wikipedia.org/wiki/List_of_messiah_claimants

[3] Ibid.

[4] http://www.dailymail.co.uk/news/article-1299099/Prince-Charles-My-duty-save-world.html

[5] London Evening Standard, May 4, 1966

[6] In recent years there has been a softening among the anti-DDT crowd and some are suggesting its re-introduction "with caution." "DDT spraying remains the most cost-effective solution for poor countries to prevent malaria." (http://www.policynetwork.net/health/media/malaria-and-ddt-story) In 2006 WHO changed its policy and now backs DDT as a way to control malaria. http://www.npr.org/templates/story/story.php?storyId=6083944

[7] Matthew 24:24

[8] 2 Nephi 25:18

[9] Review of The United States of Paranoia, Jesse Walker, Wall Street Journal, August 23, 2013, A11

[10] Ibid.

[11] D&C 123:12, 2 Peter 1:16

CHAPTER 10: CISGENDER HETERONORMATIVE CREATED HE THEM?

[1] https://www.lds.org/topics/print/satan

[2] http://www.capitolreportnewmexico.com/2014/04/supreme-court-lets-ruling-stand-on-nm-wedding-photographer-and-same-sex-couple/comment-page-1/

[3] http://www.cdc.gov/nchs/data/nhsr/nhsr064.pdf

[4] http://www.religiondispatches.org/dispatches/joannabrooks/7465/first_gay_couple_to_get_married_in_utah___love_comes_like_a_thief_in_the_night_/

[5] Wall Street Journal, March 28, 2013, A14

[6] Masha Gessen: http://savingmarriage2011.blogspot.com/2012/06/what-sort-of-marriages-do-homosexual.html

[7] Lincoln, Ibid.

[8] Isaiah 5:20

[9] 3 Nephi 3:7

[10] http://townhall.com/columnists/dennisprager/2012/10/30/why_a_good_person_can_vote_against_samesex_marriage/page/full

[11] "Examples of Righteousness," Ensign, May 2008, 65

[12] http://www.deseretnews.com/media/pdf/1294036.pdf and http://www.nationalreview.com/corner/370366/15-consequences-redefining-marriage-michael-t-worley

[13] Richard L. Larsen, A Secular Approach to Same-Sex Marriage – An Illogical Counterfeit: http://www.ldsmag.com/article/1/12524

[14] http://www.law.cornell.edu/supremecourt/text/12-307

[15] U.S. v. Windsor, Ibid, 24

[16] https://ecf.cand.uscourts.gov/cand/09cv2292/files/09cv2292-ORDER.pdf Also: http://www.washingtonpost.com/wp-dyn/content/article/2010/08/04/AR2010080400716.html

[17] Former Georgetown law professor Chai Feldblum quoted in National Review, April 21, 2014, 26

[18] Saul D. Alinsky, Rules for Radicals, New York: Vintage, 36. Incidentally, Alinsky received tutoring from Al Capone's lieutenants in the tactics of the mob. Hmm, the mob, the Gadianton robbers, the radicals. Maybe the story is in the Book of Mormon for a reason.

[19] http://www.todayifoundout.com/index.php/2010/02/how-gay-came-to-mean-homosexual/

[20] Quoted by Elder Neil L. Andersen in April 2014 General Conference

[21] Ibid.

[22] http://www.reagan.utexas.edu/archives/speeches/1984/82384a.htm

[23] Helaman 7:5

[24] Elder Dallin H. Oaks, No Other Gods, General Conference, October 2013

Chapter 11: Families Are Whatever

[1] http://www.theblaze.com/blog/2014/04/11/george-will-im-quite-confident-that-were-going-to-rebel-against-this-abusive-government/

[2] http://en.wikipedia.org/wiki/The_Family:_A_Proclamation_to_the_World

[3] http://www.cdc.gov/nchs/fastats/unmarried-childbearing.htm

[4] http://www.cdc.gov/nchs/nsfg/abc_list_p.htm#premarital

[5] http://fatherhoodfactor.com/us-fatherless-statistics/

[6] Mark Regnerus, "How Different Are the Adult Children of Parents Who Have Same-Sex Relationships? Findings from the New Family Structures Study," Social Science Research, Vol. 41, No. 4 (July 2012) and Loren Marks, "Same-Sex Parenting and Children's Outcomes: A Closer Examination of the American Psychological Associations' Brief on lesbian and Gay Parenting," Ibid.

[7] I've searched. Fifty bucks to the first person to prove this sentence wrong.

[8] http://nypost.com/2013/07/04/calif-lawmakers-pass-k-12-transgender-rights-bill/

[9] http://www.loc.gov/exhibits/archives/reps.html

[10] All quotes from http://cnsnews.com/news/article/susan-jones/sebelius-describes-federal-government-our-federal-family

Chapter 12: It Doesn't Take a Village, Idiot; It Takes a Family

[1] MSNBC April 8, 2013

[2] http://www.activistpost.com/2014/06/shock-medical-notice-we-need-to-have.html

[3] http://www.slate.com/articles/double_x/doublex/2013/08/private_school_vs_public_school_only_bad_people_send_their_kids_to_private.html

[4] Hillary Clinton quoted in the Wall Street Journal, October 30, 2013, A13

Chapter 13: Just a Blob of Unwanted Cells?

[1] http://www.catholic.org/news/international/europe/story.php?id=34602

[2] http://www.life.org.nz/bioethics/bioethics1/

[3] http://www.weeklystandard.com/blogs/obama-largest-abortion-provider-god-bless-you_719216.html

[4] Ensign January 1974

[5] Genesis 3:15

[6] http://ldsmag.com/article/1/12254

[7] Ibid

Chapter 14: The Destruction of Meaning: The Non-Divorce Divorce

[1] 2 Cor. 11:14 and 2 Nephi 9:9

[2] George Orwell, "Politics and the English Language," Horizon, 1946. Also: https://www.mtholyoke.edu/acad/intrel/orwell46.htm In that same essay he also said, "The whole tendency of modern prose is away from concreteness." The less concrete the word, the easier for mischief-makers to redefine it.

[3] Wall Street Journal, 11 Feb 2013, A11

[4] See Alma 11 for how the Nephites handled it.

[5] Matthew 11:18-19

[6] John 10:20

[7] Helaman 16:6

[8] Helaman 13:26-27

[9] http://www.washingtonpost.com/blogs/post-politics/wp/2013/01/23/nras-wayne-lapierre-says-obama-trying-to-take-away-basic-rights/

[10] http://www.goop.com/journal/be/conscious-uncoupling

Chapter 15: Ageless Emotions, Timeless Principles, A Moral Document

[1] Specifically D&C 98:4-8 and D&C 101:77-80

[2] http://www.civilwar.org/education/history/faq/

[3] Edwin Meese III, The Meaning of the Constitution, The Heritage Foundation, September 16, 2009

[4] http://famguardian.org/Subjects/Politics/ThomasJefferson/jeff1030.htm

[5] Meese, Ibid

[6] http://www.washingtontimes.com/news/2013/jan/14/defenders-of-constitution-dont-always-use-it-for-l/?page=all

[7] http://www.cnsnews.com/news/article/when-asked-where-constitution-authorizes-congress-order-americans-buy-health-insurance

Chapter 16: Old Dead White Men Versus Old Dead White Mean

[1] http://www.memritv.org/clip_transcript/en/3295.htm and http://spectator.org/blog/28797/justice-ginsburg-egypt-dont-look-us-constitution-model

[2] The Constitution is the oldest and shortest constitution of any nation today. It has 4543 words including signatures. The Affordable Care Act (Obamacare) has 363,086 words, not counting the innumerable rules and regulations it has generated. By comparison, the median word count for novels is 64,000, and only 2% of all books ever published have more words than the ACA.

[3] http://www.today.com/id/46279899/ns/today-today_news/t/obama-presidency-you-get-better-time-goes/#.UrJOkRazBHg

[4] New York Times, May 7, 1989

[5] Presentation, July 8, 2012, Great Falls, VA, private paper

[6] Max Farrand, ed., The Records of the Federal Convention of 1787, Yale University Press, 1966, vol.1, p 451

[7] To the Executive of New Hampshire, November 3, 1789

[8] P.L. Ford, ed., Essays on the Constitution, 1892, 412

[9] Federalist 37

[10] http://www.nationalreview.com/corner/351031/white-house-website-lauds-founding-founders-charles-c-w-cooke

[11] http://www.policymic.com/articles/21779/louis-michael-seidman-georgetown-law-professor-give-up-on-the-constitution and

http://www.infowars.com/georgetown-law-professor-scrap-archaic-idiosyncratic-and-downright-evil-constitution/

[12] Woodrow Wilson, diary, July 4,1876

[13] http://en.wikipedia.org/wiki/Woodrow_Wilson

[14] William E. Gladstone, as quoted by President Ezra Taft Benson: http://speeches.byu.edu/?act=viewitem&id=87

[15] http://digitalcommons.pepperdine.edu/cgi/viewcontent.cgi?article=1094&context=plr, 497

[16] Bradley C.S. Watson, Claremont Review of Books, Winter 2011-12, 78

[17] http://teachingamericanhistory.org/library/document/speech-on-the-occasion-of-the-one-hundred-and-fiftieth-anniversary-of-the-declaration-of-independence/

[18] Meese, Ibid.

[19] Charles C. W. Cooke, National Review, Feb 11, 2013, p 2

Chapter 17: Cherry Picking the Cotton-Pickin' Laws

[1] http://oversight.house.gov/wp-content/uploads/2014/02/Engelbrecht.pdf and http://www.powerlineblog.com/archives/2014/02/americas-latest-heroine-fights-back.php

[2] http://www.nationalreview.com/article/380990/federal-octopus-victor-davis-hanson/page/0/1

[3] http://www.huffingtonpost.com/2012/03/09/book-length_n_1334636.html

[4] House Judiciary Committee hearing, December 3, 2013

[5] Ibid

[6] http://dailycaller.com/2013/08/18/j-christian-adams-doj-using-the-law-to-punish-opponents-video/

[7] Daniel Henninger, Obama's Creeping Authoritarianism, Wall Street Journal, August 1, 2013, A14

[8] http://www.pbs.org/wnet/supremecourt/antebellum/history2.html

[9] http://www.foxnews.com/politics/2014/02/06/boehner-hits-brakes-on-immigration-overhaul/

[10] http://www.chamberlitigation.com/recess-appointments-litigation-resource-page

[11] Wall Street Journal, August 14, 2013, A10

[12] Bradley A. Smith, The IRS Attack on Political Speech, Wall Street Journal, August 6, 2013, A13

[13] McConnell, Ibid.

[14] Congressional testimony, February 6, 2014: http://www.law360.com/articles/479072/marriage-group-sues-irs-over-leaked-tax-return See also: http://www.powerlineblog.com/archives/2014/02/the-most-dangerous-woman-in-america.php

[15] http://www.wnd.com/2014/02/ben-carson-obama-officials-acting-like-gestapo/

[16] Wall Street Journal, Little Sisters of the Government, January 4-5, 2014, A10

[17] http://www.calt.iastate.edu/article/senators-challenge-osha's-attempts-regulate-small-farm-grain-bins

[18] http://www.nationalreview.com/article/369560/governing-pen-and-phone-victor-davis-hanson/page/0/1 and http://www.theguardian.com/world/2013/dec/19/republicans-consequences-james-clapper-testimony

[19] FCC Commissioner Ajit Pai,The FCC Wades Into the Newsroom, Wall Street Journal, February 11, 2014, A14

Chapter 18: About That Food Storage You Thought You Owned

[1] Also used by Herbert Hoover in 1928. The reverse was a hippie slogan in the 1960s.

[2] Wickard v. Filburn, 317 U.S. 111 (1942)

[3] Add in 14.6 million full-time and 4.7 part-time state and local government employees overseen, for the most part, by part-time legislators and the problem is little better outside Washington. http://www2.census.gov/govs/apes/11stlus.txt

[4] An insightful explanation how this came about may be found in Budget Battles and the Growth of the Administrative State by John Marini, Imprimis, October 2013.

[5] The bureaucracy has been solidly Democratic for decades. In the 2012 elections, for example, the American Federation of Government Employees gave 97% of its contributions to Democrats and employees at the IRS gave 94%. http://www.nationalreview.com/article/380812/bureaucrats-bureaucrats-bureaucrats-jonah-goldberg

[6] http://en.wikipedia.org/wiki/The_Nixon_Interviews

[7] Gary Lawson, Professor of Law, Boston University School of Law: Burying the Constitution Under a TARP, Journal of Law and Public Policy: http://www.harvard-jlpp.com/wp-content/uploads/2010/01/lawson.pdf

[8] A borrowed and apt phrase from Joseph Epstein and Saul Bellow.

[9] http://www.nationalreview.com/article/364080/twenty-seven-obamacare-changes-grace-marie-turner-tyler-hartsfield and http://www.galen.org/topics/at-least-27-significant-changes-already-have-been-made-to-obamacare/

[10] http://www.youtube.com/embed/yQwfPu1E3rk?feature=player_embedded

[11] January 14, 2014 Cabinet meeting: http://washington.cbslocal.com/2014/01/14/obama-on-executive-actions-ive-got-a-pen-and-ive-got-a-phone/

[12] http://www.politico.com/story/2014/01/president-obama-economy-102218.html

[13] http://www.powerlineblog.com/archives/2014/02/obama-then-and-now-3.php

[14] Kevin Williamson, The Front Man, National Review, August 5, 2013, 28

[15] David B. Rivkin Jr. and Elizabeth P. Foley, An ObamaCare Board Answerable to No One, Wall Street Journal, June 20, 2013, A21

[16] http://www.cato.org/sites/cato.org/files/pubs/pdf/PA700.pdf

[17] Ibid.

[18] The legal doctrine of penumbras "has primarily been used to represent implied powers that emanate from a specific rule, thus extending the meaning of the rule into its periphery or penumbra." http://legal-dictionary.thefreedictionary.com/penumbra

[19] http://reason.com/blog/2012/01/30/meet-roscoe-filburn-the-dead-farmer-at-t

[20] Ibid.

[21] http://abcnews.go.com/Politics/long-dead-ohio-farmer-roscoe-filburn-plays-crucial/story?id=15460050#.TycrRiNVs7A

[22] http://papers.ssrn.com/sol3/papers.cfm?abstract_id=2336213

[23] U.S. Constitution, Article I, Section 8.

[24] McCulloch v. Maryland, 1819. http://www.ourdocuments.gov/doc.php?doc=21&page=transcript

[25] Quoted in Kevin Williamson, The Front Man, National Review, August 2, 2013, 26

[26] http://www.archives.gov/federal-register/executive-orders/pdf/12919.pdf and http://www.gpo.gov/fdsys/pkg/FR-2012-03-22/pdf/2012-7019.pdf

[27] https://s3-us-gov-west-1.amazonaws.com/dam-production/uploads/20130726-1650-20490-5258/final__defense_production_act_091030.pdf

Chapter 19: The Cancerous Administrative State

[1] http://press-pubs.uchicago.edu/founders/documents/v1ch18s11.html

[2] D&C 121:39

[3] http://www.centerforsmallgovernment.com/small-government-news/agencies-of-the-federal-government/

[4] Competitive Enterprise Institute's annual survey of the regulatory state, Ten Thousand Commandments, as cited in: http://dailycaller.com/2013/05/21/the-towering-federal-register/

[5] http://www.powerlineblog.com/archives/2013/07/environmental-fraud-alert.php

[6] Claremont Review of Books, Spring 2013, p 32.

[7] http://thinkexist.com/quotation/you-will-never-understand-bureaucracies-until-you/347030.html

[8] http://www.whitehouse.gov/the-press-office/2014/03/28/fact-sheet-climate-action-plan-strategy-cut-methane-emissions

[9] http://washingtonexaminer.com/mitch-mcconnell-slaps-irs-bonuses-says-public-sector-unions-bankrupting-country/article/2532230

[10] http://www.powerlineblog.com/archives/2014/07/is-administrative-law-unlawful-1.php

[11] http://www.powerlineblog.com/archives/2014/07/is-administrative-law-unlawful-3.php

[12] http://www.powerlineblog.com/archives/2014/07/is-administrative-law-unlawful-2-july-4-edition.php

Chapter 20: Just One of the Bunch?

[1] New York Times, September 11, 2013

[2] An elaboration and quasi defense of this quote is found in http://www.washingtonpost.com/blogs/the-fix/wp/2013/09/12/american-exceptionalism-explained/

[3] 1 Nephi 13:30; Ether 2:10; 2 Nephi 3:2; and 2 Nephi 10:11

[4] 1 Nephi 22:7-11

[5] http://www.ohio.com/news/bill-ayers-defends-weather-underground-bombings-1.395109

[6] US Ambassador to the United Nations (2013-) Samantha Power, New Republic, March 2003

[7] http://www.examiner.com/article/nancy-pelosi-celebrate-obamacare-on-independence-day

[8] https://www.youtube.com/watch?v=LYY73RO_egw

[9] http://www.nationalreview.com/article/359999/response-richard-dawkins-dennis-prager/page/0/1

[10] 1 Nephi 13:12-15

[11] Alma 61:15

[12] http://www.rasmussenreports.com/public_content/politics/current_events/russia/59_think_u_s_more_exceptional_than_other_nations

[13] See 1 Samuel 8

[14] 1 Samuel, Ibid, vv 9-20

[15] WSJ, American Sovereignty and Its Enemies, July 20-21, 2013, A13

[16] Ibid

[17] Stephen J. Markman, The Coming Constitutional Debate, Imprimis, April 2010.

[18] Ibid

CHAPTER 21: MY COUNTRY, 'TIS OF ME

[1] Alma 51:8

[2] 4 Nephi 24:26

[3] 2 Nephi 28:13

[4] 3 Nephi 6:10

[5] https://www.lds.org/general-conference/1989/04/beware-of-pride?lang=eng&query=beware+of+pride

[6] Wall Street Journal, March 11, 2013, A15

[7] Quoted by George McGovern in his 1972 concession speech.

[8] http://politicalquotes.org/node/33564

[9] http://carnegieendowment.org/2013/03/01/stalin-puzzle-deciphering-post-soviet-public-opinion/fmz8#

[10] Alma 46:5

[11] Helaman 2:5

[12] Ether 6:23

[13] Mosiah 29:13

[14] Mosiah 11:5

[15] http://cnsnews.com/mrctv-blog/terence-p-jeffrey/i-me-my-obama-uses-first-person-singular-199-times-speech-vowing

[16] http://dailycaller.com/2013/08/15/obama-working-to-unilaterally-impose-cell-phonetax/

[17] April 4, 2013 http://washington.cbslocal.com/2013/04/04/obama

[18] http://www.powerlineblog.com/archives/2014/02/obama-then-and-now-3.php

[19] http://www.c-span.org/video/?320197-1/president-obama-economy

[20] http://www.whitehouse.gov/the-press-office/2013/05/05/remarks-president-ohio-state-university-commencement

CHAPTER 22: THE NEW PLAGUE OF LOCUSTS

[1] Federalist 51

[2] http://www.ncsl.org/legislatures-elections/legislatures/full-and-part-time-legislatures.aspx

[3] http://www.nbcnews.com/id/45819570/ns/us_news-life/t/new-laws-toughen-rules-abortions-immigrants-voters/#.Udstzha-hbU and http://www.politifact.com/texas/statements/2012/apr/27/

[4] http://finance.townhall.com/columnists/markbaisley/2013/07/01/the-government-monster-is-alive-n1631296/page/2

[5] Milton Friedman, Free to Choose, quoted in Wall Street Journal, March, 19, 2014, A-17

[6] Elder Ezra Taft Benson, The Constitution – A Glorious Standard, April 1976 General Conference.

[7] Bastiat, 32

[8] http://articles.washingtonpost.com/2013-06-20/opinions/

[9] http://www.americanbar.org/content/dam/aba/publications/supreme_court_preview/briefs-v2/12-10_resp_amcu_bfrl-etal.authcheckdam.pdf

[10] http://www.scotusblog.com/case-files/cases/agency-for-international-development-v-alliance-for-open-society-international-inc/

[11] For example, the Dodd-Frank Act of 2010 requires "that regulators create 2343 rules, conduct 67 studies and issue 22 periodic reports." (Niall Ferguson, "How America Lost Its Way," Wall Street Journal, June 8-9, 2013, C1)

[12] http://m.nationalreview.com/article/353869/name-bureaucrat-john-fund/page/0/1

[13] Ibid

[14] Ibid, Fund

[15] http://rt.com/usa/dhs-ammo-investigation-napolitano-645/

[16] http://www.nbcnews.com/id/45819570/ns/us_news-life/t/new-laws-toughen-rules-abortions-immigrants-voters/#.Udstzha-hbU and http://www.ncsl.org/legislatures-elections/legislatures/full-and-part-time-legislatures.aspx

[17] Rivkin and Foley, op. cit.

[18] An October 2013 Fox News Poll found that 88% say government is in charge of the people and only 8% say the people are in charge of the government.

[19] http://en.wikipedia.org/wiki/Alexis_de_Tocqueville#cite_note-twsC11r44-3

[20] 3 Nephi 6:10-11

[21] http://usatoday30.usatoday.com/money/economy/income/2010-08-10-1Afedpay10_ST_N.htm?csp=usat.me

[22] From C.S. Lewis's essay anthology "God in the Dock" 1948

[23] 1 Peter 4:14

Chapter 23: Your Friendly Speech Control SWAT Team

[1] http://www.infowars.com/nevada-governor-blasts-feds-first-amendment-area-in-bundy-dispute/

[2] Jarom 1:12

[3] http://www.thecrimson.com/column/the-red-line/article/2014/2/18/academic-freedom-justice/?page=single See also Ross Douthat, The Challenge of Pluralism, New York Times, March 19, 2014.

[4] http://www.irs.gov/irb/2013-52_IRB/ar18.html

[5] https://theconversation.com/is-misinformation-about-the-climate-criminally-negligent-23111 See also: http://dailycaller.com/2014/03/17/u-s-college-professor-demands-imprisonment-for-climate-change-deniers/

[6] http://www.rasmussenreports.com/public_content/politics/general_politics/april_2014/55_favor_government_oversight_of_political_ads_and_candidates_comments

[7] http://www.foxnews.com/politics/2013/08/02/seattle-officials-call-for-ban-on-potentially-offensive-language/

[8] http://www.languagemonitor.com/category/politically-correct-2/

[9] http://www.lifesitenews.com/news/mark-steyn-case-wakes-up-canadian-press-to-human-rights-tribunals-threat-to

[10] Helaman 7:4-5

[11] Ibid v 6

[12] Ephesians 6:12

[13] 3 Nephi 6:15

[14] Jefferson's action cannot be construed as a weakening of his firm belief in limited government and his strict construction of the Constitution. He even prepared an amendment that would have authorized his purchase, but Congress ignored it. While his action can be pointed to "as an example of the federal government's ignoring the constraints in which it was placed," according to Charles C. W. Cooke, "to claim that the lack of an amendment makes the case that there was no need for one in the first instance is nothing short of extraordinary." Refusal of the government to abide by constitutional rules does not and cannot change those rules. http://www.nationalreview.com/article/370791/against-reinterpreting-constitution-charles-c-w-cooke

[15] The Supreme Court was a little quicker to invalidate Harry Truman's attempt to nationalize all steel mills by executive order in Youngstown Steel. http://en.wikipedia.org/wiki/Executive_Order

[16] http://www.newyorker.com/online/blogs/comment/2013/08/swat-team-nation.html

[17] http://www.foxnews.com/politics/2013/09/14/armed-epa-agents-in-alaska-shed-light-on-70-fed-agencies-with-armed-divisions/

[18] http://rt.com/usa/dhs-ammo-investigation-napolitano-645/

[19] http://www.huffingtonpost.com/2013/07/10/obama-police-militarization_n_3566478.html

[20] When questioned about the purchase of 174,000 hollow point bullets, the SSA said they were for firing range practice. Trouble is, hollow points are designed to stop people; other types of bullets are usually used for practice.

[21] Alma 46 / He ripped what he sewed.

[22] http://econfaculty.gmu.edu/wew/quotes/arms.html

[23] http://www.uscis.gov/portal/site/uscis/

[24] http://www.constitution.org/fed/federa46.htm

[25] Op cit: Econfaculty.gmu.edu

Chapter 24: Power Corrupts and Profligacy Corrupts Absolutely

[1] The definitive work on this tragedy is Harrison Salisbury's The 900 Days: The Siege of Leningrad. A sobering read.

[2] http://en.wikipedia.org/wiki/List_of_conspiracy_theories

[3] "Making a Federal Case Out of It," National Review, August 19, 2013, 22

[4] Helaman 9:19-24

[5] Harvey A. Silverglate, Three Felonies a Day; How the Feds Target the Innocent, Encounter Books, New York, 2009. See especially Chapter 5, the story of Arthur Andersen & Co., "a horror story that, despite the accounting firm's eventual Pyrrhic victory in the Supreme Court, almost certainly will be repeated again and again…." p151

[6] See the SEC v Mark Cuban story in How the Feds Rig Their Prosecutions, Wall Sreet Journal, April 4, 2014, A13: http://online.wsj.com/news/articles/SB10001424052702303978304579475680731414774

[7] http://money.cnn.com/2012/08/06/news/companies/gibson-imports-wood/

[8] http://www.washingtonpost.com/opinions/george-f-will-the-heavy-hand-of-the-irs/2014/04/30/7a56ca9e-cfc5-11e3-a6b1-45c4dffb85a6_print.html

[9] http://www.washingtontimes.com/news/2014/jul/8/power-grab-epa-wants-to-garnish-wages-of-polluters/

[10] See Ether 8

[11] Joseph B. Wirthlin, "Earthly Debts, Heavenly Debts," General Conference, April 2004

[12] Conference Report, April 1938, 103

[13] Romain Hatchuel, "Central banks and the Borrowing Addiction", Wall Street Journal, June 21, 2013 A13.

[14] http://demonocracy.info/infographics/usa/us_deficit/us_deficit.html

[15] Jon Roland, Meaning of "High Crimes and Misdemeanors" at http://www.constitution.org/cmt/high_crimes.htm The word "high" does not mean more serious, but rather, because of the oath public officials have taken, a higher standard of behavior. "It refers to those punishable offenses that only apply to high persons …" who "because of their official status, are under special obligations that ordinary persons are not under, and which could not be meaningfully applied or justly punished if committed by ordinary persons." See also: http://www.nationalreview.com/article/379222/faithless-execution-andrew-c-mccarthy

CHAPTER 25: AMERICA: GREAT PROMISE, TERRIBLE CURSE

[1] Moroni 9:12

[2] http://www.powerlineblog.com/archives/2014/05/why-global-warming-alarmism-isnt-science-2.php

[3] 1 Nephi 12:18

[4] Quotes are respectively: D&C 20:9; Moroni 8:27, D&C 38:39

[5] Helaman 8:5-6

[6] Quoted by Elder David A. Bednar, December 15, 2012, BYU-Hawaii commencement address

[7] Isaiah 5:20

[8] Bastiat, 70

[9] Ether 2:12

[10] Mosiah 29:26

[11] Mosiah 29:27

[12] Ether 2:7-9

[13] http://www.cdc.gov/nchs/data/nhsr/nhsr064.pdf

[14] http://www.newsmax.com/Newsfront/54-million-abortions-roe/2013/01/22/id/472494/

[15] http://twentysomethingmarriage.org

[16] http://www.cdc.gov/nchs/nsfg/abc_list_n.htm#numberlifetime

[17] http://www.cdc.gov/nchs/nsfg/abc_list_a.htm#sexual

[18] Thanks to Dennis Prager for this litany: http://townhall.com/columnists/dennisprager/2014/07/08/america-wont-be-good-without-god-n1860008/page/2

[19] Jarom 1:10

[20] 2 Nephi 10:11

[21] https://rsc.byu.edu/archived/latter-day-prophets-and-united-states-constitution/11-harold-b-lee

Chapter 26: Stand Up, Say Something, and Don't Sit Down

[1] http://www.latterdayconservative.com/quotes/joseph-smith/

[2] http://en.wikipedia.org/wiki/United_States_Constitution#Ratification

[3] http://en.wikipedia.org/wiki/Anti-Federalism

[4] D&C 58:27

[5] Neal A. Maxwell, "Meeting the Challenges of Today," BYU Devotional, October 10, 1978

[6] President Ezra Taft Benson, Our Divine Constitution, October 1987. The full quote, including that the Constitution will "not be saved in Washington," that it "may also cost us blood," and that "the stars and stripes will be floating on the breeze" when the Savior comes can be seen here: http://www.youtube.com/watch?v=cxu-zw004jc&noredirect=1. The official conference report is here: http://www.lds.org/ensign/1987/11/our-divine-constitution. For additional reading, please see his book The Constitution; A Heavenly Banner.

[7] http://www.madisonbrigade.com/s_adams.htm

[8] Ronald Reagan Gubernatorial Inauguration Speech, 5 January 1967.

* * *

Index

Topics such as God, Jesus Christ, Satan, power, agency, freedom, justice, etc. are not listed due to their frequent mentions in the book.